LATINO STARS IN
MAJOR LEAGUE BASEBALL

LATINO STARS IN MAJOR LEAGUE BASEBALL

From Bobby Abreu to Carlos Zambrano

Jonathan Weeks

ROWMAN & LITTLEFIELD
Lanham • Boulder • New York • London

Published by Rowman & Littlefield
A wholly owned subsidary of The Rowman & Littlefield Publishing Group, Inc.
4501 Forbes Boulevard, Suite 200, Lanham, Maryland 20706
www.rowman.com

Unit A, Whitacre Mews, 26-34 Stannary Street, London SE11 4AB

British Library Cataloguing in Publication Information Available

Library of Congress Cataloging-in-Publication Data

Names: Weeks, Jonathan, author.
Title: Latino stars in major league baseball : from Bobby Abreu to Carlos Zambrano / Jonathan Weeks.
Description: Lanham : Rowman & Littlefield, [2017] | Includes bibliographical references and index.
Identifiers: LCCN 2016045966 (print) | LCCN 2017002777 (ebook) | ISBN 9781442281721 (hardcover : alk. paper) | ISBN 9781442281738 (electronic)
Subjects: LCSH: Hispanic American baseball players—Biography. | Baseball players—Latin America—Biography. | Hispanic American baseball players—History.
Classification: LCC GV865.A1 W4197 2017 (print) | LCC GV865.A1 (ebook) | DDC 796.3570922 [B] —dc23
LC record available at https://lccn.loc.gov/2016045966

Printed in the United States of America

CONTENTS

ACKNOWLEDGMENTS

As usual, I'd like to thank my editor at Rowman & Littlefield, Christen Karniski, for vastly improving the quality of my work. I'd also like to extend my gratitude to the ever-patient and helpful staff at the National Baseball Hall of Fame.

LIST OF PLAYERS

Dominican Republic

Felipe Alou
Matty Alou
Tony Batista
Jose Bautista
George Bell
Adrian Beltre
Armando Benitez
Robinson Cano
Rico Carty
Santiago Casilla
Luis Castillo
Starlin Castro
Cesar Cedeno
Bartolo Colon
Francisco Cordero
Nelson Cruz
Johnny Cueto
Edwin Encarnacion
Tony Fernandez
Julio Franco
Pedro Guerrero

Vladimir Guerrero
Juan Marichal
Pedro Martinez
Jose Mesa
Raul Mondesi
Manny Mota
David Ortiz
Tony Pena
Jhonny Peralta
Placido Polanco
Albert Pujols
Aramis Ramirez
Hanley Ramirez
Manny Ramirez
Jose Reyes
Carlos Santana
Alfonso Soriano
Sammy Sosa
Miguel Tejada
Juan Uribe

Puerto Rico

Roberto Alomar
Carlos Beltran
Orlando Cepeda
Roberto Clemente
Carlos Correa
Jose Cruz
Carlos Delgado
Juan Gonzalez
Francisco Lindor
Javier Lopez
Javy Lopez

Mike Lowell
Felix Millan
Bengie Molina
Yadier Molina
Jorge Posada
Vic Power
Ivan Rodriguez
Benito Santiago
Ruben Sierra
Danny Tartabull
Bernie Williams

Venezuela

Bobby Abreu
Edgardo Alfonzo
Jose Altuve
Elvis Andrus
Luis Aparicio
Tony Armas
Miguel Cabrera
Chico Carrasquel
Dave Concepcion
Alcides Escobar
Andres Galarraga
Freddy Garcia
Carlos Gonzalez

Ozzie Guillen
Felix Hernandez
Victor Martinez
Miguel Montero
Magglio Ordonez
Salvador Perez
Martin Prado
Francisco Rodriguez
Johan Santana
Manny Trillo
Omar Vizquel
Carlos Zambrano

Cuba

Jose Abreu
Bert Campaneris
Jose Canseco
Jose Cardenal
Leo Cardenas
Yoenis Cespedes
Aroldis Chapman
Mike Cuellar
Jose Fernandez
Tony Gonzalez
Livan Hernandez
Orlando Hernandez
Dolf Luque

Minnie Minoso
Kendrys Morales
Tony Oliva
Rafael Palmeiro
Camilo Pascual
Tony Perez
Yasiel Puig
Alexei Ramirez
Cookie Rojas
Tony Taylor
Luis Tiant
Zoilo Versalles

Panama

Rod Carew
Carlos Lee
Hector Lopez
Omar Moreno
Ben Oglivie

Mariano Rivera
Carlos Ruiz
Manny Sanguillen
Rennie Stennett

Mexico

Bobby Avila
Vinny Castilla
Yovani Gallardo
Jorge Orta

Aurelio Rodriguez
Joakim Soria
Fernando Valenzuela

Colombia

Orlando Cabrera
Jose Quintana
Edgar Renteria

Julio Teheran

Nicaragua

Dennis Martinez

Curacao

Kenley Jansen

Andruw Jones

Jonathan Schoop

Andrelton Simmons

Honduras

Gerald Young

Brazil

Yan Gomes

INTRODUCTION

A Defining Moment in History[1]

October 12, 1963

Polo Grounds, New York

Billed as a charity event to benefit a new Latin American Hall of Fame, two teams composed of Latino players squared off in the first and only Latino All-Star Game on October 12, 1963. It was an important moment in baseball history, signifying the "arrival" of Latin Americans as a legitimate force in Major League Baseball.

The crowd of 14,000 must have appeared rather sparse considering that the Polo Grounds had a capacity of 56,000. But in spite of the low turnout, players took the game very seriously. "It didn't matter that it was for charity and that it wasn't a real 'All-Star Game,'" Hall of Famer Orlando Cepeda remembered years later. "When you put on your uniform, you played hard and you tried even harder to win."

In addition to Cepeda, three other Hall of Famers played that day: Juan Marichal, Roberto Clemente, and Luis Aparicio. Marichal stole the show, pitching four scoreless innings and striking out six in a game

---

1. Robert Dominguez, "The Forgotten All-Star Game: Fifty Years Ago, Baseball's Latin Legends Played in Polo Grounds' Last Game," *New York Daily News*, July 10, 2013, http://www.nydailynews.com/news/national/forgotten-all-star-game-50-years-baseball-latino-legends-played-polo-grounds-game-article-1.1395064 (retrieved April 23, 2016).

won by the National League squad, 5–2. It was the last game ever played at the Polo Grounds.

✿ ✿ ✿

Some of the best players in major-league history were born outside the United States. According to an ESPN article, Latin American ballplayers held 27 percent of major-league contracts and 40 percent of minor-league contracts in 2013. In fact, Latino players represent one of the fastest-growing ethnicities in baseball. But the road to "The Show" has not been easy for many.

MLB's dreaded color barrier prevented many of the greatest players of all time from competing on baseball's grandest stage. Although Cuban luminaries Cristobal Torriente, Martin Dihigo, and Jose Mendez were elected to Cooperstown, none of them saw major-league action. The abolishment of the color barrier did little to alleviate other problems faced by Latin American ballplayers. Many grow up in poverty using improvised materials (for example, milk cartons for gloves and tree branches for bats) to learn the rudiments of the game. Language barriers leave many feeling isolated and misunderstood once they reach the United States.

Recognizing the depth of the talent pool in Venezuela, major-league teams began establishing training camps there during the 1990s. At one point, 23 major-league clubs had set up operations in the South American country. But by 2016, only four camps remained. Economic troubles, political unrest, food shortages, and rising crime rates have made it difficult for the surviving facilities to function.

An entirely different dilemma is faced by players from Cuba, where the Communist government prohibits prospects from signing with major-league teams. Desperate to realize their dreams, many players risk life and limb to escape the country. Dodgers outfielder Yasiel Puig was held hostage by the criminals who smuggled him out of Cuba. White Sox first baseman Jose Abreu nearly drowned in 15-foot waves.

The struggles faced by numerous Latin American players make their stories all the more triumphant. And as the diversity of baseball continues to grow, the quality of play is enhanced exponentially. At the time of this writing, there were 10 Latino players enshrined at the National Baseball Hall of Fame in Cooperstown. Many others have played on major-league All-Star Teams, led their respective leagues in various statistical categories, won prestigious awards, and guided their clubs to the postseason. The most successful Latino stars are profiled in the pages that follow.

I

THE DOMINICAN REPUBLIC

ORIGINS OF BASEBALL IN THE DOMINICAN REPUBLIC

Baseball is said to have appeared in the Dominican during the 1870s, when many Cubans fleeing the Ten Years' War migrated to the country, bringing the sport with them. Professional ball got its start in the 1890s, with the establishment of the Ozama and Nuevo Club teams. In 1907, the Santo Domingo-based Tigres de Licey was founded. The club became so dominant that three competing teams were inspired to combine their best players to form a single star-studded squad known as Escogido (which translates to "chosen one").

During the reign of dictator Rafael Leonidas Trujillo, many stadiums were built. In 1937, Trujillo assembled a superteam composed of the top Negro League and Latin American stars of the era. Trujillo's roster included such legendary figures as Cool Papa Bell, Josh Gibson, and Satchel Paige. To meet Trujillo's challenge, two rival squads (Estrellas Orientales and Aguilas Cibaenas) were formed with various imported stars, among them Cuban luminaries Luis Tiant Sr. and Martin Dihigo. The cost of building these dream teams was immense, and, as a result, the new league collapsed at season's end. Professional baseball remained dormant in the Dominican for more than a decade.

Founded in 1951, the Dominican Winter League is alive and well today. Commonly referred to by its Spanish acronym, LIDOM, the circuit features six teams that compete in a 50-game round-robin schedule that begins in mid-October and runs until the end of December.

The two top teams meet in a best-of-nine series to determine the national champion. The winners advance to the Caribbean Series to face teams from Mexico, Venezuela, Cuba, and Puerto Rico. As of this writing, Dominican teams have won 19 of those meetings. In addition, a Dominican national team, composed partially of major leaguers, competes in the Pan American Games, the World Cup, and the World Baseball Classic.

Beginning with Ozzie Virgil Sr., who joined the New York Giants in 1956, the Dominican Republic has been stocking the majors with exceptional players for many decades. The Dominican Summer League, comprised of more than 30 farm teams with ties to Major League Baseball franchises, has been a bountiful source of talent. In 2013, more than a quarter of the available major-league roster spots were filled with players born outside the United States. Ten percent of those slots were occupied by Dominicans. Perhaps for the first time in history, MLB's World Series is truly deserving of its name.

MAJOR STARS OF THE PAST

Felipe Alou

Outfielder

Felipe Alou was born in Bajos de Haina. He was the oldest of three brothers to play in the majors. His father was a carpenter and blacksmith who barely made enough money to support the family. Felipe attended high school in Santo Domingo and was a good student. Athletically inclined, he made the Dominican national track team, competing in running events, as well as throwing the discus and javelin. He played baseball on the side for local amateur teams.

Alou's parents wanted him to escape poverty by becoming a doctor, but it was not to be. While attending the University of Santo Domingo as a pre-med student, he helped the school's baseball team to a collegiate championship. Assigned to the national team, he gathered four hits in the Pan American Games finale versus the United States. The Dominicans captured a gold medal, and Alou received multiple offers from major-league clubs. Although his parents were not enthusiastic at first, they realized that a signing bonus would tremendously benefit the family. Felipe joined the Giants organization.

In his first minor-league season, Alou hit .377. He was promoted to Triple-A in 1957, but the outfielder slumped at the plate. Assigned to the Pacific Coast League the following year, he posted a .319 average and was called to San Francisco. He was not at all intimidated to be in the majors. "Guys from the Dominican Republic don't know fear," Alou once said. "People from the Dominican try to cross the Atlantic in boats to get to the United States. The only thing on their minds is to give it all they've got." Although he competed for playing time with the likes of Leon Wagner, Orlando Cepeda, and Hank Sauer, he was appearing regularly in the lineup by 1960. Fellow countryman Manny Mota gave Alou credit for opening the door for other Dominicans. "He was an inspiration to everybody," Mota proclaimed.

In 1960, Alou was joined by his brother Matty in San Francisco. They combined for a .265 batting average that year. In 1963, Jesus—the youngest Alou—made it a trio. On September 10, 1963, the three men appeared in the outfield together at the Polo Grounds, forming the first tandem of its kind. They were retired in order in the same inning when they batted against Mets hurler Carlton Willey.

As the years wore on, Felipe began to distinguish himself as the most powerful of the siblings. He had a breakout season in 1962, slamming 25 homers, while hitting .316. He would top that average twice—in 1966 and 1968, when he led the National League in hits. He was selected for the All-Star Team in all three campaigns.

Alou played at each outfield station and performed competently. He spent a majority of his time in right field, finishing among the top five in range factor three times and fielding percentage twice. Demonstrating his versatility, he served as first baseman in more than 400 games.

Alou wore several different uniforms through the course of his 17 seasons as a big-league player. Traded by the Giants after the 1963 slate, he had stints with the Braves, A's, Yankees, Expos, and Brewers. He reached the pinnacle of his career with the Braves, hitting .295 in six seasons. He retired as a player after the 1974 slate.

In 1976, Alou took a job as a spring-training instructor for the Expos. He liked it, beginning a minor-league managerial career the following year. After managing five different farm clubs in 12 seasons, he received an offer from the Expos, which he accepted. Between 1992 and

1996, he finished among the top three in voting for Manager of the Year four times. He won the award during the ill-fated 1994 campaign, when the Expos finished first but missed out on the postseason due to a players strike. He was chosen to manage the NL All-Star Team when play resumed in 1995.

Despite a steadily declining talent pool, Alou kept his job in Montreal until 2001, when he was replaced by Jeff Torborg. He took the helm in San Francisco before the 2003 slate, leading the club to a division title. For several years, he held the record for most wins by a manager born outside the United States (broken by Bruce Bochy, who was born in France). Expos general manager Dan Duquette later lamented his decision to cut Alou loose, saying, "The biggest mistake I've made in my career was not recognizing [Alou's] ability to be a terrific major-league manager. He's one of the best in the league."

Alou had the opportunity to manage his son for a couple of years in San Francisco. Moises, who was born in the United States, had a distinguished career, hitting .303 in 17 seasons, with more than 300 homers. "It's a family legacy," said Felipe in 2005. "I see all of us together being a force through this game and still going." When the Giants posted a 76–85 record in 2006, Alou was let go. In 26 professional seasons, he piloted his clubs to a .521 winning percentage. He was inducted into the Latino Baseball Hall of Fame, Canadian Baseball Hall of Fame, and Caribbean Baseball Hall of Fame.

Matty Alou

Outfielder

Mateo Rojas Alou was a middle child. He and his two brothers were inseparable while growing up, spending a majority of their time working with their father or playing baseball. The family was poor, and the Alous sometimes substituted coconuts for balls, tree branches for bats, and canvas strips for gloves. Mateo dropped out of school in the eighth grade to help out his parents. He hoped to forge a career as a sailor someday.

By the age of 17, "Matty" was playing for the Dominican Air Force team alongside future major-league standouts Juan Marichal and Manny Mota. The club was presided over by General Ramfis Trujillo—son of Dominican dictator Rafael Trujillo. Games were taken seriously. After losing a doubleheader one afternoon, Trujillo accused his players of drinking alcohol and threw them in jail for five days.

Following in his brother Felipe's footsteps, Matty signed with the Giants in the winter of 1956–1957. His minor-league career spanned portions of five seasons. He hit .291 at various levels between 1957 and 1960, earning a call-up in the latter campaign. After serving as a platoon player in his first two full major-league seasons, he hurt his knee in spring training and ended up back in the minors. He returned to the Giants in 1964, but found himself competing for outfield time with his younger brother Jesus and a slew of other stars, including Willie Mays and Willie McCovey. He was batting .219 when he sustained a broken wrist after being hit by a Bob Veale pitch at Forbes Field. He returned to action in July, eventually hiking up his average to .264. After a lackluster offensive showing the following year, he was traded to Pittsburgh. It was there that he turned his career around.

Working with former batting champ Harry "The Hat" Walker, Alou learned to stop pulling the ball. Walker gave Alou a heavier bat and advised him to choke up, slash down on pitches, and take advantage of his exceptional speed. The results were miraculous. After hitting just .260 in portions of six seasons with the Giants, Alou fashioned averages above the .330 mark for four consecutive campaigns. He won a batting title in 1966, with a .342 effort. Alou had a habit of hitting off of his front foot and blooping balls into center field with a flick of his wrists. Ted Williams felt that Alou's style was ugly but effective. "He violates most of the principles I teach," said Williams, "but somehow he manages to get on base." Steve Carlton described Alou as the "worst .300 hitter" he had ever seen.

Alou's most productive season came in 1969, when he led the NL with 231 hits and 41 doubles. He scored a personal-best 105 runs that year, while accruing a .331 batting average. When that mark fell 34 points the following year, he was traded to the Cardinals. Alou continued to hit for steady averages between 1971 and 1973, although he changed uniforms several times. He finished his big-league career in 1974, with a .307 lifetime mark. The Alou brothers combined for a total of 5,094 hits—topping the record previously held by the DiMaggios (Joe, Dominic, and Vince).

After falling from the major-league ranks, Alou played in Japan. "I didn't like playing there really," he admitted. "I played there because I had to. I had three kids to support." The grueling workouts and frequent travel took a toll on him, and he retired after three seasons. When his playing days were over, Matty served as a Tigers scout and managed in the Dominican Summer League. He was duly recognized for his accomplishments in 2007, when he was inducted into the Hispanic Heritage Baseball Museum Hall of Fame. The occasion was celebrated at San Francisco's AT&T Park. He died four years later from complications of diabetes.

Tony Batista

Infielder

Tony Batista was born in Puerto Plata—one of the busiest trading ports in the Dominican Republic. Bordered by the Atlantic Ocean to the north, the city is known for its many resorts. There are more than 100,000 hotel beds available to travelers. Batista attended Liceo Juan de Jesus High School and was just 17 years old when the A's signed him as an amateur free agent. He would eventually gain experience at every infield station except pitcher and catcher. On the farm, the A's experimented with him mostly at shortstop. Called to the majors in 1996, he was assigned second- and third-base duties, fielding the latter position below the league average. He was moved back to short the following year—again faring below expectations defensively. When his batting average dropped to .202 that season, he was left unprotected in the Expansion Draft. The Diamondbacks selected him in the first round.

Batista began to demonstrate some power in Arizona, but manager Buck Showalter already had his infield positions filled. Batista was traded to the Blue Jays in June 1999. Without him, the Diamondbacks advanced to the National League Division Series. In Toronto, Batista emerged as a reliable power hitter, slamming 26 homers in 98 games. He finished the 1999 campaign with 31 home runs and 100 RBIs.

There were several features that set Batista apart from other ballplayers. First and foremost was his odd batting stance. A right-handed hitter, he stood with his left foot outside the batter's box facing the pitcher, while holding the bat directly in front of him. When he saw a pitch he liked, he would step toward the plate with his lead foot and swing ferociously. He was rather indiscriminate about his pitch selection throughout the years, averaging a strikeout per every six at-bats. Another interesting aspect of Batista's game was his defense. He had a casual fielding style that was described by one writer as a "scoop and lob" procedure. He liked to get rid of the ball quickly without putting much velocity on his throws.

In addition to his unorthodox batting and fielding techniques, Batista was prone to erratic behavior on the diamond. One day, after narrowly beating out a throw from third base, he ran past the bag all the way to the outfield wall at the SkyDome. He then walked leisurely back to first. While playing in the Japanese Pacific League, he was plunked on the elbow by Yakult Swallows pitcher Masanori Ishikawa. Batista sprinted toward the mound and abruptly peeled off toward first base, scaring Ishikawa half to death. The diminutive hurler actually turned tail and ran. When he realized Batista was only bluffing, he smiled in obvious relief. The game's broadcasters were highly amused, as were many of Batista's Japanese teammates. One Japanese beat writer referred to Batista as "Mr. Nonchalant," in reference to his casual style and cool temperament.

Batista enjoyed his most productive major-league season in 2000, with the Blue Jays, scoring 96 runs and driving in 114. He also reached career-high marks in home runs (41) and total bases (322). Serving exclusively as a third baseman, he led players at his position in double plays, while finishing second in putouts and assists. Despite his impressive numbers, the Blue Jays finished third in the highly competitive American League East.

In 2001, Batista's salary nearly tripled. When he got off to a .207 start at the plate, he was traded to the Orioles. He remained in Baltimore for portions of three seasons, averaging 23 homers and 76 RBIs per year. In 2004, he was added to the Expos roster. He was the club's most productive player, with 110 RBIs. The Expos left Montreal after the season, and when no major-league team was able to meet his salary needs, Batista signed a contract worth $15 million with the Softbank Hawks in Japan. Although he finished among the league leaders in multiple statistical categories, the Hawks were looking for younger talent and released him before the second year of his contract was fulfilled. Batista ended up with the Twins in 2006, and the Washington

Nationals the following year. He played in the Nationals farm system in 2008, but was not promoted. His last experience in organized baseball was in the Dominican Winter League. He closed out his professional career with 313 home runs. He held the Caribbean Series record for RBIs until it was surpassed by Miguel Tejada.

Deeply religious, the two-time All-Star envisioned himself as a Christian missionary during his career. "God uses me," he told a reporter in 2006. "Everywhere I go, I talk about Him and the Power He has." While playing for Toronto, Batista donated a large percentage of his earnings to charities and churches. He also made himself imminently available to fans, signing autographs before games. "You get the feeling that he is truly a man at peace," one Minnesota writer remarked. "He seems genuine, sincere, and even a little innocent."

George Bell

Left Fielder

To some, George Bell embodied the stereotype of the hot-tempered Latino ballplayer. But others have described him more flatteringly as "colorful" and "competitive." Blue Jays coach John McLaren once said, "George simply hates to lose. Sometimes you wonder what he's doing and sometimes he may try too hard, but he plays to win." There were times when Bell's passion landed him in hot water. Brushed back by Red Sox pitcher Bruce Kison in June 1985, he stormed the mound and landed a flying karate kick. Razzed by Toronto fans after a tough defensive showing in the outfield, he told a reporter after the game that the hecklers could "kiss [his] purple butt." Among Dominican-born players, Bell reportedly holds the record for ejections, with 13. (Felipe Alou was thrown out of 17 contests but only one as a player.)

Bell can trace his roots to San Pedro de Macoris—one of the largest cities in the Dominican Republic. Located in the southeastern region of the country, it is home to Universidad Central de Este, an esteemed private college. The city has produced an unusually high number of major leaguers—more than 30 to date.

Bell was originally signed by the Phillies in 1978, and began his minor-league career at the age of 18. The Blue Jays acquired him in the 1980 Rule 5 Draft and promoted him the following year. After putting up mediocre numbers in his debut, he was sent back to the farm. In 1983, he had a breakout season with the Syracuse Chiefs and was again summoned to Toronto. He ended up sticking around for the next seven seasons.

Bell had an interesting hitting style, rocking backward before the pitch and exploding toward the ball. He was a free swinger, drawing no more than 43 walks in any given season. A reliable run producer, he gathered 86 or more RBIs in nine straight campaigns, reaching the century mark four times. Even his outs were productive. He finished among the top 10 in sacrifice flies on six occasions, and his lifetime total is among the top 100 marks of all time.

Bell reached the summit of his career in 1987, blasting 47 homers while driving in a league-high 134 runs. His 47 long balls served as a team record that stood for more than 20 years. Given the outstanding performances turned in by several of Bell's rivals that year, his selection as Most Valuable Player was questioned by some. Mark McGwire set a rookie record for home runs, with 49. Wade Boggs hit .363, and Don Mattingly tied a major-league record with home runs in eight consecutive games. The Yankees first baseman also raised the bar for grand slams in a season, with six. But it was Alan Trammell who presented the biggest challenge to Bell's candidacy, gathering 12 first-place votes. In the end, Bell captured the honor with 85 percent of the total share.

By 1988, Bell was suffering from knee and shoulder problems. When manager Jimy Williams announced that he would serve as a designated hitter that season, the slugger openly revolted, refusing to bat in a spring-training game against the Red Sox. On Opening Day, he hit three home runs and then snarled at a reporter after the game, declaring, "I got too many things on my mind right now to be happy." Williams relented, penciling Bell into 149 games in the outfield.

After the 1990 campaign, when Bell sat out 20 games due to ongoing physical issues, he was traded to the Cubs. He appeared regularly in the lineup, hitting .285, with 25 homers—a performance that earned him his third and final All-Star selection. In the offseason, he was traded to the other Chicago team for Sammy Sosa. It has been referred to as one of the worst trades in White Sox history. Sosa became one of the great sluggers of the modern era. Bell drove in 112 runs in his Chicago debut and suffered a statistical collapse the following year. He was finished in the majors by the age of 34.

Bell worked as a hitting coach for the Blue Jays during the 2000s. In 2013, he began serving as a club consultant. He was elected to the Canadian Baseball Hall of Fame that same year. Summing up his career, one reporter remarked, "He was volatile, unpredictable, and a great hitter. It was hard not to like him, and Toronto fans loved him."

Armando Benitez

Pitcher

Armando Benitez grew up in Ramon Santana—a small municipality in the province of San Pedro de Macoris. His parents split up during his formative years, and he was raised by his mother, who made a living hand-washing clothes. There were four children, and money was tight. Benitez began playing ball when he was in his early teens. Although he was more than six feet tall by the age of 15, he weighed just 140 pounds. During his prime playing years, he was significantly heavier. Originally an outfielder and third baseman, his strong arm prompted a positional switch.

Signed by the Orioles in 1990, Benitez began his pro pitching career the following year in the Gulf Coast League. He was used in every capacity—as a starter, setup man, and closer. He fared well, with a 2.72 ERA, before experiencing a disappointing follow-up campaign, averaging more than four earned runs per nine innings. He kept plugging away and, by 1995, was ranked number 11 among major-league prospects.

The O's promoted Benitez in 1994, liking what they saw, and the team retained his services the following year. He struggled mightily and was demoted to the minors. It was more of the same in 1996, as he made the team out of spring training, only to be sent to the farm for more conditioning. Returning in August, he allowed just three earned runs in his last 14 appearances. He was effective in the 1996 American League Division Series against the Indians but struggled in the American League Championship Series against the Yankees. It was Benitez who gave up the infamous game-tying homer to Derek Jeter in the series opener (although replays proved it wasn't actually a homer—a young fan named Jeffrey Maier reached over the wall and grabbed the ball before outfielder Tony Tarasco could catch it). Benitez returned to the mound in the fourth game and this time had no excuse for coughing up a two-run blast to Darryl Strawberry that put the Yankees ahead, 8–4.

But better days were ahead for Benitez. In 1997, he struck out 106 batters in 73.1 innings, while serving primarily as a setup man. He posted an economical 2.45 ERA that year. In 1999, he was even better, averaging 14.8 strikeouts per nine innings for the Mets, while recording a dazzling 1.85 ERA. From 2000 to 2002, he was the primary closer for the Mets, picking up 117 saves and 278 strikeouts. He put up his finest numbers with the Marlins in 2004, notching a league-leading 47 saves, while accruing a pristine 1.29 ERA. He made his second consecutive All-Star appearance and received some MVP consideration.

Benitez's fastball was routinely clocked in the high 90s. He had a hard-biting slider to go with it. A fierce competitor, he got into trouble in 1998, when he hit slugger Tino Martinez with a pitch, inciting a bench-clearing brawl. Benitez insisted he hadn't done it on purpose but received an eight-game suspension anyway. The fiery hurler had plunked Martinez several years earlier after giving up a grand slam to one of Martinez's teammates.

Traded to the Giants before the 2005 campaign, Benitez embarked on a brief and star-crossed career in San Francisco. During his debut season, he missed several months of action after tearing tendons in his right hamstring. Upon returning, he began to suffer periodic melt-downs in crucial situations. The media jumped all over him, and he lost his appeal to fans. Giants GM Brian Sabean admitted that Benitez had become a "whipping boy." One sportswriter observed that Benitez "in-curred the wrath of San Francisco fans with his perceived attitude, as well as his performance. . . . He maintained his tendency to shrug off accountability for poor performances, prompting the crowds at AT&T Park to boo him after the slightest lapse."

Benitez's career wound down quickly after leaving the Bay Area in 2007. Out of the majors in 2009, he gave up four straight homers during an outing for the Round Rock Express—the Astros' Triple-A affiliate. Although he showed vast improvement the following year in the Mar-lins farm system, he was not promoted. In 21 professional seasons, Benitez gathered 71 wins and 372 saves, with a highly respectable 3.08 ERA. His 289 major-league saves are among the top totals of all time.

Rico Carty

Left Fielder/Designated Hitter

Born in San Pedro de Macoris, Rico Carty originally aspired to be a pro boxer but found the allure of baseball irresistible. He traded his boxing gloves for a catcher's mitt and played so impressively, he ended up signing 10 different minor-league contracts. This was, of course, against the rules, and National Association president George Trautman was forced to intervene. "I was just a dumb kid," Carty remarked years after the fact. "I just wanted to play ball." Since Carty had not accepted money from any of the clubs he had signed with, Trautman ruled that Carty could go wherever he wished. In the end, he chose the Braves.

Carty was among the earliest wave of Dominicans to play American baseball, following the Alou brothers. Under close scrutiny, Carty's defensive skills behind the plate didn't hold up, and he was converted to an outfielder. He hit .366 at the Class B level in 1962, before putting himself on a fast track to the majors with a .327 follow-up in the Texas League. Shortly before making his big-league debut, he was transferred to the Braves Triple-A affiliate in Toronto, where he hit two home runs during the same at-bat. When the first one was disallowed because time had been called, Carty stepped back in and lifted another ball into the seats.

A magnetic character, Carty's career was controversial and plagued by injury. He traveled extensively, spending time with six different clubs. In 1965, he missed part of the season with a bad back. In 1967, he suffered multiple shoulder separations. In 1968, he sat out the entire year with tuberculosis. A knee injury derailed his 1971 campaign. Since these misfortunes befell Carty in his prime, one can only speculate what his numbers would look like had he stayed healthy. As it stands, he was a .299 lifetime hitter.

Stories of Carty's personal clashes abound. While on a team flight with the Braves, he was speaking loudly in Spanish with some of his Latino comrades. Hank Aaron, who was sitting nearby, suspected that Carty was talking about him and provoked an argument. Carty cursed at Aaron, prompting baseball's future home-run king to take a wild swing that reportedly put a dent in the wall of the airplane. Carty ended up landing a punch to Aaron's face. It was not the first time the fiery

Dominican would clash with Atlanta teammates. Before his trade to the Rangers, he had a run-in with pitcher Ron Reed as well.

By the time Carty arrived in Texas for the 1973 campaign, the team's trainer remarked he had seen "better knees on a camel." Manager Whitey Herzog was a little spooked by Carty's intensity. "I think he's practicing voodoo or something," the Texas skipper commented to a reporter. "Check out his eyes. Rico's crazier than a peach orchard sow." Herzog had reason to be uncomfortable. After striking out one afternoon and arguing with the umpire, Carty stormed into the dugout and screamed at Herzog for his lack of support. The two men had to be separated by teammates. Herzog arranged for Carty to be traded to Chicago, where he clashed with star third baseman Ron Santo. He was subsequently shipped to Oakland, finishing the season there.

Despite his personal struggles, fans loved Carty for his persistent smile and charismatic personality. Known to some as the "Beeg Mon" (a nickname he gave himself), he once made the All-Star Team as a write-in candidate. He was later named Man of the Year in Cleveland.

When healthy, Carty was one of the most prolific hitters in the majors. Typically appearing fourth or fifth in the batting order, he topped the .300 mark in eight seasons. After finishing second in Rookie of the Year voting to Dick Allen in 1964, he won a batting title with a .366 average in 1970. His 25 homers, 101 RBIs, and league-leading .454 on-base percentage earned him serious MVP consideration that year.

After the regrettable events of 1973, Carty had a career revival in Cleveland. Serving primarily as a designated hitter, he averaged 15 homers and 76 RBIs per year between 1975 and 1977. Shipped to Toronto in 1978, he was traded yet again in August. He finished the season with 31 homers—a major-league record for a DH (since broken). Granted free agency, Carty resigned with the Blue Jays for the 1979 campaign. It was his last season in the majors. He hit .256 in 132 games and became the oldest player to reach the 200-homer mark—at 39 years of age.

Carty has stayed away from organized baseball in his retirement. He has spent many years serving as a mentor to young players in San Pedro de Macoris. Alfonso Soriano and Robinson Cano were among his star pupils. Carty was made an honorary general in the Dominican army and was elected mayor of his hometown—although he ultimately lost that

election after a recount. "I didn't like politics anyway," he told a
MLB.com reporter. "You have to lie too much."

Luis Castillo

Second Baseman

Luis Castillo was yet another fine player to hail from San Pedro de
Macoris. He graduated from Colegio San Benito Abad and is the only
alumnus to reach the majors to date. Castillo entered the Marlins farm
system at the age of 18. Before establishing full-time playing status in
Florida, he was called up and sent back down on multiple occasions.
During the Marlins' championship season of 1997, he appeared on the
roster from April through July, finishing the campaign in Charlotte. He
is the only Marlins player to appear in both of the club's championship
seasons without being traded in between. When Florida won the World
Series in 2003, Castillo was the starting second baseman. Interestingly,
it was Castillo who hit the infamous foul ball that was deflected by a fan
at Wrigley Field in the National League Championship Series. At the
time, the Cubs were five outs away from clinching their first pennant in
decades. Moises Alou appeared to have a shot at catching Castillo's foul
before a spectator named Steve Bartman got in the way. Castillo ended
up drawing a walk and scoring during the ensuing eight-run Florida
rally.

Castillo has been described by one writer as an "adequate defender
who could get on base and run like the wind." It's true that he was fast.
He gathered 20 or more steals on eight occasions and led the league
twice. But in regard to Castillo's defense, "adequate" is not a sufficient
expression of his skills. In 2007, he set a major-league record with 143
consecutive appearances at second base without an error. Prior to that,
he captured three straight Gold Gloves (2003–2005). "What he does
defensively doesn't surprise me anymore," said Marlins fielding coach
Perry Hill. "His defense saves so many runs, it's like he gets what I call
'defensive RBIs' every game." Hill worked extensively with Castillo to
improve his defense. In a gesture of gratitude, the slick-fielding second
baseman gave Hill his first Gold Glove as a gift.

Serving primarily as a leadoff hitter, Castillo had little to no power.
He collected just 28 homers in 1,720 games and averaged a meager

total of 19 extra-base hits per year in portions of 15 seasons. But he put up steady batting averages, with numbers ranging from .263 to .334 during seasons in which he made at least 120 appearances. A streaky hitter, he compiled a 35-game skein in 2002—the longest by a second baseman (since matched by Chase Utley). He had a 22-game hitting streak in 1999.

There are many who would agree that Castillo is the greatest second baseman in Marlins history. At the start of the 2016 campaign, he held franchise records for hits, triples, walks, and stolen bases. Moreover, he set the Marlins single-game record for steals, with four. He was named team MVP by the South Florida chapter of the Baseball Writers' Association of America twice—in 1999 and 2002. A three-time All-Star, Castillo remained with the club until December 2005, when he was traded to Minnesota. He helped the Twins to a postseason appearance in 2006, and was hitting .304 at the time of his transfer to the Mets midway through the 2007 campaign.

Beset by injuries during most of his tenure in New York, Castillo had an excellent season in 2009, hitting .302, with a .387 on-base percentage. Plagued by foot problems the following year, he ended up being released before the 2011 campaign. He signed a minor-league contract with the Phillies but was cut in spring training. He was finished as a player after that. In 2016, he became eligible for the Hall of Fame in Cooperstown but received no votes.

Cesar Cedeno

Center Fielder/First Baseman

Cesar Cedeno was a 16-year-old unknown from Santo Domingo when he was discovered by Houston scouts Pat Gillich and Tony Pacheco in the fall of 1967. After combing the island looking for talent, the duo invited Cesar to attend a tryout in San Pedro, which was roughly 60 miles from Cedeno's home. When Gillich learned that a $1,000 offer from a St. Louis scout had already been rejected by Cesar's father, he seduced the elder Cedeno with a $3,000 bid. As the story goes, Gillich encountered the Cardinals scout outside of the Cedeno home immediately after inking the deal. "You're a few minutes too late," he gloated.

Cedeno's father didn't have much use for baseball. He wanted Cesar to help out at home and in the family store in Santo Domingo. But Cesar's mother was more supportive, allowing him to sneak off before his chores were complete. She secretly bought him a glove and shoes to play ball with.

Cedeno was only 17 years old when he joined the Appalachian League. He hit .374 and moved quickly up the ladder. In 1970, the Astros were considering sending him to a Triple-A affiliate when a member of Houston's farm staff advised against it, insisting that Cedeno was "too good for Triple-A." The Astros found out firsthand when he hit .373, with 61 RBIs in 54 games, at Oklahoma City. Cedeno earned a call to the majors at 19 years of age.

The speedy outfielder arrived as a five-tool player, hitting for average and power, stealing bases in bunches, and drawing a fair amount of walks. He also had wide range and a powerful arm in center field. Comparisons to the all-time greats were inevitable. Leo Durocher claimed that Cedeno was better than Willie Mays. Harry "The Hat" Walker asserted that he would outshine Roberto Clemente. Yogi Berra insisted that he would lead Houston to a World Series someday. Although none of those predictions proved accurate, Cedeno had an outstanding career.

Between 1972 and 1976, Cedeno made four All-Star appearances and won five consecutive Gold Gloves. He stole at least 50 bases in six straight seasons, peaking at 61 steals in 1977. Sportswriters and fans began referring to the Astrodome as "Cesar's Palace." But an ugly incident before the 1974 slate altered Cedeno's career trajectory.

After hitting .320 with 25 homers and 56 steals during the 1973 campaign, Cedeno spent a portion of the winter in Santo Domingo. He met his mistress at a seedy hotel one day and, after consuming an ample portion of alcohol, got into a dispute about a gun he had purchased for protection. The woman was carelessly playing with the pistol when Cedeno tried to wrestle it away from her. In the ensuing struggle, the weapon accidentally discharged, killing the woman. Instead of notifying the authorities, Cedeno panicked and fled the scene, waiting several hours to turn himself in. Because he was a famous ballplayer who invoked a sense of national pride, he was given a ridiculously lenient sentence—20 days in jail and a $100 fine. Although the incident was kept under wraps by Houston's PR department, word slowly spread.

Cedeno was heckled by fans sporadically for years. He finally lost his composure in 1981, climbing into the stands to assault a man who had been shouting insults at him for several days.

While Cedeno set career highs in homers (26) and RBIs (102) during the 1974 slate, he never came close to matching the .320 average and 69 extra-base hits he had accrued two seasons earlier. In 1977, sportswriter Peter Gammons wrote, "[Cedeno] will end up with decent statistics, but statistics are for people who don't know anything. He's never been the same hitter since that incident." As Cedeno's numbers began to fall back to earth, teammate Bob Watson offered an alternate theory about the slugger's slow decline, explaining, "He altered his swing trying to hit homers. After that, maybe pitchers adjusted, and he hasn't readjusted himself." In 1977, the outfield fences in the Astrodome were moved back to discourage home runs, and a string of injuries curtailed Cedeno's production. In 1978, Cedeno tore a ligament in his knee. In 1979, he contracted hepatitis. The following year, he broke his ankle. The Astros finally gave up on him, trading him to the Reds in December 1981.

Even in the latter stages of his career, many of the five tools Cedeno possessed were still evident. In 1984, he gathered seven assists in 77 outfield appearances, putting him on pace to challenge the league leaders had he played full time. In August 1985, the Cardinals picked up Cedeno from the Reds to fill in for the injured Jack Clark at first base. It would prove to be one of the greatest late-season acquisitions in history, as Cedeno hit .434, with six homers and 19 RBIs down the stretch, helping St. Louis to a World Series appearance. The following year, Cedeno was signed by the Blue Jays and released after spring training. He ended up joining the Dodgers but was cut loose in June. It was his last major-league season.

Cedeno played in the Senior Professional Baseball Association in 1989–1990. He later served as a minor-league coach for the Washington Nationals and Astros. He also worked as a hitting instructor in the Dominican Winter League and Venezuelan Winter League. In his *Historical Baseball Abstract*, renowned statistician Bill James assigns Cedeno an all-time ranking of 21st among center fielders.

Francisco Cordero

Pitcher

Francisco Cordero can trace his origins to Santo Domingo—the Dominican's capital city. He attended Colegio Luz Arroyo Hondo High School and was signed by Detroit at the age of 19. Enamored with his mid-90s fastball and hard slider, the Tigers experimented with him as a starter in the minors. It was an epic fail, and by 1997, Cordero was appearing exclusively in relief. He picked up six wins and 35 saves in the Midwest League that year, warranting a promotion to the Double-A level.

Cordero, known to many as "CoCo," made his big-league debut in 1999. He entered 20 games, averaging a strikeout and a hit per inning. Before he could get comfortable in Detroit, he was packaged in a nine-player deal and shipped to Texas. It was there that he emerged as a star.

After struggling to find the plate in 2000 and 2001, Cordero learned to spot his pitches. In 2002, he posted a 2–0 record, with 10 saves and a 1.79 ERA. When closer Ugueth Urbina faltered in 2003, manager Buck Showalter began turning to Cordero to get the job done. By 2004, Cordero had assumed full-time closing responsibilities. He had an All-Star season, collecting 49 saves—second in the league to Mariano Rivera. Although he was passed over for the All-Star Team the following year, Cordero had another excellent campaign, averaging more than 10 strikeouts per nine innings and gathering 37 saves—the sixth-best mark in the AL. He struggled in the spring of 2006, losing his job to Akinori Otsuka. In late July, he was traded to the Brewers. The change of scenery worked wonders, as he went 3–1, with a 1.69 ERA the rest of the way.

In 2007, Cordero set a franchise record for saves with 44, earning his second All-Star selection. Granted free agency at season's end, the Reds outbid the Brewers for his services. The four-year, $46 million deal was one of the most lucrative ever offered to a reliever. Cordero didn't disappoint, averaging 38 saves per year during the life of the contract. He entered 283 games and compiled a highly creditable 2.96 ERA. His best year with the Reds came in 2009, when he compiled a 2.16 ERA and made his third All-Star appearance. He pitched a scoreless ninth for the NL squad, retiring Brandon Inge, Carl Crawford, and Justin Morneau in order.

By 2012, Cordero was in his late 30s and had put on a significant amount of weight. His fastball had lost a lot of its pop, topping out at 90 miles per hour, as opposed to the 94 he had consistently reached earlier in his career. The Blue Jays signed him but let him go in July of that year. The Astros followed suit in September. Determined to play another season, Cordero went on a strict diet and lost two pants sizes. In the 2013 Dominican Winter League, he compiled a 2.13 ERA in 16 appearances. It was enough to spark the interest of the Red Sox, who signed him to a minor-league contract. "I got released and said to myself, 'If I can pitch, this isn't the way to go,'" Cordero told a reporter during spring training. "I don't want to leave the bad taste in my mouth." His comeback attempt ultimately failed, as the BoSox released him shortly before the 2014 campaign.

During the height of his career, Cordero purchased a five-story townhouse that offered views of downtown Cincinnati. In 2014, he sold the 6,600-square-foot home at a significant loss. He waited until 2015 to announce his retirement. He entered 800 games for six major-league teams and left with a 3.38 ERA. He ranks second in games finished (575) and first in saves (329) among Dominican-born players.

Tony Fernandez

Shortstop

Hailing from the baseball mecca of San Pedro de Macoris, Tony Fernandez was discovered by Blue Jays scout Epy Guerrero in 1979, and signed as an amateur free agent. In the Toronto farm system, he exceeded the .300 mark at the plate for three straight seasons, earning a 1983 call-up. With veteran Alfredo Griffin at shortstop, there was little chance of Fernandez becoming a full-time player. But the Jays were a team on the rise, and manager Bobby Cox was always looking for new talent. Promoted again in May 1984, Fernandez served mostly as Griffin's understudy. He also made a few appearances at third base—a position he would occupy full-time late in his career.

By 1985, the shortstop job was Fernandez's to lose. He played in 161 games, and showing off some of the skills that would eventually net him four Gold Gloves, he led the AL in assists. He also established himself as one of the best ninth-slot hitters in the league, fashioning a .289

average. Eventually, his bat would be deemed too valuable to bury at the bottom of the order. The Jays finished first in the AL East, taking on the Royals in the ALCS. Fernandez chipped in with eight hits and a pair of RBIs as Kansas City edged Toronto in seven games.

From 1986 to 1989, Fernandez established himself as one of the best shortstops in the league both offensively and defensively. He hit .294 in that span, while averaging 47 extra-base hits and 67 RBIs per year. He also stole 20 or more bases three times. Prior to 1986, the Gold Glove Award had been monopolized by Alan Trammel. Fernandez knocked Trammel off of his perch, capturing the honor in four consecutive seasons.

Fernandez was a tough customer, often playing through injuries. At one point, he appeared in 403 consecutive games—a Blue Jays record. In September 1987, he sustained a fractured elbow on a hard slide by Detroit's Bill Madlock. The two teams were locked in a tight pennant race that season, and the slide was characterized by some as "dirty." Without him in the lineup, the Jays faltered down the stretch, finishing second. In April 1989, Fernandez was involved in a terrifying on-field incident. After launching a grand slam in a game against the Rangers, he was subsequently hit in the face by a Cecilio Guante pitch. He underwent reconstructive surgery and was out for a month. He admitted that the two injuries sapped his courage a bit. "I think I am a more conservative shortstop now," he said years later.

Fernandez narrowly missed the Jays' championship season of 1992. He was traded to the Padres, along with Fred McGriff, in a blockbuster deal that brought Roberto Alomar and Joe Carter to Toronto. The Blue Jays reacquired Fernandez midway through the 1993 campaign, and he hit .306 down the stretch, helping the club to a second-straight pennant. Fernandez was among the most productive postseason hitters that year, driving in 10 runs as Toronto disposed of the White Sox and Phillies on their way to a repeat championship.

Fernandez became a nomad after that, playing for five different teams over his next six seasons. He sat out the entire 1996 slate with an elbow injury before returning for another stint in Toronto. Proving he could still hit with the best of them at 37 years of age, he carried a .400 average for three months. The Toronto press dubbed him "Mr. Gadget" for the odd-looking array of workout equipment he used. "This guy is a marvel," said manager Jim Fregosi. "When I was 37, I was D-U-N."

Fernandez finished the season at .328 and then defected to the Japanese Pacific League after a dispute with management. "Latin players should unite so we don't get stepped on in the United States," he griped to a reporter. "A player of my status, who's been in the game as long as I have, should be respected more." Despite those blustery words, the Toronto brass brought him back for a final curtain call in 2001. He hit .305 in 48 games.

Fernandez spent portions of 12 seasons with the Blue Jays. Through 2016, he was the franchise leader in hits and triples. He compiled a .333 postseason average while wearing a Toronto uniform. Recognized for his accomplishments, he was inducted into the Canadian Baseball Hall of Fame.

Julio Franco

Infielder/Designated Hitter

Julio Franco loved baseball so much, he kept playing it into his late 50s. In 2015, he signed a contract with a semipro team in Japan—the Ishikawa Million Stars. Serving as player-manager, he appeared in 10 of the club's first 14 games. "I wasn't planning on playing this much, but one of my best hitters got hurt, so I have to play first base or DH," said the 56-year-old Franco. "I want to play until I'm 66," he added. "That's the goal."

To get a better idea of just how long Franco has been around, one only needs to look at the beginning and end points of his major-league career. When he made his big-league debut with the Phillies in 1982, he was sharing a clubhouse with Pete Rose, Steve Carlton, and Sparky Lyle. By the time he made his last appearance in "The Show" at age 49, his teammates included Mark Teixeira, Jeff Francoeur, and Brian McCann. Only six men have appeared in a major-league game at a more advanced age. None were everyday players. In 2004, Franco surpassed Cap Anson as the oldest regularly appearing positional player in history. To date, his baseball career has spanned five decades.

Franco was born in Hato Mayor del Rey—a cattle-raising district. His family moved to Consuelo when he was still a child. Like many Dominican youths, he dreamed of making it to the big leagues. He took his first significant step in that direction when he joined the Phillies organization in 1978. After spending the better part of five seasons in the minors, he was invited to Philadelphia. He hit .276 in a 16-game stint and was packaged in a six-player deal that landed him in Cleveland for the 1983 campaign. By the time he was finished, he had played for more than a quarter of the teams in the majors.

Franco gained a lot of attention throughout the years for his unusual batting style. In 2013, when he became eligible for the Hall of Fame in Cooperstown, one journalist suggested that his batting stance should be inducted as a separate entity. A right-handed hitter, Franco stood pigeon-toed at the plate with his feet apart and his knees close together. He crouched slightly, holding the bat high above his head and pointing in a straight line toward third base. "From the side, Franco's stance always made it look like he needed to use the bathroom immediately," remarked the aforementioned reporter.

Strange as it was, the stance served Franco well during his 23 seasons in the majors. A three-time All-Star and five-time recipient of the Silver Slugger Award, he hit .286 or better for eight straight seasons. He enjoyed his finest year at the plate in 1991, with the Rangers, when he won the AL batting crown with a .341 mark. A serious knee injury kept him out of action for most of the 1992 slate, dropping his average to .234, but he reached the .300 plateau four more times after that. Franco had moderate power, peaking at 20 homers in 1994. He also had good speed, stealing 30 or more bases on four occasions. Proving he could still run well for an older guy, he swiped 15 bases at the age of 38.

Defensively, Franco was as versatile as they come, spending time at six different positions. He played more than 500 games at three stations—shortstop, second base, and first base. He was competent at each, although he led the AL twice in errors as a shortstop. As he began to age out, he spent most of his time as a designated hitter. He also served extensively as a pinch-hitter, accruing a lifetime .277 average in that role.

Franco's postseason experience was rather extensive. Although he never appeared in a World Series, he played in the NLCS twice—once with the Braves and again with the Mets. In 31 playoff contests, he reached base by hit or walk 28 times. He had a few memorable All-Star moments as well. His two-run double off of Rob Dibble in the 1990 All-Star Game accounted for all the AL's runs and netted him MVP honors.

Franco completed his last major-league season in 2007, before traveling far and wide. He managed in the Gulf Coast League, Mexican League, and Venezuelan Winter League. He also played professionally in Japan and Korea. If he continues until age 66, as he jokingly predicted, he will finally hang up his spikes in 2025.

Pedro Guerrero

Infielder/Outfielder

Guerrero (no relation to Vladimir) was born in San Pedro de Macoris. The community was impoverished, and most residents could only aspire to a career in the sugar cane fields. Guerrero left school in his early teens to harvest cane for the country's rum industry. His paltry salary of $3 per week helped support his divorced mother and siblings. The grueling work made him durable and muscular.

On weekends, Guerrero played in local youth baseball leagues, serving mostly as a third baseman. As word of his talent began to spread, he was scouted by Reggie Otero of the Indians. Otero was a bit put off by Guerrero's slender frame but knew the youngster would eventually fill out. In late 1972, Guerrero accepted a $2,500 signing bonus. He hit .255 in his Gulf Coast debut at the age of 17. In April 1974, he was traded to the Dodgers.

In the Los Angeles farm system, Guerrero began crushing the ball. Between 1975 and 1978, his averages ranged from .305 to .403. Proving he could handle major-league pitching, he went 5-for-8 in a 1978 September call-up. Guerrero was capable at first and third base, but the Dodgers were well stocked at those positions, with Steve Garvey and Ron Cey making perennial All-Star appearances. Guerrero's .333 showing in the PCL during the 1979 slate prompted the Dodgers to promote him again. He would remain in LA for the next eight seasons.

In 1980, Guerrero was used at six different positions. By 1981, he found himself splitting time between the outfield and third base. During his 15 years in the majors, Guerrero manned every outfield station at least 100 times. He had extensive range in his younger years and finished among the top five in fielding percentage twice. He was less skilled at the hot corner, where he led the league with 30 errors in 1983.

Guerrero became a staple in the LA lineup after his masterful performance in the 1981 World Series. He hit .333, with four extra-base hits and seven RBIs, as the Dodgers avenged consecutive losses to the Yankees in 1977–1978. Guerrero was named MVP of the Series.

The hard-hitting Dominican would go on to establish himself as one of the most productive hitters of the 1980s. Renowned statistician Bill James once referred to him as the "best hitter God has made in a long time." A five-time All-Star, Guerrero hit .300 or better in seven seasons. A reliable RBI man, he reached the century mark in that category three times. He enjoyed his finest all-around campaign in 1985, when he compiled a .320 average while leading the league in on-base and slugging percentage. He also clubbed a career-high 33 homers that year, finishing third in MVP voting—a position he would occupy three times during his career.

In 1986, Guerrero ruptured a tendon in his knee on the last day of spring training. He sat out most of the season. Upon returning to full-time duties the following year, he suffered from limited mobility. This prompted a defensive switch to first base. Guerrero ended up clashing with his outfield replacement, Kirk Gibson, who was known for his cockiness. Bad chemistry in the Dodgers clubhouse incited the club to trade Guerrero to the Cardinals in August 1988. In his first full season with the club, Guerrero hit .311, with 117 RBIs. He also led the NL with 42 doubles. He had two more productive seasons with St. Louis before going into decline. He was out of the majors after the 1992 slate. He continued in the minors through 1995, hitting .302 at the age of 39.

When his playing days were over, Guerrero managed briefly in the Pacific Association. He suffered a cerebral hemorrhage in 2015, but fully recovered, joining the Ogden Raptors coaching staff the following year. He also coached the Dominican national team in the 2015 Pan American Games.

Vladimir Guerrero

Right Fielder

Vladimir Guerrero has nine siblings. He and his brother Wilton ascended to the majors in the same season and were teammates for three years. Vladimir hung around the majors much longer and assembled a far more impressive resume. Born in Nizao, in the southern region of the Dominican Republic along the coast, Guerrero's initial tryout was memorable. Since his family was too poor to provide him with proper equipment, he showed up in street clothes. After taking a few swings and making solid contact, he pulled a hamstring running to first. Despite the mishap, scout Arturo DeFreites offered him a contract. The Expos weren't sure what to do with their new prospect, so they tried Guerrero at several positions, including pitcher. He eventually settled in the outfield.

Named Minor League Player of the Year in 1996, Guerrero was included in a wave of September call-ups. He hit poorly in a nine-game trial but fared so well in spring training the following year, the Expos traded budding slugger Cliff Floyd to make room for him. Floyd had several excellent seasons elsewhere, while Guerrero became one of the most celebrated players in Expos history. Referred to by some as "Vlad the Impaler," Guerrero had little patience at the plate, averaging just 46 walks per year during his 16 seasons in the majors. A notorious "bad-ball hitter," he swung at anything he could reach and was known to make contact with balls in the dirt.

Guerrero's years with the Expos coincided with the club's slow decline. The front office was unwilling or unable to build a solid team around him, and he ended up carrying the club for the better part of six seasons. He is the Expos' all-time leader in home runs, batting average, and slugging percentage. He also holds the record for most homers at Olympic Stadium, with 126.

With the exception of the 2003 campaign, when Guerrero sat out 50 games, he drove in more than 100 runs each year from 1998 to 2007. He exceeded the .300 mark at the plate in 12 straight seasons and was a 30/30 man twice. He narrowly missed joining the 40/40 club in 2002, finishing with 39 homers and 40 steals. In game 161 of the season, he hit a ball that caromed off the top of the center-field wall and back onto the field. Remarkably, the 2002 campaign wasn't even Guerrero's best. He hit .337 with the Angels in 2004, leading the league in runs scored (124) and total bases (366). He was named MVP on the strength of that performance. Guerrero enjoyed numerous accolades throughout the years, including nine All-Star selections and eight Silver Slugger Awards. He was named Player of the Week on 10 occasions. In 2010, he

received the Edgar Martinez Award, which is given to the best designated hitter in the majors.

Guerrero left the Expos in 2004, taking a slight pay cut. He won the
2007 Home Run Derby. Two years later, he delivered an Opening Day
RBI (the 19th of his career), breaking a record he had shared with
Frank Robinson and Jeff Kent. Traded to Texas in 2010, he put forth
his last 100-RBI effort. He played for the Orioles the following year,
becoming the all-time hits leader among Dominican-born players. His
lifetime total has since been surpassed by Adrian Beltre.

Guerrero was out of the majors in 2012 and 2013. The Angels signed
him to a one-day contract the following year so he could retire as a
member of the club. He was chosen to throw out the first pitch on
Opening Day, but the ceremony was marred by an unfortunate incident, when coach Don Baylor, who was assigned to catch Guerrero's
toss, twisted his leg in the process and sustained a broken femur.

Guerrero never played for the Dominican national team. Shortly
before the 2006 World Baseball Classic, he lost three cousins in a car
accident and took a leave of absence. He removed himself from the
roster in 2009, which was an injury-plagued season for him. In February
2016, he competed in a home run derby during the Caribbean Series.
Although he lost in the first round, he was a big hit with fans and
members of the Cuban team, many of whom wanted their pictures
taken with him. Guerrero's son, Vladimir Jr., is a top prospect in the
Blue Jays organization. In addition, three of his cousins are minor leaguers. If Guerrero makes the Hall of Fame in Cooperstown, he will
likely be inducted as a member of the Angels since the Expos are
defunct. He became eligible in 2016.

Juan Marichal

Pitcher

Describing Juan Marichal's unique pitching style, one researcher offered the following words: "First the leg . . . the glove . . . the hand . . .
the pitch. Like a cobra mesmerizing a mongoose, Juan Marichal hypno-
tized hitters with a striptease-like delivery that made his pitches difficult to follow, much less hit." He had five pitches in his arsenal and was
not in the habit of studying his opponents' weaknesses. "I don't know

any hitters," he once said. "Catcher, he tells me what to do. I can get anything I want over the plate." His artful delivery and pinpoint control earned him the nickname the "Dominican Dandy."

Born in the farming village of Laguna Verde, Marichal was the youngest of four children. The house he grew up in had no electricity. When he was just a boy, he fell into a coma for nine days and was not expected to live. His family nursed him back to health with steam baths. Doctors attributed the illness to poor digestion. From the age of six, Marichal dreamed of forging a career as a ballplayer. He claimed to have mastered a curve by the time he was 10. He began as a shortstop but switched to pitching when he saw Dominican national team standout Bombo Ramos perform. Marichal was enamored with Ramos's sidearm style and adopted it as his own. He dropped out of school in 1956, to play for the United Fruit Company team. He was signed by the Giants the following year.

While pitching for the Class A Springfield Giants, one of Marichal's coaches suggested he try throwing overhand. Marichal was hesitant at first, but when the same coach assured him he would be more effective against lefties, he was willing to give it a shot. The only way he felt comfortable was to add a high leg kick, which became his signature move. He began the 1960 campaign at the Triple-A level, and after compiling an 11–5 record in 18 games, he was added to San Francisco's roster. A sign of the wonderful things to come, he tossed a one-hit shutout against the Phillies in his July debut. He would remain at the major-league level for the next 15 seasons.

At the peak of his career, Marichal had a diverse array of offerings that included a fastball, change, curve, screwball, and late-breaking slider. Extremely durable, he completed 53 percent of his lifetime starts. There were stretches in which Marichal was virtually unhittable. He won 10 consecutive decisions in 1966 and 1968. His no-hitter against the Dodgers in June 1963 was the first by a Giant since Carl Hubbell's 1929 gem. On July 2 of that season, he squared off against Warren Spahn in what many consider to be the greatest game ever pitched. Only 16,000 fans were on hand at Candlestick Park to see Spahn and Marichal match zeroes for 15 innings. Willie Mays finally ended the epic duel with a walk-off homer. Marichal's 16-inning shutout will likely be the last of its kind in the majors.

From 1963 to 1969, Marichal was a 20-game winner on six occasions. He led the league twice in victories and made the All-Star Team each year during that span. He was named MVP of the 1965 Midsummer Classic and compiled a 0.50 ERA in 18 innings of All-Star action. Despite his success, however, he never captured a Cy Young Award. Even in 1966, when he posted a 25–6 record, with a 2.23 ERA, he was overlooked. Among Dominican-born players, Marichal is the all-time leader in wins, complete games, and shutouts. He ranked second in strikeouts at the time of this writing (although Bartolo Colon is approaching his lifetime mark).

During the 1960s, the Giants and Dodgers engaged in tight pennant races almost every year. In 1965, the two front-runners were slugging it out yet again, and tempers were wearing thin. Facing the Dodgers on August 22, Marichal issued a pair of knockdown pitches in the early innings. When he came to bat against Sandy Koufax, catcher John Roseboro called for retaliation. Koufax refused, but Roseboro deliberately fired a ball back to the mound that grazed Marichal's ear. The Giants ace went ballistic, clubbing Roseboro over the head with his bat and opening up a cut that required stitches. Marichal was suspended for nine games and fined a modest $1,750. The incident haunted him for years.

In 1970, Marichal had a severe reaction to penicillin that caused him chronic back pain and severe arthritis. He bounced back in 1971, but began a rapid decline after that. Without the velocity of his earlier years, he compiled an 11–15 record in 1973. He made sporadic appearances during the next two seasons and finished his career with his old rivals—the Dodgers.

Eligible for the Hall of Fame in 1981, Marichal was passed over on the first two ballots. Fearing the ugly incident of 1965 had permanently blemished his reputation, he asked for help from John Roseboro, who made a personal appeal to the BBWAA. It must have worked, because Marichal was elected on the next try. The hurler thanked Roseboro during his induction speech. When Roseboro died in 2002, Marichal was an honorary pallbearer. "Johnny's forgiving me was one of the best things that happened in my life," Marichal told the assembly of mourners. "I wish I could have had John Roseboro as my catcher."

After his playing days, Marichal worked as a broadcaster for Spanish radio. His number 27 was retired by the Giants. In 2005, a statue of him was erected outside AT&T Park in San Francisco. In addition to Cooperstown, Marichal was inducted into the Hispanic Heritage Baseball Museum Hall of Fame.

Pedro Martinez

Pitcher

Born in Manoguayabo, a suburban neighborhood in Santo Domingo, Pedro Martinez is the fifth of six children. His family lived in a tin-roofed house with dirt floors. Martinez's parents were manual laborers, and as soon as he was old enough, Pedro landed a job as a mechanic to help out financially. Baseball ran in the Martinez family's blood. Pedro's father had been a star pitcher in the Dominican Republic during the 1950s. And his older brother Ramon arrived in the majors when Pedro was in his mid-teens.

In 1990, Ramon had a breakout season with the Dodgers, collecting 20 wins and leading the league with 12 complete games. By then, Pedro had made his pro debut with a Los Angeles affiliate in the Pioneer League. Ramon boasted to manager Tom Lasorda about his brother's pitching prowess, but Lasorda was ambivalent on account of Pedro's smallish frame. Ramon was no imposing figure himself, at 6-foot-4, 165 pounds, but Pedro weighed roughly the same and was much shorter.

In 1992, Pedro joined his older brother in Los Angeles. It was a tough year for Ramon, as he sustained a late-season injury and sat out the final month of the season. Pedro debuted in late September, making one relief appearance and one start—a quality outing against the Reds. The Dodgers staked him to a single run, and he absorbed the loss.

The 1993 season was busy for the Martinez brothers. Together, they entered 97 games and gathered 20 wins. Ramon struggled with his control, leading the league in walks. Pedro pitched almost exclusively out of the bullpen, posting a 2.61 ERA and averaging 10 strikeouts per nine frames. The Dodgers finished fourth that season and, looking to strengthen their infield, traded Pedro Martinez to the Expos for second baseman Delino DeShields.

Inserted into Montreal's starting rotation, Martinez developed a reputation as a hothead. In 24 games, he hit 11 batters (a league high) and was ejected 12 times. He also got into several fistfights. During one of his starts, he carried a perfect game into the eighth before hitting Reds outfielder Reggie Sanders with a pitch. Sanders charged the mound and was subsequently ejected. Martinez finished the strike-shortened season at 11–5, with a 3.42 ERA. Montreal fans loved his competitive spirit and adopted him as their own.

On June 3, 1995, Martinez pitched nine perfect innings against the Padres. Had the Expos not waited until the top of the 10th to score a run, the game would have been historic. But Martinez gave up a double to Bip Roberts in the bottom of the frame and settled for a one-hit shutout.

Martinez's best season in Montreal came in 1997, when he led the NL with a 1.90 ERA and 13 complete games. His 17 wins couldn't prevent the Expos from finishing fourth, but he was rewarded for his efforts with the first of three Cy Young Awards. Having officially "arrived," Pedro knew he deserved a significant pay raise. Unable to meet his needs, the Expos traded him to the Red Sox for two top pitching prospects. Martinez eventually inked a six-year deal with Boston worth $75 million—the most lucrative contract ever offered to a pitcher at the time.

Pedro enjoyed his prime years with the Red Sox, winning 117 games in a seven-year span. He captured a Triple Crown in 1999, with a 23–4 record, a 2.07 ERA, and 313 strikeouts. He followed with a second-straight Cy Young season, posting a career-best 1.74 ERA. He missed out on the MVP Award that year in a controversial election. Although he received more first-place votes than Rangers catcher Ivan Rodriguez, he was left off of two ballots.

Martinez's success with the Red Sox was remarkable given that Fenway Park has long been considered an ideal hitter's venue. In fact, before Martinez, only two other Boston players had captured a Cy Young—Jim Lonborg and Roger Clemens. Martinez employed a tailing fastball, an elusive changeup, and a biting curve. He threw from a low angle and hid the ball well from opponents. Renowned for his intensity, he wasn't shy about throwing inside. "Some people are a little afraid of Pedro, and that helps him," said Cubs manager Lou Piniella. Yankees first baseman Jason Giambi was always a bit leery about where he stood in the box when facing Martinez. "If you lean over the plate, he'll stick one up your nose," the slugger groused. Despite his intense on-field persona, Pedro was pretty easygoing. "He stares at hitters and pumps his fist when he pitches," observed pitcher Tom Glavine, "but that's all part of his competitive nature. After the game, he's back to being humble."

During Pedro's days in Boston, the Yankees finished ahead of the Red Sox in the standings each year. Boston hadn't won a World Series since 1918, and there was incessant talk about a Babe Ruth curse. Asked about it one day, Pedro snapped, "I don't believe in any damn curses. Wake up the damn Bambino and have me face him. Maybe I'll drill him in the ass." Feelings of frustration boiled over in game three of the 2003 ALCS, when Pedro got into a tussle with 72-year-old Yankees coach Don Zimmer. During a bench-clearing brawl, Zimmer came rushing at Martinez, who promptly threw the older man to the ground.

There were times when Martinez was dominant against the Yankees, but he took his share of tough losses as well. After a disappointing outing against the Bombers late in the 2004 campaign, Martinez provided fodder for fans when he remarked, "I just tip my hat and call the Yankees my daddy." The quote was widely circulated, and after that, whenever Pedro pitched in the Bronx, chants of "Who's your daddy?" filled the stadium. Martinez insisted that the cool reception from Yankees fans made him feel important. "[If] you reverse the time back 15 years ago, I was sitting under a mango tree without 50 cents for a bus," he commented. Although he yielded nine runs to the Yankees in the 2004 ALCS, the season ended on a high note when the Red Sox finally captured a championship. Facing the Cardinals in Game Three of the World Series, Pedro tossed seven brilliant innings, getting the win. It was his last appearance with Boston.

Martinez spent portions of five more seasons in the majors after that, nursing injuries a great deal of the time. He assembled a 37–24 record, with an un-Pedro-like 3.86 ERA, from 2005 to 2009. His last big-league appearances came against the dreaded Yankees in the 2009 World Series. He turned in a quality start for the Phillies in Game Two but lasted just four innings in the sixth contest, getting saddled with his second loss of the Series. Discounting those two performances, Pedro was 6–2 in postseason play, with a highly serviceable 3.40 ERA.

After his retirement, Martinez joined the Red Sox as a special assistant to GM Ben Cherington. He was elected to the Cooperstown Hall of Fame in 2015. That same year, he was hired as a studio analyst for the

MLB Network. His autobiography, *Pedro*, was coauthored by *Boston Herald* writer Michael Silverman. An eight-time All-Star, Martinez holds the lifetime record for strikeouts per nine innings among players with a minimum of 1,500 innings pitched (10.20). He also has the highest career winning percentage among hurlers with at least 200 decisions. He is the only pitcher in history to gather 3,000 strikeouts in less than 3,000 innings.

Jose Mesa

Pitcher

The literal translation of Jose Mesa's name—"Joe Table"—became his nickname. Born in Pueblo Viejo, he was signed by the Blue Jays at the age of 15 and came to the United States in 1982. Groomed as a starter in the minors, he suffered through some serious control problems. Playing for the Kinston Jays in 1985, he averaged 6.7 walks per nine innings. Two years later, while stationed in the Atlantic League, he issued 104 free passes in 193 innings. He continued his path to the majors nevertheless.

Mesa remained a starter during his first five big-league seasons. He was not terribly effective in the role, compiling a 27–40 record, with an inflated ERA. He was traded twice in that stretch, eventually ending up in Cleveland. At the beginning of the 1994 slate, the Indians were still reeling from the tragic loss of relievers Steve Olin and Tim Crews in a boating accident the year before. With the bullpen in a transitional state, manager Mike Hargrove decided that Mesa might be more effective in smaller doses. He was spot-on in that assessment.

After posting the lowest ERA of his major-league career during the 1994 slate, Mesa followed with one of the finest seasons ever by an Indians reliever. He led the league in games finished (57) and saves (46), while posting a minuscule 1.13 ERA. The Indians clinched the division title that year, and Mesa closed three of four victories over Seattle in the ALCS. He picked up a win and a save in the World Series, but it wasn't enough, as the Braves prevailed in six games. The blow was softened somewhat for Mesa when he was named Rolaids Relief Man of the Year. *Sporting News* also recognized him as the AL's top reliever.

Mesa made his second career All-Star appearance in 1996, as the Indians coasted to a first-place finish, earning the right to face the Orioles in the ALDS. With his team on the brink of elimination in game four, Mesa was called upon to protect a 3–2, ninth-inning lead. He faltered, yielding a game-tying single to Roberto Alomar. Having emptied out his bullpen at that point, Mike Hargrove left Mesa in the game. After pitching two scoreless innings, the big right-hander got burned again by Alomar, who launched a game-winning homer. It was a disappointing finish to an otherwise successful season.

The 1997 campaign was even more frustrating for Mesa. While he posted a stellar 2.40 ERA during the regular season, he blew saves in consecutive games of the ALCS. His performance in the World Series wasn't much better. With the Indians on the verge of capturing their first championship in 50 years, he allowed the Marlins to tie the game in the ninth. He pitched a scoreless 10th before giving way to Charles Nagy, who promptly surrendered the winning run. Some chose to dwell on Mesa's epic fail. In his autobiography, *Omar! My Life on and off the Field*, former teammate Omar Vizquel remembers the moment as follows: "The eyes of the world were focused on every move we made. Unfortunately, Jose's eyes were almost vacant. Completely empty. Nobody home. Jose's first pitch bounced five feet in front of the plate and, as every Cleveland fan knows, things got worse from there." Mesa took exception to those words and vowed to hit Vizquel every time he faced him. He made good on the threat more than once and has not spoken to Vizquel since the book's publication.

When he got off to a 3–4 start with a 5.17 ERA in 1998, the Indians traded Mesa to the Giants, who let him go at season's end. He saved 33 games for the Mariners the following year, but after a weak encore in 2000, he again was cast adrift.

For a large portion of his career, Mesa sported a long, black goatee. During the height of his popularity, he had a fan club known as "Mesa's Faces," who wore fake goatees and danced when he struck out a batter or saved a game. While playing for the Phillies in 2001, he won back the appreciation of fans when he saved 42 games. Proving it was no fluke, he added 45 saves in 2002. But the notoriously fickle fan base in Philly let him have it the following year when he stumbled to a 5–7 record, with a 6.52 ERA. As the boos rained down on Mesa, manager Larry Bowa stopped using him during home games.

The Pirates acquired Mesa at a bargain-basement price before the 2004 slate. Again, the veteran reliever revived his career, gathering 43 saves (fifth best in the league), while compiling a respectable 3.25 ERA. He was off to a hot start in 2005, with 21 saves, before the All-Star break but ultimately lost the closer's job when he slumped down the stretch.

In 2006, the Rockies lured Mesa to dreaded Coors Field—an infamous hitter's park. At 40 years of age, he made 79 appearances and posted a 3.86 ERA—not bad for Colorado. The following year, he became the 11th hurler to appear in 1,000 games. His last season in the majors was spent with the Tigers and Phillies. His 7.11 ERA proved he had little left to offer. At the time of his retirement, he was ranked 12th on the all-time saves list. He was the all-time leader among Dominican-born players until Francisco Cordero surpassed him in 2011.

Raul Mondesi

Outfielder

Born in San Cristobal, Raul Ramon Mondesi Avelino was signed by the Dodgers in 1988, but he did not appear in the minors until two seasons later, when he was 19 years old. He climbed quickly through the Dodgers system and earned Rookie of the Year honors during the strike-shortened 1994 campaign. Mondesi was almost the complete package, hitting for power and average, while demonstrating good speed and an exceptionally strong arm. He was lacking a bit with a glove, however, leading the league in errors three times.

Mondesi hit the peak of his career in Los Angeles, averaging 29 homers and 90 RBIs between 1995 and 1999. His batting averages ranged from .253 to .310 during that span. He became the first Dodgers player to join the 30/30 club, which he accomplished in 1997, duplicating the feat two years later. He narrowly missed in 2001, finishing with 27 homers and 30 steals.

Despite his occasional lapses in the outfield, Mondesi was renowned for his rifle-like arm. He led the league in assists three times and finished with double-digit figures during five campaigns. His lifetime total is among the top marks of all time. A majority of the players ahead of him on the list played in the 1950s or earlier. Recognized for his defensive efforts, Mondesi won Gold Gloves in 1995 and 1997.

Before the 2000 slate, Mondesi was traded to the Blue Jays. He was off to a prodigious start before a ligament injury to his throwing arm forced him out of action. There was talk about him losing the most important aspect of his defensive game, but he successfully rehabbed, returning in late September. He finished the season with 24 homers and 67 RBIs in 96 games, which would have put him on target for a 40-homer, 100-RBI campaign had he remained healthy.

After another industrious season in 2001, his numbers tapered off. Looking to boost their outfield production, the Yankees signed him in July 2002. In 71 games, he gathered 11 homers and 43 ribbies, while demonstrating his powerful arm on occasion. Although he got off to a hot start in April of the following year, he eventually fell into a slump and was periodically benched by manager Joe Torre against certain pitchers. Mondesi griped to the press about losing playing time and said he did not want to be in New York as part of a platoon. After being pinch-hit for in a July game against the Red Sox, he stalked to the clubhouse, showered, and went home. He then skipped the team's West Coast flight the following day. Two days later, he was traded. Explaining the move, Yankees GM Brian Cashman said, "He was upset he was pinch-hit for, and he didn't stay and root [his teammates] on versus our rivals. He played hard between the lines, but I need our players to respect the manager's decision, even if they don't play." Mondesi finished the season with the third-place Diamondbacks, hitting .302 in 45 games.

Granted free agency after the 2003 slate, Mondesi signed with the Pirates. He was released in May after getting off to a somewhat slow start. Picked up by the Angels, he managed a feeble .118 average in eight appearances. The Braves took him on as a project in 2005, but ultimately gave up. Mondesi was out of the majors at the age of 34. He appeared on the Dominican national team roster for the Pan American Games in 2007, but didn't play.

Mondesi hit no fewer than 24 homers in nine consecutive seasons (1995–2003), putting him in elite company. In that same span, only Sammy Sosa, Barry Bonds, Jim Thome, Rafael Palmeiro, and Manny Ramirez turned the trick. Mondesi returned to his home country upon retiring and was later elected mayor of San Cristobal. Two of his sons played professionally, although neither had reached the major-league level at the time of this writing.

Manny Mota

Outfielder/Pinch-Hitter

Born in Santo Domingo, Manuel Rafael Mota Geronimo was the sixth of eight children. Mota's father was a soldier in the Dominican army and died when Manny was quite young, leaving him with the enduring nickname of "El Chory" (which translates loosely to "Shorty" or "Pee Wee"). Mota carried that nickname throughout his career in the Dominican Winter League, which spanned 20 seasons—the longest stretch of service in the circuit's history. His lifetime batting average of .333 was still the highest ever recorded at the time of this writing.

Manny attended a Catholic secondary school and became a devout Christian. Although he wasn't terribly serious about baseball as a kid, he ended up on the Dominican Air Force team, along with Juan Marichal and Matty Alou. The team was strictly run, and Mota said that he became a more disciplined player because of it.

In 1957, Mota was signed by the Giants. He hit .314 in the Midwest League that year and was promoted to the Class B level. Serving mostly as an outfielder, he dabbled a bit at second base. His minor-league career spanned portions of seven seasons and ended with a .304 batting average. Mota had an unsuccessful trial with the Giants in 1962, and was traded to the Houston Colt .45s in November. The following April, Houston dished him to the Pirates for an outfielder of little note. Mota got his first significant stretch of major-league playing time with Pittsburgh.

In 1963, Mota participated in the only Latin All-Star Game, which was the last game held at the Polo Grounds in New York. He picked up a pair of RBIs as the NL Hispanic Stars prevailed, 5–2. That winter, he won a Dominican batting title (one of several) with a .379 mark.

During his time in Pittsburgh, Mota became close friends with Hall of Famer Roberto Clemente, who identified with Mota's struggle to make a name for himself in American baseball. Clemente worked tirelessly with Mota on his hitting and fielding. Mota got a chance to show off what he had learned in 1964, entering 115 games and compiling a

.277 average primarily out of the second slot in the order. When manager Danny Murtaugh stepped down due to ill health, Mota got a chance to work with former NL batting champ Harry "The Hat" Walker. Walker taught him to keep the ball low and spray it to all fields. The results were noticeable, as Mota hit at a combined .326 pace in 1966–1967.

Mota was the Expos' second pick in the 1968 Expansion Draft, which took place in October. He was off to a .315 start at the plate in 1969, when Montreal traded him to Los Angeles, along with Maury Wills, for Ron Fairly and Paul Popovich. The righty-swinging outfielder would remain with the Dodgers organization for more than four decades.

After finishing the 1969 slate at .321, Mota kept his average above the .300 mark for the next four seasons. By 1974, the Dodgers lineup was packed with stars, and the starting outfield slots were all taken. At 36 years of age, Mota was still useful as a pinch-hitter. He remained in that role for the rest of his career and gained a reputation as one of the best. Dodgers fans loved him for his ability to come off the bench and drive in runs during the late innings of close games. Broadcaster Vin Scully once remarked that Mota could wake up on Christmas morning and hit a line drive to center field. Los Angeles sportswriter Jim Murray quipped that if you woke Mota up at 2 a.m., handed him a toothpick, and then tossed an aspirin tablet at him, he would hit it into right field for a single.

Teammates were amazed by Mota's durability. "He's scary," first baseman Steve Garvey once said. "I wish just one spring he would show up with one gray hair." In September 1979, Mota was called upon to hit for pitcher Jerry Reuss in a game against the Astros. At 41 years of age, he delivered a single—the 146th pinch hit of his career. It broke a long-standing record held by Smoky Burgess (although it has since been broken). Mota was invited to the White House that October to meet President Jimmy Carter.

The ageless Mota added three more pinch hits to his lifetime total before he retired as a player. In 497 pinch-hit appearances, he hit .300, with 115 RBIs. By way of comparison, baseball's current pinch-hit leader, Lenny Harris, hit .264, with 90 RBIs, in 883 appearances.

When his playing days were over, Mota served as a Dodgers coach until 2013. He remained with the Dodgers organization as a broadcaster for Spanish-language feeds of SportsNet LA. Mota and his wife run the Manny Mota Foundation, which has been providing assistance to disadvantaged Dominican youths and their families for more than 30 years. In 2003, he was inducted into the Hispanic Heritage Baseball Museum Hall of Fame and honored in a pregame ceremony at Dodger Stadium. Mota has four sons who played professionally. Jose and Andy made it to the majors. Gary was named MVP of the South Atlantic League in 1992. Tony had a brief and uneventful minor-league career.

David Ortiz

Designated Hitter

It was once believed that a designated hitter would never make it to the Hall of Fame. But Paul Molitor and Frank Thomas contradicted that assumption when they were inducted. Both spent significant portions of their careers in the DH slot. With the barrier officially removed, it's a safe bet that David Ortiz will follow Molitor and Thomas to Cooperstown. Plainly speaking, he was the best the game has ever seen.

Ortiz was born in Santo Domingo. The oldest of four children, he took inspiration from his father, who played extensively in the Dominican leagues. Ortiz's parents said he was the calmest, most easygoing member of the family. While attending high school at Estudia Espallat, he became a multisport star, focusing his efforts on baseball and basketball.

When the Seattle Mariners signed Ortiz in 1992, they incorrectly listed him as David Arias. Arias was his maternal family name. Although he accepted the moniker during his days in the Seattle farm system, he set the record straight after joining the Twins in September 1996. Ortiz was trained as a first baseman in the minors and proved to be a rather inept one. He made 20 errors in the PCL during the 1999 slate. In addition to his sloppy defensive play, he sustained wrist injuries in 1998 and 2001. The Twins promoted him several times in that span, but when he added knee problems to his list of maladies, they released him.

In 2002, the Red Sox employed a tandem of designated hitters. The most frequently used—Carlos Baerga—hit .286 in 73 games, with modest power numbers. Realizing they needed a little more punch, the Sox took a chance on Ortiz, who was still virtually unknown at the time.

After sitting out most of April and May, Ortiz hit eight homers in July and 11 in August, securing the starting job.

During the course of his long career, Ortiz's value to the Red Sox has been immense. "I know that great players are great, are supposed to be great in any moment," Boston GM Ben Cherington once said, "but it's hard to see [Ortiz] in those moments and not think there's something different about him . . . I can't add anything more to the legend that's already there. He keeps writing more chapters on his own."

Entering the 2016 campaign, Ortiz held multiple all-time records for designated hitters, including most hits, home runs, and RBIs. His 54 long balls in 2006 were the most by a Red Sox player at any position. Like the iconic BoSox greats before him (for example, Jimmie Foxx and Ted Williams), Ortiz made his homers count. Between 2003 and 2013, he launched 12 walk-off blasts. Two of them came in the postseason in extra innings, prompting Red Sox majority owner John Henry to label Ortiz the "greatest clutch hitter" in team history.

A 10-time All-Star, Ortiz reached the 100-RBI threshold on 10 occasions, leading the league twice. A measure of the respect given to him by opposing pitchers, he was intentionally walked 194 times through the 2015 slate. Although he struck out fairly often, he had a good feel for the strike zone, drawing 70 or more walks in eight consecutive seasons. When he crossed the plate after hitting a homer, Ortiz would point at the sky in memory of his mother, who passed away in 2002, at the age of 46.

After going without a championship for more than 80 years, the Red Sox captured three World Series titles during Ortiz's career. It was no coincidence, as the big slugger (6-foot-3, 230 pounds) put up gaudy numbers in the postseason—especially in the World Series. His performance in the 2013 Fall Classic is among the most impressive in history. During Boston's six-game win over the Cardinals, Ortiz went 11-for-16 at the plate, with seven runs scored and six driven in. He was named MVP. Entering the 2016 campaign, Ortiz was a .455 hitter in World Series play.

Had Ortiz been an ordinary hitter during his career, he still would have attained a measure of popularity in Boston. With his warm personality and engaging smile, he remained approachable to the press and fans throughout his career. After hitting a game-winning homer against the Yankees at Fenway Park in April 2016, he stopped to hug several youngsters who were sitting close to the field before returning to the dugout. In 2007, Ortiz started his own Children's Fund to support various causes in the Dominican and the United States. After the Boston Marathon bombing in 2013, he inspired local residents with the following statement: "This is our fucking city and ain't nobody going to dictate our freedom. Stay strong!"

Known affectionately to many as "Big Papi" or "Cookie Monster," Ortiz announced his impending retirement before the 2016 slate. John Henry showed his appreciation for everything Ortiz has done for the city, remarking,

> For the community, he has been the hero providing leadership off the field in ways that consistently make a difference—often completely unseen. And for those of us who have had the honor of knowing him all these years, he has been exactly what you hope to see in a man that has been the face of the organization.

Tony Pena

Catcher

Tony Pena's mother was a star softball player in the Dominican, and he gives her credit for teaching him how to play. He was raised in Monte Cristi, in the coastal lowlands near the border of Haiti. Surrounded by desert-like terrain, most of the town's inhabitants make their living farming or fishing.

Pena was signed by the Pirates as an amateur free agent in 1975. He came to the United States the following year and hit just .214 in the Gulf Coast League. A strong defensive prospect, his hitting came around in 1979, when he compiled a .313 batting average in 134 Eastern League games. Promoted to the PCL the following year, he swung the bat at a .327 clip, earning a summons to Pittsburgh. Aside from a brief rehab stint in 1987, he would remain at the major-league level for nearly two decades.

Pena had an unusual catching style. He sat on the ground with one knee tucked to the side and the other leg extended. He had a powerful arm and could throw out would-be basestealers without moving from that position. Throughout the years, he gained a reputation as one of the finest strategists in the sport. Few catchers called games as masterfully as Pena. He was behind the plate in 1,950 contests—sixth on the all-time list.

Pena was extremely enthusiastic about the sport, showing consistent hustle even when his teams slumped in the standings. Gracious and accommodating, he was popular among fans. His energy behind the plate netted him three consecutive Gold Glove Awards from 1983 to 1985. In 1991, he landed on a short list of catchers to capture the honor in both leagues. To date, Bob Boone is the only other backstop to turn the trick.

Pena hit for decent averages at the beginning of his career. As the Pirates' full-time catcher from 1981 to 1986, his marks ranged from .249 to .301. He had moderate power, putting up double-digit home run totals in six seasons. Even when he wasn't producing offensively, he found his way into the lineup. In 1993, manager Butch Hobson penciled him into 126 games despite his .181 batting average. Pena helped four different teams reach the postseason. His October numbers were impressive, especially in 1987, when he tagged opposing pitchers for 17 hits. In eight postseason series, Pena racked up a .338 batting average.

After spending time with six clubs in 18 seasons, Pena finally called it quits. His postplaying career has been quite eventful so far. He served as a minor-league manager for the White Sox and Astros. In 2002, he took over the helm of the Kansas City Royals, replacing John Mizerock before the All-Star break. The team fared poorly that year, but Pena turned things around in 2003, steering the club to a respectable third-place finish. His efforts did not go unnoticed, as he was named Manager of the Year.

Pena liked to keep his players loose. During a five-game losing streak in April 2004, he went into the showers in full uniform and soaped himself up. "I had to do something—make them laugh," he told reporters. As it turned out, laughter was not the best medicine, as the club lost 104 games, putting Pena's job in jeopardy. After an 8–25 start the following year, he voluntarily stepped aside as manager. Without him, the team crashed and burned, setting a new franchise record with 106 losses.

Pena was elected to the Latino Baseball Hall of Fame in 2012. He managed the Dominican national team to a perfect record in the 2013 World Baseball Classic. In 2016, he was elected to the Caribbean Baseball Hall of Fame. Tony and his wife Amaris have three children. Their son, Tony Jr., had brief stints with the Royals and Braves. Their other son, Francisco, made the majors as a catcher in 2014. Their daughter Jennifer is a beauty queen who won the Miss Dominican Republic pageant in 2007.

Placido Polanco

Second Baseman/Third Baseman

Placido Polanco was born in Santo Domingo—the largest city in the Dominican. He attended high school there and moved on to college at Miami Dade University. He didn't get much attention from scouts and ended up being signed by the Cardinals in a late round of the 1994 Amateur Draft.

While Polanco was skilled at both middle-infield stations, the Cardinals had those positions filled with veterans as he was climbing up the ladder. A youth movement in 1999 saw 22-year-old Edgar Renteria installed at shortstop. Polanco, just 23 years old, was platooned with Joe McEwing at second base. By 2000, Polanco had assumed full-time responsibilities. He hit .300 in two consecutive seasons and was off to a .284 start before the Cardinals dealt him to the Phillies with two other players in July 2002. Polanco had two separate stints in Philadelphia during his 16-year career. He also played for the Tigers and Marlins before retiring.

Although Polanco appeared in nine postseason series with three different teams, he managed to fly under the radar for most of his career. A free-swinger, he hit for high averages and rarely struck out, averaging one whiff per every 13 at-bats. While he was capable of hitting for power, peaking at 17 homers in 2004, more than 70 percent of his lifetime hits were singles. He was well-suited to the second spot in the batting order, where he logged most of his at-bats. He was a .301 hitter in that capacity. His best season at the plate came in 2007, with the Tigers, when he hit .341 (third best in the league) and stroked a career-high 36 doubles. It was a year of firsts, as he earned his first All-Star selection, his only Silver Slugger Award, and the first of three Gold Gloves.

Primarily a second baseman, Polanco appeared in more than 700 games at third. He led the league in fielding percentage three times at each station, and his lifetime mark is the highest at both. He is one of only two major leaguers to win a Gold Glove at two positions (Darin Erstad is the other). Detroit manager Jim Leyland once commented on Polanco's all-around ability, declaring, "He's obviously a sure-handed guy. I can't say it any better than what I've said: He's a true baseball player in every sense of the word. Some guys are athletes. Some guys are players. Sometimes, you've got a little bit of both."

Polanco was a vital component of three division-winning squads. He carried a .375 postseason average into the 2006 World Series with Detroit before falling into an 0-for-17 slump against Cardinals pitching. He was named MVP of the ALCS that year. In 38 playoff games, he reached base 50 times (excluding fielder's choices), scoring 11 runs and driving in 13.

Polanco celebrated his 38th birthday in 2014. Granted free agency by the Marlins, he was unable to land a contract with a major-league team. As of 2015, he considered himself "90 percent" retired, although he expressed his openness to a possible coaching position. In 2008, he became a naturalized U.S. citizen, taking his oath at Comerica Park before a game. Polanco's former teammate Albert Pujols is godfather to his son.

Aramis Ramirez

Third Baseman

Hailing from Santo Domingo, Aramis Ramirez is the only Aida Cartagena Portalatin High School alumnus to reach the majors to date. Signed by the Pirates in 1994, he made his pro debut at the age of 18, hitting .305 in the New York–Pennsylvania League. He was called up in 1998 and 1999, but failed both auditions. He enjoyed a breakthrough season in 2001, hitting an even .300 for Pittsburgh, with 74 extra-base hits and 112 RBIs.

In 2003, the Pirates were looking to trim costs, trading Ramirez and Kenny Lofton to the Cubs in July for three marginal players and cash. The longest-suffering franchise in the majors, the Cubs pinned their hopes on Ramirez and a handful of other young players. He entered the prime of his career between 2003 and 2008, helping the club to three playoff appearances. In 2003, the Cubs came within five outs of clinching their first pennant since the 1940s before an improbable Marlins rally turned the tide of the series. Ramirez had four homers and 10 RBIs in 12 postseason games that year.

A three-time All-Star, Ramirez was invited by NL manager Bruce Bochy to replace Placido Polanco at third base in the 2011 Midsummer Classic. He declined on account of plans he had made with his family. In addition to his three All-Star selections, Ramirez was named player of the week five times and finished among the top 10 in MVP voting on three occasions.

Ramirez's best offensive season came in 2006, when he gathered 80 extra-base hits and drove in a career-high 119 runs. Injuries plagued him throughout his career. He finished the 2005 season on the disabled list with a severe quadriceps strain. In 2009, he missed half the year with a dislocated shoulder. The following season, a bruised thumb kept him out of action for more than a month and dropped his fielding percentage to .939—the lowest among major league third basemen. The maladies didn't end there, as a sprained knee in 2013 sapped his power and eventually led to his retirement.

Ramirez put up strong offensive numbers despite his injuries, reaching the 100-RBI mark in seven seasons. He averaged 28 homers per year between 2001 and 2012. In the latter campaign, he led the NL with 50 doubles while playing for Milwaukee. Defensively, Ramirez improved throughout time, finishing among the top five in fielding percentage on six occasions. He led the league twice in that category.

After sitting out 70 games in 2013, Ramirez got off to a hot start the following year. His production stalled after the All-Star break, however, raising questions about the health of his knee. He announced his impending retirement before the 2015 campaign, and when he failed to return to form that year, the Brewers traded him back to the Pirates. In one of his last appearances at Wrigley Field, the Cubs honored him by presenting him with a number-16 placard from the center-field scoreboard (he had worn the number when he played in Chicago). "Any time they do something like that, you have to appreciate it," Ramirez said after the game. "That means they appreciate what I did here for a long time." He retired as a member of the Pirates. He has mentioned the possibility of returning to the game as a coach, but as of this writing, an opportunity has yet to materialize.

Manny Ramirez

Left Fielder

Manny Ramirez (no relation to Aramis) was one of the most colorful and enigmatic players of his generation. His puzzling behavior, which baffled fans and insiders for years, came to be known as "Manny Moments." But despite his involvement in a handful of regrettable incidents, he provided enough clutch performances to fill several highlight reels.

Manuel Aristides Ramirez Onelcida was born in Santo Domingo and spent 13 years of his childhood there. He was reportedly obsessed with baseball while growing up. In 1985, he moved with his family to Washington Heights in Manhattan. Although he lived a short distance from Yankee Stadium, he cheered for the Blue Jays. Ramirez spent five years in high school and never graduated. Described as a modest kid who avoided the spotlight, he led the George Washington High School baseball team to three division championships. The Indians were sufficiently impressed, picking him in the first round of the 1991 Amateur Draft.

Ramirez was a September call-up in 1993. While he hit just .170 in 22 games, manager Mike Hargrove saw his potential. In 1995, Ramirez formed a potent slugging tandem with fellow outfielder Albert Belle. Together, they launched 81 homers as the Indians made their first World Series appearance in four decades. Ramirez would help keep the team in contention throughout his tenure in Cleveland, which ended after the 2000 campaign.

During portions of 19 seasons in the majors, Ramirez clubbed 30 or more homers 12 times. He not only hit them often, but also far. He was particularly successful at the SkyDome in Toronto (now known as the Rogers Centre), where he hammered three balls that traveled in excess of 460 feet. On June 3, 2001, his shot off of Chris Carpenter reached the fifth deck in left field and was estimated to have sailed 493 feet. Incredibly, it wasn't even his longest home run of the year. On June 23, he launched a titanic 501-foot drive at Fenway Park—the second-longest drive in the stadium's storied history. Ramirez was enamored with his own blasts and would often loiter at the plate watching them. It was not uncommon to see him flip his bat, extend his arms dramatically, and saunter up the first-base line—habits he was widely criticized for.

Ramirez's swagger at the plate was not the only thing he was admonished for. The "Manny Moments" began occurring with frequency after he had established himself in Cleveland. In 1997, he received four tickets during a single traffic stop, the last one coming when he left the scene via an illegal U-turn. During the Red Sox championship seasons of 2004 and 2007, he skipped both team visits to the White House. Johnny Damon covered for Ramirez the first time, but when he failed to honor the second invitation, President George W. Bush remarked sarcastically, "I guess his grandmother died again." Other incidents were more comical—like the time he hauled in a drive by Orioles first baseman Kevin Millar at full speed and then climbed up the wall, high-fived a fan, and threw in time to double up Aubrey Huff. He was also known to regularly disappear inside the Green Monster at Fenway Park during mound conferences or pitching changes. One day, he allegedly failed to reemerge until a pitch was in mid-flight.

Despite the controversy, Manny kept being Manny at the plate. After gathering a career-high 165 RBIs with Cleveland in 1999, he spent seven full seasons with Boston, reaching the century mark in ribbies for six straight years. In 2004, he captured World Series MVP honors in Boston's four-game sweep of Colorado. He hit his 500th career homer in 2008, but clashed with teammate Kevin Youkilis and traveling secretary Jack McCormick, whom he pushed to the ground. His public apology did not prevent him from being traded to the Dodgers after the All-Star break.

In 2009, Ramirez received a 50-game suspension for using banned substances. His numbers went into decline, and he was traded to the White Sox partway through the 2010 campaign. He tried to avoid a second PED suspension the following year by announcing his retirement, but when Oakland signed him to a minor-league contract in 2012, he was mandated to sit out for 50 games. The A's never promoted him anyway.

Ramirez was active in the Dominican Winter League in 2012 and 2014, hitting at a combined .305 clip, with 10 homers in 66 games. In 2014, he served as a player-coach for the Iowa Cubs. He was hired by the parent club as a spring-training instructor in 2015, receiving praise from manager Joe Maddon for his work with young players. "I love having him here," said Maddon. "He's a positive, upbeat kind of guy and so he's a really nice fit."

Alfonso Soriano

Second Baseman/Left Fielder

While some major-league players migrate to Japan at the end of their careers, Alfonso Soriano got it backward. He was born in the baseball hotbed of San Pedro de Macoris and began playing ball at the age of six. In the Dominican youth leagues, he was nicknamed the "Mule" because of his awkward footwork when fielding ground balls. Soriano's uncle, Hilario, was a catcher in the Dodgers farm system and would regale Alfonso with his diamond tales. Alfonso dreamed of becoming a big-league shortstop, but as many of his friends began to sign contracts with major-league clubs, there were no suitors for his own services aside from the Hiroshima Carp of the Japanese Central League. The team had a small academy in Santo Domingo and invited Soriano to train there. Following his uncle's advice, he accepted the offer.

Before long, the Carp summoned Soriano to Japan, where he instantly felt isolated and alone. During his first two months overseas, he ate only foods he recognized, subsisting mostly on fruit, candy, and ice cream. Assigned to the Japanese minors (known as "ni-gun"), he began to excel on the field, earning a promotion to the Hiroshima squad in 1997. He fared poorly in nine games and began questioning his decision to play in Japan.

Disenchanted with the grueling workouts that are a staple of Japanese baseball, Soriano hired an agent to navigate a way out of his contract. When his efforts were blocked, he temporarily retired before seeking the attention of major-league clubs—a maneuver that had worked for Hideo Nomo a few years earlier. But executives from Nippon Professional Baseball had toughened their stance against such actions, and a legal battle ensued. Commissioner Bud Selig threw his hat into the ring, endorsing the development of a posting system that allowed players to be transferred from Japan to the United States providing that the Japanese clubs were adequately compensated. Thanks to this new arrangement, Soriano entered the Yankees farm system as a 23-year-old rookie. When Chuck Knoblauch developed throwing difficulties in 2000, the door was opened for Soriano. By 2001, he was the club's starting second baseman.

Throughout the course of 16 major-league seasons, Soriano didn't win much acclaim for his defense. He spent significant portions of time in left field and at second base. Although he had an exceptionally strong arm, he led the league in errors for five straight seasons as an infielder. When he joined the Washington Nationals in 2006, he lost his job to incumbent second baseman Jose Vidro. Moved to left field, he was slow to master the position, placing among the top three in errors for six straight campaigns. He had his act down pat by 2012, however, posting the highest fielding percentage in the NL.

Offensively, Soriano demonstrated a pleasing combination of power and speed. He gathered 30 or more homers in seven seasons and was a 40/40 man with the Nationals in 2006, joining Jose Canseco, Barry Bonds, and Alex Rodriguez as the only players to accomplish the feat. Soriano came close while playing for the Yankees in 2002, finishing the year with 39 homers and 41 steals. In addition, he led the league in runs scored (128) and hits (209). An eminent threat on the basepaths, he swiped 30 or more bags five times, averaging 18 thefts per year.

The Rangers thought so highly of Soriano in 2004, they were willing to trade Alex Rodriguez to obtain his services. He spent two seasons there before moving to Washington. In 2007, he began his longest consecutive stretch with a single team, patrolling left field for the Cubs through the 2012 slate. At 37 years old, the Chicago brass felt he was no longer worth the money they were paying him. In late July 2013, he was traded back to the Yankees, finishing the season with 34 homers and 101 runs batted in, the fourth time he had reached the century mark in RBIs.

In August 2013, Soriano nearly tied a Yankees team record with 13 RBIs in a two-game span. He ended up just shy of the franchise mark (15) set by Tony Lazzeri in 1936. Mired in a horrible slump in July 2014, he was released by the Yankees. Soriano admitted to being surprised and disappointed by the club's decision. He announced his retirement the following year, commenting, "I've lost the love and passion to play the game. Right now, my family is the most important thing. Although I consider myself in great shape, my mind is not focused on baseball."

Soriano and his wife have six children—three boys and three girls. During the span of his major-league career, he netted an estimated $157 million. He has donated a significant portion of his earnings to Dominican children in need.

Sammy Sosa

Outfielder

Born in Consuelo, a small town near San Pedro de Macoris, Sammy Sosa's parents were extremely poor. After Sammy's father passed away, the family lived in an abandoned hospital. Sammy helped support his mother and siblings by selling oranges and shining shoes. He started playing baseball in his early teens. Like many underprivileged Dominican youths, he and his comrades used tree branches for bats and milk cartons for gloves.

The Phillies tried to sign Sosa at the age of 15, but the transaction was blocked because he didn't meet the minimum age requirements. He was working out at the Toronto Blue Jays camp in 1985, when Rangers talent hawk Omar Minaya offered him a contract. Sosa's scouting report said that he was "malnourished."

Sosa spent portions of four seasons in the Rangers farm system, showing little of the slugging ability that would later earn him the nickname "Slammin' Sammy." In 1989, he was packaged in a multiplayer deal that landed him in Chicago with the White Sox. Manager Jeff Torborg penciled him into 33 games. He hit .273, with virtually no power.

Sosa's earliest baseball cards depict him as being tall and lean. In one, he is actually laying down a bunt. The White Sox had no idea he would blossom into a hulking slugger. In his first two full seasons, he hit at a collective .222 pace, while averaging just one homer per every 37 plate appearances. He demonstrated excellent speed and solid fielding, however, stealing 45 bases in that span, while leading the AL in multiple defensive categories. Looking for more power in their lineup, the White Sox dealt him to the Cubs for fellow countryman George Bell.

Sosa's transformation from a singles hitter to a prodigious slugger didn't happen overnight. He was used sparingly in 1992, gathering 17 extra-base hits in 67 games. In 1993, he gave Cubs fans a preview of things to come, launching 33 homers and driving in 93 runs. Two years later, he made the All-Star Team and reached the century mark in RBIs for the first time. He would remain a 100-RBI man for nine consecutive seasons.

While other players were bulking up on steroids, Sosa claimed to be clean throughout his career. In 2005, he testified before Congress alongside Rafael Palmeiro, Jose Canseco, and Mark McGwire. Speaking through his lawyer, he told the congressional panel, "I have been tested as recently as 2004, and I am clean." Although the *New York Times* reported in 2009 that Sosa was on a list of players who had tested positive, a spokesman from Commissioner Bud Selig's office declined to comment, stating that MLB did not have a copy of those results. The charge was never proven, but Sosa's physical makeup during his prime slugging seasons raised a few doubts. He gained a lot of muscle mass throughout the years and generated close to 50 percent of his lifetime homers in a five-year span. In 2003, he was ejected from a game when umpires discovered he was using a corked bat. He claimed to have accidentally grabbed the bat, which he admitted to using during batting practice. Major-league officials tested more than 70 of Sosa's other bats, and they all came up clean. Still, this left lingering doubts about his integrity.

Regardless of those suspicions, Sosa was tremendously popular in Chicago. Affable and energetic, he would literally sprint onto the field to his right-field station. It became his trademark. While he was already a good player by the end of the 1997 slate, he became a household name the following year, when he engaged in an epic home-run duel with Cardinals masher Mark McGwire. Sosa hit 20 home runs in June of that year—the most ever in a single month. Even so, he lagged behind McGwire during the season and cheered on his rival with great enthusiasm, winning the admiration of fans throughout the sport. Both players broke Roger Maris's single-season home-run record, and although it was McGwire who won the highly publicized "chase," it was Sosa who came away with MVP honors. His 158 RBIs were the most by a NL player since 1930. At season's end, Sosa further endeared himself to the masses by raising money for hurricane victims in the Dominican Republic. President Leonel Fernandez dubbed him "Hurricane Sosa" and awarded him a prestigious national medal. When Sosa returned to the United States, thousands of people showed up in the rain to welcome him back. A parade was held to honor him in New York.

Unlike McGwire, who had one good slugging season left before he would succumb to injuries, Sosa continued to pound the ball for several more years. He reached the 60-homer mark twice more, while averaging 50 long balls per season from 1999 to 2004. In the latter campaign, he sustained a fluke injury when a violent sneeze landed him on the disabled list. He missed 36 games but still finished with 35 homers. It was his last year with the Cubs.

As of 2016, Sosa still held the single-season franchise records for slugging percentage and home runs. His 545 blasts in a Cubs uniform placed him ahead of the most popular Chicago player of all time— Ernie Banks.

Traded to Baltimore in 2005, Sosa failed to earn his exorbitant salary. He finished the season at .221, with just 14 homers, prompting the O's not to renew his contract. Out of the majors in 2006, he returned with the Rangers the following year, reaching several career milestones. On April 26, he homered in his 45th major-league park—a new record. On June 20, he became the fifth man in history to reach 600 homers. It came in an interleague game versus the Cubs, giving him a homer against every active major-league team. He tried out for the Dominican national squad in 2009, but was not selected. He officially retired that year and currently holds the record for most home runs in a 10-year span (479 between 1995 and 2004).

Despite his many positive attributes, Sosa's bid for the Hall of Fame has been steadily losing steam. In his first year of eligibility, he garnered just 12.5 percent of the vote. In 2016, he barely remained on the ballot, with 7 percent. He has one more shot in 2017, before his name is removed.

Miguel Tejada

Shortstop

Miguel Tejada made his first major-league appearance with Oakland in 1997. He didn't make an impression with a bat until 1999, when he clubbed 21 homers and scored 93 runs. He was among a wave of young and offensively gifted shortstops that included Derek Jeter, Alex Rodriguez, and Nomar Garciaparra. Once upon a time, shortstops were not expected to hit much. Tejada helped redefine the position, along with his contemporaries.

One writer referred to Tejada as "baseball's version of Forrest Gump, an observer and participant in some of baseball's most defining moments of the era." He was a vital component of Billy Beane's "Moneyball" scheme, which altered the way some teams assemble their rosters. And like many players who became immersed in MLB's so-called Game of Shadows, he suffered a humiliating fall from grace. But somehow he found the strength to carry on. "The negative things in my career made me realize that in life sometimes difficult things can happen," he said in 2013. "I thank God for keeping me strong mentally to get past these things. And also to be an example to show people that despite all these things happening, I didn't let it affect me in my life or in my career."

Born in Bani—a commercial and manufacturing center in the southern region of the Dominican—Tejada's family suffered a tragedy in 1979, when their home and belongings were destroyed by Hurricane David. They moved to the outskirts of the city, where they took up residence in a three-room shack without running water or electricity. Miguel did whatever was necessary to help out. By age six, he was shining shoes. His mother died when he was in his early teens, and he found work in a garment factory.

Miguel's brother Juansito was a fine player who might have gone pro had he not suffered a broken leg that was set improperly. Miguel learned to play his defensive station using discarded milk cartons as gloves. He was not an elegant athlete and worked hard to perfect the fundamentals. As fate would have it, he was discovered by one of the Dominican's most beloved diamond heroes, Hall of Fame pitcher Juan Marichal, who was working as an A's scout. Tejada signed for $2,000, which seemed like a fortune to him at the time.

In 1994, Tejada joined the Dominican Summer League, getting his first real taste of top-shelf competition. In 1995, the A's sent him to the Northwest League. By 1998, he was Oakland's starting shortstop. Nicknamed "Miggy" or "La Gua Gua," Tejada was solidly built, at 5-foot-9, 220 pounds. During the early part of his career, he weighed much less. Although he was never recognized with a Gold Glove, he had one of the strongest arms at his position, leading the league in assists seven times. A reliable partner around second base, he turned more double plays than his peers on three occasions. His range factor per game was among the top five marks in 10 seasons.

Offensively, Tejada measured up against the best sluggers in the league. He gathered 80 or more RBIs in nine consecutive seasons, leading the AL with 150 in 2004. He collected 30 or more doubles for eight straight years. During his 13 seasons as a full-time player, he averaged 23 home runs per year. He also hit for average during his prime, exceeding the .300 mark five times.

The fact that Tejada made six All-Star Teams is impressive given the stiff competition at the time. In 2004, he won the annual Home Run Derby that precedes the All-Star Game, setting a short-lived record with 15 dingers in one round. Tejada was named Player of the Week six times and captured a pair of Silver Slugger Awards, but his most prestigious honor came in 2002, when he was named AL MVP. He had an even better statistical year in 2004, but finished fifth in the voting.

Tejada's career took an unfortunate turn in 2005, when Rafael Palmeiro claimed that his own steroid violation had been caused by a vitamin B-12 mixture given to him by Tejada. In his book *Juiced*, which came out the same year, Jose Canseco speculated that Tejada was likely using steroids. Tejada was absolved of any wrongdoing until 2007, when he was mentioned in the infamous Mitchell Report. Interviewed by a congressional committee, he was subsequently indicted for lying about his PED usage. Instead of the maximum sentence of one year in a federal penitentiary and deportation, he was sentenced to a year of probation. He continued to play, but his numbers tapered off. Out of the majors in 2012, the Royals signed him as a utility infielder the following season. On August 17 of that year, he was suspended for amphetamine use. He had previously been given medical permission to use the drug Adderall for a presumed attention-deficit disorder, but that authorization had expired. The suspension effectively put an end to his major-league career. He attempted a comeback with the Marlins in 2014, but never made it past the Double-A level.

Tejada played for six teams during his big-league tour, spending his longest stretch with the A's and Orioles from 1997 to 2007. His streak of 1,152 consecutive games played is the fifth longest in history. When he first arrived in the majors, he knew little English and was extremely quiet. Veteran teammates in Oakland, like Jason Giambi, encouraged him to speak by learning a new vocabulary word every day. By the end of his career, Tejada had become an outspoken team leader in spite of his transgressions. Baltimore GM Jim Beattie once said, "You try to find players like [Tejada] . . . guys who are not only good, but players who make everyone else around them better." Pitcher Bruce Chen, who played with Tejada in Baltimore and Kansas City, echoed that sentiment. "He's one of the best teammates I've ever had," commented

Chen, "and not only in his leadership and presence. The attitude he brings just makes everyone better." Although Tejada will undoubtedly be remembered by some in an unfavorable light, many who played alongside him still harbor a deep respect for him. And he remains a popular figure in his native country. As of this writing, he holds the all-time Caribbean Series record for homers and RBIs.

NOTABLE ACTIVE PLAYERS

Jose Bautista

Right Fielder

Bautista was born in Santo Domingo and grew up in Bani. An amazing coincidence, Bani was also home to a major league pitcher with the same name. Jose's parents were both gainfully employed—his mother as an accountant and his father as the owner/proprietor of a poultry farm. Jose helped out with the chickens from time to time while growing up. He attended a private school and reportedly excelled in math and science.

In addition to baseball, Bautista tried his hand at basketball as a boy. Though he preferred the latter, it was the former sport in which he showed superior skills. To qualify for the major league draft, Bautista enrolled at Chipola Junior College in Florida. He had a fine year in 2000 and ended up being drafted by the Pirates in the 20th round. He began his pro career with Williamsport the following year.

Bautista was unreasonably hard on himself. Instead of focusing on his strengths, he had a tendency to ruminate over mistakes he made on the field. He could be difficult to coach at times, ignoring the advice of superiors. Extremely high-strung, he was pulled from multiple minor league games due to emotional lapses. The Orioles took a chance on him in 2003, acquiring him from Pittsburgh in the Rule 5 draft. He was promoted in 2004 and then placed on waivers in June. He became the property of three other teams that season before returning to Pittsburgh in a multi-player deal.

Extremely slow in developing, Bautista bounced up and down from the majors to the minors until 2008. He hit .242 with 12 homers in 107 games for Pittsburgh that year and ended up being traded to Toronto, where his career finally took off.

In 2009, Blue Jays hitting coach Dwayne Murphy spotted a flaw in Bautista's hitting mechanics. After making numerous adjustments, the Dominican veteran began to show marked improvement. He began the 2010 campaign as the Jays starting right fielder. By mid-June, he had already established a new career-high for homers. After making his first All-Star appearance, he became the third Toronto player to collect at least 10 home runs in two different months of a season. On September 17, he set a new franchise record with 48. He finished with a league-best 54—a figure that earned him a Silver Slugger Award and a five-year contract extension.

As Bautista's slugging ability surfaced, pitchers began to work carefully around him. He drew 100 walks in 2010 and 132 the following season—tops in the AL. This included a franchise record 28 walks in April. He won his second consecutive home run crown in 2011, going deep 43 times. Additionally, he led the league in slugging percentage and intentional walks. Recognized for his efforts, he finished third in MVP voting.

2012 proved to be disappointing for the hard-hitting right fielder as a wrist injury prompted him to undergo season-ending surgery. He was on pace for a 40-homer 100-RBI effort. He sat out more than 40 games the following year, but kept his streak of All-Star appearances alive with his fourth consecutive selection.

In 2014, Bautista reached base safely in 37 straight games from the start of the season—yet another franchise record. He received the highest number of votes for the All-Star team that year. On September 8, he joined George Bell, Carlos Delgado, and Vernon Wells as the only Blue Jays players with 200 career homers.

The emergence of Bautista as a major star coincided with the Blue Jays rise to contention. The Jays made their first postseason appearance in more than twenty years during the 2015 slate. Bautista generated some controversy in Game 5 of the ALDS against Texas. After hitting a 3-run homer that held up as the series-clinching blow, he stood at home plate and flipped his bat high in the air. Rangers players complained afterward that the gesture was unsportsmanlike. Bautista found himself in hot water again during the 2016 slate. Hit by a pitch in a game against the Rangers, he executed an illegal slide into Rougned Odor at second base. Odor punched Bautista and a bench-clearing brawl ensued. Bautista received a one-game suspension for his actions.

A wrist injury in 2016 sidelined Bautista for more than 50 games. He hit just .234, but maintained a high on-base percentage. A free agent at seasons'end, the Jays decided it would be imprudent to let him go. Bautista signed a one-year contract with options for the following two seasons. Entering the 2017 slate, he ranked among the Blue Jays top five in homers, RBIs, walks, and runs scored.

Adrian Beltre

Third Baseman

Adrian Beltre was born in Santo Domingo. He has ties to the Alou family through marriage, and his uncle was a minor-league player in the Cardinals system. In the early part of his youth, Beltre's favorite sports were basketball and tennis. It wasn't until the age of 12 that he became seriously involved with the game that has made him famous. Originally a middle infielder, he became enamored with third baseman Ken Caminiti and sought to master the same position.

At Liceo Maximo High School, Beltre was spotted by Dodgers scouts. He was signed at the age of 15, which was against major-league rules. His forged birth certificate would land the Dodgers organization in hot water years later. They ended up paying a hefty fine, although they were allowed to keep him on their roster.

After a phenomenal debut in the Dominican Summer League, Beltre traveled to the United States to join the Savannah Sand Gnats in 1996. He would have the opportunity to meet his boyhood idol during the annual Hall of Fame exhibition game the following year. Beltre still remembers the moment clearly—how he wanted so badly to tell Caminiti that he had been an inspiration but ended up starstuck and tongue-tied. In the years that followed, Beltre would have that effect on others.

After hitting .321 in 64 games with the San Antonio Missions in 1998, Beltre was called to Los Angeles. His offensive contributions increased each year. In 2004, he led the NL with 48 homers, while finishing fourth in RBIs (121) and batting average (.334). He was runner-up for MVP behind Barry Bonds. The Dodgers made it to the

NLDS that year but ended up being swept by the Cardinals. It was Beltre's only postseason appearance with LA.

Granted free agency at season's end, Beltre decided to test his skills in the AL, signing with the Mariners. Although he was a veteran of seven major-league seasons by that point, he still had not earned an All-Star selection or captured a Gold Glove. The latter honor was finally bestowed upon him in 2007, when he finished among the top 10 in numerous defensive categories. He would claim the award three more times in the next five seasons. Beltre didn't earn his first All-Star selection until 2010—a season in which he hit .321 and led the AL with 49 doubles. By the end of the 2015 slate, he had four All-Star selections and four Silver Slugger Awards to his credit.

Beltre is one of the best-kept secrets in the majors. Despite receiving only moderate attention through the years, he stacks up nicely against the greatest third basemen in history. Through 2017, only 11 third basemen are in the Hall of Fame. Among those players, Beltre ranks second in RBIs, third in homers, and fourth in runs scored. Not even 40 years of age, he is closing in on the 3,000-hit mark—a plateau reached by few players at his position. He is also on pace for 600 doubles, which would put him in an elite group numbering less than 20. Although his home-run production has tapered off in the last few seasons, he may still hit 500 during his career, assuming he remains healthy.

Beltre likes to swing the bat, never drawing more than 61 walks during any season. A frequent strikeout victim early in his career, he has made adjustments. He has not been victimized more than 100 times in a season since 2007. He plays aggressively on defense. Describing his style, he once said, "I don't like to play slow or softly. I like to play hard. Always." Possessing the confidence of an accomplished veteran, he has been careful not to get carried away with himself. "I'm confident, but not so confident I'm cocky," he explained.

Currently property of the Rangers, Beltre is signed through 2018. As he continues to put up consistent numbers year after year, his name has begun to surface in Hall of Fame discussions more frequently. A 2016 Sporting News article proclaims he will be an "easy" selection to Cooperstown and ranks him among the all-time greats. Anyone who takes the time to carefully examine his career can only draw the same conclusion.

Robinson Cano

Second Baseman

Cano was born in San Pedro de Macoris. As an infant, he went without a name for several weeks as his parents debated the options. In the end, he was named after his father's favorite player—Jackie Robinson. Cano's dad was a minor-league pitcher who got a brief call-up with the Astros in 1989. By the time his father's career was winding down, Cano had become one of the best young players in the Dominican League. Having spent the seventh through ninth grades in the New Jersey school system, Cano is fluent in English. He finished high school in the Dominican Republic, excelling at basketball, as well as baseball.

Cano impressed local scouts with his hitting skills, which he had polished under his father's tutelage. In January 2001, he signed with the Yankees organization. Although he hit just .230 in his pro debut, he led the team in RBIs.

Given trials at third base and shortstop, Cano eventually found a niche at second base. The Yankees lineup was difficult to break into, but Cano landed himself a permanent roster spot in 2005. His debut was spectacular, as he hit .297, with 52 extra-base hits and 62 RBIs. He finished second in Rookie of the Year voting.

During the next several seasons, Cano established himself as one of the best offensive second basemen in the majors. He spent nine years with the Yankees, averaging 23 homers and 91 RBIs per season. His batting average ranged from .271 to .342. Beginning in 2009, he kept his average above the .300 mark for six straight seasons.

Defensively, Cano improved over time. He led the league in putouts on five occasions between 2007 and 2012. He also topped the circuit in double plays and assists three times apiece in that span. Duly recognized for his efforts, he received a pair of Gold Gloves.

Before signing with the Mariners prior to the 2014 slate, Cano helped the Yankees to seven postseason appearances. He gathered 45 hits and 14 walks in 51 playoff games. His finest performance came in the 2010 ALCS against the Rangers, when he slammed four homers in six games. He won a World Series ring with the Yankees in 2009.

In his three seasons with Seattle (2014, 2015, and 2016), Cano has been one of the team's most reliable hitters. In 2014, he posted the highest batting average among regulars. He ranked third in homers and runs scored the following year. Popular among voters, Cano received five consecutive All-Star selections beginning in 2010. Entering the 2016 slate, he had won five Silver Slugger Awards.

Many experts agree that Cano is the best of his generation. Among active second baseman, he is the leader in putouts, assists, and double plays. His sabermetric scores compare favorably to Hall of Famers Ryne Sandberg and Bobby Doerr. Immensely proud of his Dominican heritage, Cano feels he owes a debt of gratitude to the United States. "We all should be proud of the U.S.," he said. "For those of us that came from the Dominican, we've been able to come here, work here, make money, and become somebody in our lives. We've gotten a huge opportunity in the U.S."

Santiago Casilla

Pitcher

Born in San Cristobal, Santiago Casilla forged documents to make him look three years younger at the time of his signing. A's scouts Bernardino Rosario and Raymond Abreu invited him to join the Oakland organization under the assumed name of Jairo Garcia. Casilla carried the pseudonym until spring training 2006. By then, he had appeared in seven major-league games and compiled a cumbersome ERA of 9.35.

A right-hander, Casilla throws a two-seam fastball in the low to mid-90s. He also has a hard-breaking slider, a curve, and a changeup. He has struggled with control at times, averaging close to four walks per nine innings in portions of 13 seasons in the majors. He counters his sporadic wildness with high strikeout totals. He has fanned more batters than innings pitched during several seasons.

Groomed as a starter in the minors, Kane County Cougars manager Dave Joppie decided Casilla was more effective in relief during the 2004 slate. The hard-throwing right-hander compiled a 0.30 ERA in 25 Midwest League games that year. Casilla's first three calls to the majors were unsuccessful. In 2006—the year he finally revealed his true identity—he averaged close to eight walks per nine innings. The A's finally gave up on him after the 2009 slate, allowing him to sign with San Francisco. There, his fortunes changed dramatically.

Casilla appeared in 52 games for the Giants in 2010, notching a 7–2 record and 1.95 ERA. He appeared in four postseason games that year, allowing just one run in 4.2 innings as San Francisco won the World Series. During the next five seasons, Casilla would be used in various roles—as a middle reliever, setup man, and closer. From 2011 to 2015, his ERA never exceeded 2.84. He was in the low twos or better three times. His efforts propelled the Giants to two more World Series titles, in 2012 and 2014. Through the 2016 campaign, Casilla had recorded a 0.92 ERA in 25 postseason appearances.

Casilla is rarely asked to pitch more than an inning at a time. He is most effective against right-handers and is sometimes used in tight spots to get one or two crucial outs. Since a single run can seriously damage a reliever's ERA, the statistic can be somewhat deceiving. For instance, in 2012, when Casilla posted a 2.84 ERA, he actually had a streak of 14 consecutive appearances without an earned run. In 2015, when his ERA was 2.79, he had similar streaks of 12 and 13 games.

Converted to a full time closer in July 2014, Santiago has saved 88 regular season games since then. He registered his 100th career save in 2016. In May of the previous year, he pitched an immaculate inning against the Reds, striking out all three batters he faced on three pitches.

Starlin Castro

Shortstop/Second Baseman

Born in Monte Cristi, Starlin Castro is the oldest of five children. He began his pro career with the Cubs organization in 2007, at the age of 17. He matured quickly, spending time in four different leagues during the 2009 campaign. He went 4-for-4, with an inside-the-park homer in the Florida State League All-Star Game that year.

Prior to 2010, Castro was ranked 16th among major-league prospects. Called to Chicago in May, he made a spectacular entrance, slamming a three-run homer in his first at-bat. He added a bases-clearing triple later in the game. His six RBIs were an all-time record for a debut performance. At 20 years of age, he was the youngest shortstop in Cubs history. He was also the first player born in the 1990s to appear in the majors.

Solidly built, at 6-foot-2, 230 pounds, Castro's development at short-stop was somewhat slow. After leading the league in errors for three straight seasons, he was benched briefly by Cubs manager Joe Maddon and then moved to second base. He has remained there ever since. Improvement has been evident. Castro has a strong arm and makes a reliable double-play partner.

Offensively, Castro has speed and power. He also hits for average, posting a mark of .283 or higher four times between 2010 and 2014. In 2016, he completed a string of six consecutive seasons with double digit home run totals. He paced the circuit with 207 hits in 2011.

A three-time All-Star, Castro was traded to the Yankees before the 2016 slate. He got off to a hot start with seven hits and eight RBIs in his first three games. He finished the season with 21 homers and 70 RBIs. In a facetious promotional ad, Castro and shortstop Didi Gregorius vowed to become best friends on account of their shared interest in love ballads, dinosaurs, and karate.

Bartolo Colon

Pitcher

Bartolo Colon was raised in the small town of Altamira, which is located in the Puerto Plata province. His childhood home had no electricity, running water, or indoor plumbing. Bartolo worked long hours picking beans and fruit alongside his siblings and father. With insufficient funds to purchase baseball equipment, the family substituted milk cartons for gloves and tightly wound rags for balls.

Colon is one of the game's ageless wonders, having played for three decades. Thanks to an experimental procedure on his shoulder, he won 14 games for the Mets at the age of 42 and was still on the roster the following year. His efforts to remain active were not always on the level, however. In 2012, he was suspended for 50 games after testing positive for testosterone—one of MLB's banned substances. He apologized and accepted responsibility for his actions. Although his name was linked to the dreaded Biogenesis Laboratories scandal of 2013, evidence of his involvement was inconclusive, and he received no punishment.

Signed by the Indians as an amateur free agent in 1993, Colon spent four seasons in the minors before receiving a summons to Cleveland.

His debut was a bit rocky, but the Indians brought him back the following year. It was a good move, as he won 14 games—second most on the staff—and reduced his ERA by nearly 2 runs. He was rewarded with the first of four All-Star selections.

From 1999 to 2001, Colon was one of the most reliable members of the Cleveland rotation. He ate up no less than 188 innings per year while averaging 16 victories. The Indians made two postseason appearances in that span, and Colon was right in the thick of it, making four starts. His best outing came against the Mariners in the first game of the 2001 ALDS. He scattered six hits in eight innings and struck out 10.

Colon has traveled extensively during his career. At the beginning of the 2017 campaign, he will be wearing his ninth different uniform. He posted winning records in six of the cities he called home, gathering at least 15 victories in eight seasons. He reached the 20-win threshold twice—in 2002 and 2005.

A big right-hander, at 5-foot-11, 285 pounds, Colon has four effective pitches in his arsenal. His four-seam fastball was regularly clocked in the mid-90s and occasionally reached 100 miles per hour in the early part of his career. As he began to lose velocity, he introduced a two-seamer. He also employed a changeup and slider. He stayed in the strike zone most of the time and, as a result, gave up a fair amount of hits.

Traded to the Mets in 2014, Colon became immensely popular among fans for his enthusiasm. Teammates referred to him as "Big Sexy." Commenting on his personality, one writer remarked hyperbolically that he was the "living embodiment of joie de vivre, whose at-bats are as whimsical and unexpected as Wes Anderson films and whose pitching style could be described as crafty wizardry that will be practiced until the sun devours planet earth." In September 2015, Colon added another gem to his growing list of highlight-reel plays with a behind-the-back relay to first that nabbed Justin Bour of the Marlins by a step. He pitched a complete-game shutout that day.

Anchoring a young pitching rotation, Colon helped the Mets reach the World Series in 2015. He appeared in seven postseason games, compiling a 2.08 ERA. Proving that age is only a state of mind, he was offered a $7.25 million contract with the Mets before the 2016 campaign. Colon has made more than $100 million during his major-league career, which is still going (although winding down) at the time of this writing. Among Dominican-born players, Colon ranks second in wins and third in strikeouts. The players ahead of him on the list are both in the Hall of Fame.

Nelson Cruz

Right Fielder

Unlike many of his fellow countrymen, Nelson Cruz was raised in a prosperous Dominican neighborhood. He attended the same high school where his father taught history. He idolized Michael Jordan growing up and, at one point, considered putting all his energy into basketball. During his teen years, he shined shoes for extra money and worked as a mechanic helper at a tractor factory.

In 1998, Cruz signed with the Mets. He labored in the minors for quite some time and switched organizations twice before getting a call to the majors. His big-league debut came in 2005 with the Brewers. He put up mediocre numbers and was traded to the Rangers in a six-player deal.

Asked about Cruz's potential, Dominican League manager Felix Fermin said, "He's serious, and most important, he is a hard worker . . . very dedicated to his profession. He won't make the Rangers look bad if he is given the opportunity." That opportunity finally came in 2009, when he slammed 33 homers and made the All-Star Team.

Cruz picked up the nickname "Boomstick" for his ample power. Between 2010 and 2015, he averaged 31 homers and 89 RBIs per year. He made three All-Star appearances in that span. Reliable in the clutch, he had eight grand slams to his credit entering the 2016 campaign. He had also compiled a .282 average with runners in scoring position. Swinging from the right side of the plate, he assembled back-to-back 40 homer seasons in 2014 and 2015.

Cruz's efforts have propelled the Rangers and Orioles to four playoff appearances. He was named MVP of the 2011 ALCS against Detroit on the strength of his six homers and 13 RBIs. Through the 2016 campaign, he had yet to win a World Series ring, although he has appeared in two Fall Classics. In December 2014, he became property of the Mariners and is signed through 2018. He logged his third consecutive 40 homer season in 2016.

Johnny Cueto

Pitcher

Johnny Cueto can trace his roots to San Pedro de Macoris. He was signed by Reds scout Johnny Almaraz at the age of 18. His ascent to the majors was laborious, as he appeared in five different minor leagues before earning a call to Cincinnati. Listed at 5-foot-10, many believe that Cueto is actually two inches shorter. His physical stature interfered with his path to stardom. "Some told me I was too short," Cueto said. "Others thought I was in fact older than the age that appeared in my papers." Despite his somewhat stout appearance (he weighs 220 pounds), Cueto was named Reds Minor League Pitcher of the Year twice before he appeared in the majors.

Cueto is a bit theatrical on the mound. He has long dreadlocks that hang well over his shoulders. He pivots toward second base before delivering to the plate, reminding some of Luis Tiant. He often finishes with his leg in the air and his arms flailing. A high-energy player, Cueto celebrates important strikeouts emphatically and uses a variety of deliveries to keep batters on their heels. He has a knack for adjusting to hitters' weaknesses on the spot. With a variety of breaking balls and a sharp slider, he induces a lot of ground-ball outs. Giants manager Bruce Bochy once said, "[Cueto's] got great savvy out there with great stuff. He's one of those guys who can turn it up a notch out there when he needs to."

After posting a won–loss record below .500 and an ERA above the 4.00 mark in his first two seasons, Cueto found his groove in 2010, posting a 12–7 record, with a 3.64 ERA. Injuries in 2011 and 2013 significantly shortened his seasons, but he had a stellar campaign in 2012, winning 19 games and finishing third in the league with a 2.78 ERA. He placed fourth in Cy Young voting that year.

Following his first 20-win campaign in 2014, which earned him an All-Star selection, Cueto was off to another hot start before a July trade sent him to Kansas City. The Royals went to the World Series despite his substandard 4–7 record down the stretch. Cueto fared well in Game Five of the ALDS but was knocked out of the box in his only start of the ALCS. He redeemed himself in the World Series against the Mets, tossing a two-hitter in the second game and getting the win.

Granted free agency after the Royals' five-game victory over New York, Cueto's 2016 return to the NL was magnificent. He posted an 18-5 record with a 2.79 ERA for the Giants, making his second All Star appearance. His 5 complete games were tops in the circuit. Speaking through a translator, he assured reporters that he was "having fun" in San Francisco.

Edwin Encarnacion

First Baseman/Third Baseman

Born in La Romana, Edwin Encarnacion grew up in the modest barrio of Rio Salado. His father was an athlete who later became a track-and-field coach. As a boy, Encarnacion picked mangoes from a tree in his backyard and sold them. He and his two brothers played a variation of baseball known to Dominican kids as "Vitilla." In the popular street game, sticks are used as bats and bottle caps serve as balls. The cap is spun like a Frisbee, causing it to dart in various directions like a big-league breaking ball.

Encarnacion played high-school ball in Caguas. He was chosen in a late round of the 2000 MLB Draft by the Rangers. Although he proved himself to be competent offensively, his defense left something to be desired. The Rangers quickly gave up on him, trading him to the Reds in June 2001. Encarnacion made his major-league debut in 2005, hitting just .232 in 69 games. He raised his average to .289 in 2007, and followed with excellent power numbers in 2008, gathering 56 extra-base hits—his highest total to that point.

Encarnacion began his career as a third baseman, but it was a rocky road. He finished among the top five in errors three times and posted a cumulative fielding percentage more than 20 points below the league average. Demoted to the minors for a spell in 2009, the Reds ended up trading him to Toronto. Encarnacion remembers his struggles with the glove vividly. "I tried to do the best I could," he said. "But it got in my head—and when that gets in your head, it's hard to get out. I got frustrated a little bit. I couldn't hit because I was thinking about defense."

The Blue Jays were patient with Encarnacion, trying him out at various positions before reassigning him to first base. He spends a significant amount of time as a DH as well. Beginning in 2012, Encarnacion emerged as one of the most reliable sluggers in the AL. He blasted 42 homers that year and drove in 110 runs. During the next three campaigns, he averaged 36 homers and 104 ribbies per season. He has an odd way of celebrating after his home runs, extending his right elbow like a wing and "gliding" around the bases. Fans in Toronto love it.

Encarnacion's success at the plate coincided with Toronto's 2015 ALCS appearance—their first since 1992. The right-handed slugger hit .333 in the ALDS against Texas. He reached base by hit or walk seven times in the ALCS as the Jays bowed to the Royals in six games. As of 2016, Encarnacion was Toronto's franchise leader in walk-off homers. He also ranks among the top 10 in RBIs, slugging percentage, and runs scored.

Jhonny Peralta

Shortstop

Although Jhonny Peralta hasn't gained a lot of acclaim during his career, he has been one of the most reliable shortstops in the majors for more than a decade. In 2013, he accepted a 50-game suspension for his involvement in the dreaded Biogenesis Laboratories PED scandal. Cut loose by the Tigers, he signed a contract with the Cardinals worth $53 million. Questioned about the move, St. Louis GM John Mozeliak said, "Character and makeup are something we weigh into our decision-making. In [Peralta's] case, he admitted what he did. He took responsibility for it. I feel like he paid for his mistakes." Peralta stayed clean and pulled his weight in 2014–2015, helping the Cardinals to consecutive playoff appearances.

Peralta was born in Santiago, an independent component city with a population of approximately 150,000. He attended high school at Colejo Pedagogico and was signed by the Indians as an amateur free agent in 1999. He began his pro career at the age of 18. Within five years, he had developed into a power-hitting shortstop. He accrued a .326 average with the Buffalo Bisons in 2004. His 44 doubles were a team record for the modern era. Named MVP of the International League that year, he also received the Lou Boudreau Award, which is given to the Indians' top minor-league player.

Peralta was called to the majors in 2003 and 2004, but he didn't earn a permanent roster spot until the following year. He hit .292 in his first full season, with 24 homers and 78 RBIs. With the exception of the ill-fated 2013 campaign, he appeared in at least 141 games in the next 11 seasons, finishing with double-digit home-run totals each year. He gathered no fewer than 71 RBIs eight times during that span.

Defensively, Peralta covers a lot of ground. His range factor was tops in the league on two occasions. Few shortstops have fielded their position as flawlessly as Peralta. He has placed among the top five in fielding percentage seven times, and his lifetime mark was the ninth highest in history entering the 2016 campaign.

Peralta has aided the Indians, Tigers, and Cardinals in achieving playoff berths, but despite his many positive attributes, he did not become an All-Star until he was in his ninth major-league season. He has never won a Gold Glove. Moved to third base in 2016, he had multiple stints on the disabled list and competed for playing time with the highly capable Matt Carpenter. By late-August, he was back in the lineup full time. He finished the season with a .260 batting average, scoring and driving in a combined total of 66 runs in 82 games.

Albert Pujols

First Baseman

Albert Pujols was born into a poor family. His father was in and out of his life during his formative years, and his grandmother assumed a majority of the maternal responsibilities. The family lived in a communal setting in Santo Domingo that, according to one source, "resembled a campsite." Pujols's grandmother was devoutly religious, and he remains a deeply spiritual man, donating his time to a host of charities.

Young Albert grew up idolizing Julio Franco. During the early 1990s, his family began immigrating to the United States. After a handful of unsavory episodes in New York City, they moved to Independence, Missouri. During the summers, Albert played American Legion ball. He started out as a shortstop. Assisted by a tutor, he mastered English in high school and excelled academically.

After drawing the attention of scouts during his junior year, Pujols was recruited to play at nearby Maple Woods Community College.

Unlike many of his teammates, he preferred wooden bats over the aluminum ones that were widely used at the college level. He became the team's starting shortstop, hitting 22 homers, with 80 RBIs, in his debut. Drafted in the 13th round, Pujols turned down a $10,000 signing bonus from the Cardinals. He opted for the Jayhawk League instead—a Kansas-based circuit for college-age players. When the Cardinals increased their offer to $60,000, he accepted. It was the beginning of a fruitful professional career.

Pujols ascended to the majors after just one season on the farm. In his 2001 debut, he captured Rookie of the Year honors and a Silver Slugger, and also made the All-Star Team. His 130 RBIs and 88 extra-base hits were a record for NL rookies. He would reside among the game's greatest players for the next decade, winning three MVP Awards and reaching a host of other milestones, including most consecutive seasons of 30 or more homers from the start of a career (12). During his first 11 campaigns, he accumulated more homers than any player in the same span, with 445. At the end of the 2016 campaign, he was poised to join the elite 600-homer club, which currently has eight other members.

Pujols's extraordinary talents prompted glowing praise from contemporaries. Angels manager Mike Scioscia said, "He's a once-in-a-generation player. There's no doubt he's the gold standard for what guys [do] not only in the batter's box but on the field." Cardinals manager Tony La Russa echoed that sentiment, saying, "It's so obvious and evident if you watch him closely that, from his rookie year to today, he has played the game to win. . . . He's a perfect player in all categories of the game—hitting, running, defense, cheerleading, being a mentor—you see Hall of Fame greatness." With so much natural ability, Pujols has always felt comfortable on the diamond. "There's no pressure," he once said. "I just concentrate and do the best I can. I try to do my best every day and help the team win any way I can."

Pujols has become accustomed to winning. The Cardinals made seven postseason appearances during his tenure in St. Louis. Entering the 2017 campaign, he had appeared in three World Series and captured two rings. Granted free agency before the 2012 slate, he signed with the Angels, guiding the club to an ALDS berth in 2014.

Pujols has been so successful at the plate, his defense is often overlooked. He leads active players in multiple statistical categories, including putouts, double plays, and range factor. In 2009, he set a single-season record for first basemen with 185 assists. He has received two Gold Gloves.

Although Pujols's batting averages have declined during the past few seasons, he continues to be a reliable clean-up hitter. In 2016, he logged his thirteenth 100 RBI season. His sabermetric similarity scores compare him favorably to the all-time greats, including Jimmie Foxx, Hank Aaron, and Willie Mays.

Hanley Ramirez

Infielder

Hanley Ramirez was born in Samana. His father supported the family working as an auto mechanic. Hanley's idols while growing up were Tony Fernandez and Pedro Guerrero. He entered his first organized league at the age of five. His parents hoped he would study engineering one day, but baseball eventually preempted his academic pursuits.

Hanley began attracting scouts at about age 15. Red Sox talent hawk Levy Ochoa believed that Ramirez might be a five-tool player someday and offered him a contract in July 2000. Ramirez joined the Dominican Summer League the following year and topped .400. In 2003, Ramirez received a 10-game suspension for flipping his own Florida State League teammates the bird. Despite his obvious need to mature, he appeared to be ready for big-league action. Unfortunately, the BoSox had acquired veteran Edgar Renteria to play shortstop, and Ramirez's path to the majors was blocked. There was talk of moving him to another position before a trade sent him to the Marlins in November 2005. Having lost Alex Gonzalez to free agency, the Marlins had an immediate opening at short.

In his first full season, Ramirez hit .292 primarily out of the leadoff spot, with 46 doubles and 51 stolen bases. His seven leadoff homers were a franchise record. He was also the first Marlins player to reach double digits in homers, triples, and steals. He was named Rookie of the Year on the strength of those numbers.

Ramirez's follow-up campaign was phenomenal, as he scored 125 runs (second in the NL) and hit .332. His 83 extra-base hits (a career high) were fourth best in the circuit. Before the 2008 campaign, the

Marlins traded two of their cornerstone veterans—Dontrelle Willis and Miguel Cabrera. Ramirez assumed the role of team leader, pacing the league in runs scored in 2008, and following with a batting title in 2009. He was the first NL shortstop to claim the honor since Dick Groat in 1960.

Ramirez's career took a downward turn in 2010. While he hit an even .300, he missed several games with a sore elbow and shoulder. He also clashed with manager Fredi Gonzalez, who benched Ramirez for loafing after a ball he accidentally misplayed. In 2011, Ramirez aggravated his shoulder diving for a ball in an August game against the Mets. He was out for the rest of the year.

Mired in a slump the following season, Ramirez was shipped to Los Angeles in exchange for pitching prospect Nathan Eovaldi. Free from the pressures of carrying a club, he finished the season with 57 extra-base hits and 92 RBIs.

Ramirez's tenure in LA was plagued by more injuries. In 2013, he tore a thumb ligament and sat out most of April. A subsequent hamstring injury sidelined him for another month. He posted a stellar .345 batting average in 86 games that year. In the final season of his contract with the Dodgers, he suffered a slew of ailments that kept him out of 34 games. Questioning his ability to remain healthy, the Dodgers allowed him to sign with the Red Sox.

In Boston, Ramirez was moved to the outfield. Injured after crashing into the left-field wall, he was assigned to first base. In 2016, he slugged 30 homers while driving in 111 runs. He had three All-Star selections and a pair of Silver Slugger Awards to his credit at the start of the 2017 campaign.

Jose Reyes

Shortstop

Born in Villa Gonzalez, Jose Reyes grew up on the outskirts of Santiago in a northern-lying village known as Palmar Arriba. His parents were not especially wealthy. The family lived on an unpaved road near a banana grove, and their only bathroom was an outhouse. Jose did not become interested in baseball until the age of 10. Because his parents had no cash to buy him a glove, he sometimes fielded his position bare-handed.

Reyes was the first player from his village to aspire to the majors. He became a switch-hitter around the age of 16 and attended the Mets' tryout camp in 1999, uninvited. Scout Eddy Toledo was captivated by Reyes's defensive skills and enthusiasm. Although he was undersized at 130 pounds, the Mets signed him anyway. He was sent to the Appalachian League in 2000.

Reyes hit .307 for the Capital City Bombers of the South Atlantic League in 2001. By 2003, he was playing at the Triple-A level. The Mets were having a terrible year, and manager Art Howe began combing the minors for help. Reyes got the call in early June. His season ended when he sprained an ankle breaking up a double play, but his numbers were excellent. He compiled a .307 average in 69 games, with 32 RBIs and 21 extra-base hits.

A pulled hamstring in 2004 kept Reyes out until mid-June. He put up decent stats until a back injury again landed him on the disabled list. Entering the 2005 campaign, there were serious doubts about Reyes's ability to remain on the field. He silenced his detractors by staying healthy for the next four seasons. He enjoyed his most productive stretch in New York from 2005 to 2008, leading the league in triples and steals three times apiece. He also paced the circuit in hits during the latter campaign.

A two-time All-Star at that point, Reyes suffered a calf injury in 2009, limiting him to 36 games. He returned to top form in 2011, capturing a batting title with a .337 mark. But the honor was shrouded in controversy. A strained hamstring had kept him out of action for more than a month, and after bunting for a single in his first at-bat of game number 162, he asked manager Terry Collins to remove him from the lineup. Collins complied, giving Reyes a two-point lead over Ryan Braun of the Brewers. Braun went 0-for-4, and Reyes earned a batting title in 126 games—the fewest since Manny Ramirez claimed the honor in 120 games during the 2002 slate.

During his last several seasons, four different teams have taken a chance on the injury-prone Reyes. He has played well whenever he has been healthy—particularly in 2014, when he scored 94 runs and stole 30 bases for the Blue Jays. Dealt to Colorado in 2015, he was suspended for violating the major-league domestic violence policy. He rejoined the Mets in July 2016, stealing 9 bases in 11 attempts while hitting .267.

Carlos Santana

Catcher/First Baseman/Designated Hitter

Born in Santo Domingo, Carlos Santana shares his name with an iconic Mexican guitarist. His ability to switch-hit served him well during his youth, and by the age of 18, Dodgers scout Andres Lopez was eager to sign him. In the Los Angeles farm system, Santana filled many roles, including second base, third base, and outfield. He had been given a trial at catcher in his Gulf Coast League debut, and it became his primary station with the Inland Empire 66ers in 2008. A late July trade that year shifted him to the Indians organization. He was named Minor League Player of the Year the following season.

Prior to his 2010 debut, Santana was ranked among the top 10 prospects in baseball. He was called to Cleveland in early June, forming a platoon with catcher Lou Marson. The incumbent Marson hit just .195, as Santana trumped him with a .260 mark. Santana would remain the Indians' first-string backstop through 2012. Injuries and defensive shortcomings eventually prompted a switch to first base in 2014.

Although Santana has fielded his first-base position several points above the league average, he is known more for his aptitude with a bat. He has ample power, slugging 20 or more homers in four of his six seasons as a full-time player. He averaged 55 extra-base hits and 80 RBIs between 2011 and 2015. Often appearing as a cleanup hitter, he generates most of his power from the left side of the plate. Through August 2016, he had compiled a .338 average with the bases loaded. Santana is an aggressive hitter and strikes out at the rate of once per every five at-bats. Unlike some of the other big whiffers in the game today, he draws a lot of walks as well. He peaked at 113 free passes in 2014 (a league high) and has finished among the top five on six occasions.

Santana slugged a career-high 34 home runs in 2016, helping Cleveland to a World Series berth. He added 3 more long balls in the postseason as the Indians ultimately lost to the Cubs in seven games.

Juan Uribe

Infielder

Juan Uribe was born and raised in Bani, the capital of Peravia. The city has produced more than a dozen major leaguers to date. Uribe's second cousin was a shortstop for the San Francisco Giants and would entertain young Juan with stories from the big leagues. Uribe focused his energies on baseball and was spotted by a Rockies scout in 1997. He signed for $5,000.

Uribe moved up the minor-league ladder each year. He started the 2001 campaign with Colorado and was sent back down multiple times before the Rockies traded veteran Neifi Perez. Uribe had a fine rookie season overall, playing in 72 games and hitting .300. His 11 triples tied a club record set by the aforementioned Perez and Juan Pierre.

Uribe was Colorado's starting shortstop in 2002. He assembled a 17-game hitting streak in April and May but slumped in the second half. He also played sloppily in the field, leading the team with 27 errors. Injured in spring training the following year, the Rockies experimented with him in the outfield and at second base. Although improvement was evident both offensively and defensively, he was traded to the White Sox.

During the next several seasons, Uribe spent a significant amount of time at second and third base, in addition to shortstop. He never finished among the top 10 in errors after 2002. In fact, he led the league in putouts, double plays, and assists once apiece. Despite his somewhat portly stature (he stands six feet tall and weighs roughly 250 pounds), he still has excellent range.

Uribe peaked offensively between 2004 and 2010, when he averaged 74 RBIs per year during each season in which he appeared in at least 132 games. He put forth his best offensive effort in 2004, batting .283, with 60 extra-base hits (including 23 homers). Given the chance to play every day, Uribe demonstrates power at the plate. His 162-game average (through the 2016 slate) included 29 doubles and 18 home runs. He does have a tendency to strike out, piling up more than 80 K's in eight seasons.

In 2006, Uribe was accused of wounding a farmer named Antonio Gonzalez Perez with a pellet gun. Despite a conspicuous lack of evidence, the case went to court. Uribe was cleared of any wrongdoing and insisted that the plaintiff was attempting to extort money from him.

As of 2016, Uribe was 37 years old and approaching the end of his career. He has played for seven clubs, helping four of them reach the playoffs. In the 2005 ALDS against the Red Sox, he hit .400, with a homer and four RBIs. He was almost as good in the 2013 NLDS, raking Atlanta pitching at a .375 clip. His teams won two of the three World Series he appeared in. He drove in eight runs and scored six in 10 Fall Classic games.

2

PUERTO RICO

ORIGINS OF BASEBALL IN PUERTO RICO

Baseball first appeared on the shores of Puerto Rico in the late nineteenth century. It was introduced by Cubans and native Puerto Ricans who had traveled abroad. The sport was poorly received by some initially, but others were enamored with its intricacies. In time, it became one of the country's favorite pastimes.

In 1897, the first teams were founded. The earliest organized game took place the following year in Santurce, with Borinquen defeating Almendares. When Puerto Rico became a U.S. territory in the wake of the Spanish–American War, American soldiers stationed on the island organized their own team. In November 1900, the Alimendares club destroyed the U.S. Second Regiment by a score of 32 to 18.

During the 1920s, teams from Puerto Rico began traveling to New York City to take on professional clubs from the United States. At the same time, Puerto Rican players began immigrating to the Negro Leagues. By 1938, a semipro league had been founded in Puerto Rico. One of the league's top pitchers, Hiram Bithorn, was drafted by the Cubs, opening the door for the 200-plus players who followed.

Today, the Liga de Beisbol Profesional Roberto Clemente (formerly known as the Puerto Rico Baseball League) is the top professional circuit on the island. Champions compete in the Caribbean Series against other Latin American countries. Through 2015, Puerto Rican teams had won 14 Caribbean Series titles. The brightest stars from the island territory are featured on the pages that follow.

MAJOR STARS OF THE PAST

Roberto Alomar

Second Baseman

Roberto Alomar was born in Ponce, an important trading and distribution center on Puerto Rico's southern coastal plain. At the time of his birth, Alomar's father, Sandy Sr., was entering his fifth major-league season. Raised in Salinas, "Robbie" was a precocious child who reportedly tried out his father's batting stance at the age of two and played in his first Little League game when he was only six years old. He would later give credit to his father for teaching him everything he knew about the game.

Roberto entered high school at the age of 13 and led his Double-A Juvenile team to a national championship in 1985. That same year, he joined the Padres organization. Roberto's older brother, Sandy Jr., had signed with San Diego two seasons earlier. The two were united in the minors at Wichita in 1987, and Las Vegas the following year. Although they both appeared on the Padres roster in 1988–1989, they would not play together full-time in the majors until the 2000 campaign. When Roberto joined his brother in Cleveland before the 1999 slate, Sandy told reporters that their reunion was a "dream come true."

Padres GM Joe McIlvaine once referred to Alomar as "Dr. J in cleats." A self-professed student of the game, the slick-fielding second baseman surprised himself at times. "Some plays just come out of me, just on instinct," he once said. "I'll make a play and wonder, 'How did I do that?'" Few players were as dedicated to their profession. When he was with the Blue Jays, Alomar lived in a hotel that was literally attached to the SkyDome. His love of the game made him one of the best players of his generation.

Described by multiple sources as an "acrobat" at second base, Alomar's speed and agility allowed him to go deep in the hole to snare hard-hit grounders. His long, precise throws to first base frustrated many opponents throughout the years. He led the American League in fielding percentage four times and captured 10 Gold Glove Awards—more than any second baseman in the history of the game.

The same quickness that made Alomar a superior defensive player aided him offensively as well. During his 17 seasons in the majors, he averaged 28 stolen bases per year. He collected 30 or more steals on eight occasions, peaking at 55 in 1993. Hitting most often out of the second spot in the order, he was reliable in the clutch, compiling a .314 average with runners in scoring position. He reached the century mark in RBIs twice. Not just a singles hitter, he generated close to 800 extra-base hits. He also hit for average, topping the .300 mark during nine campaigns.

A measure of his value to the clubs he played for, Alomar made seven postseason appearances with three different teams—the Blue Jays, Orioles, and Indians. He was named Most Valuable Player of the 1992 American League Championship Series with Toronto. He was a prime candidate for World Series MVP the following year, when he hit .480 against the Phillies, but he ended up losing out to Paul Molitor. Alomar had postseason hitting streaks of 12 (1993 to 1996) and 11 (1991 to 1992) games.

Although he is remembered by many for an unfortunate run-in with umpire John Hirschbeck, Alomar made amends and later became friends with the arbiter. After Alomar missed out on the Hall of Fame in his first year of eligibility, Hirschbeck made an appeal to the Baseball Writers' Association of America. A 12-time All-Star, Alomar was enshrined at Cooperstown in his second year on the ballot.

In 2010, Alomar was inducted into the Canadian Baseball Hall of Fame. He was hired by the Blue Jays the following year as a special assistant to baseball operations in Toronto. He designed a clothing line, "second2none," which was marketed at the Rogers Centre. His uniform number was the first to be retired by the Jays.

Orlando Cepeda

First Baseman

Orlando Cepeda's father was a power-hitting shortstop who carried the nickname "Perucho," which translates to the "Bull." Referred to as the

"Babe Ruth of the Caribbean," Perucho's tremendous talent almost drove young Orlando away from the game. "I said to hell with baseball," Orlando recalled. "They kept saying, 'you'll never be as good as your father,' so I stopped playing." Orlando turned to basketball briefly and missed a full year of athletics after he tore cartilage in his right knee.

Determined to make a success of his son, Perucho put Orlando through a rigorous training routine. When Orlando dropped a fly ball during a Puerto Rican amateur championship game, Perucho told him he would not be welcome at home if he didn't atone for the error. Despite his father's harsh approach, Orlando eventually matured into a fine young player, earning the nickname "Baby Bull."

Shortly after he signed with the New York Giants, Cepeda's father died of malaria. The loss was extremely hard on Orlando. In the Mississippi–Ohio Valley League, manager Walt Dixon recognized Cepeda's personal struggles. With the proper amount of support, Cepeda hit .393 in his minor-league debut. During the next two seasons, he gathered 351 hits (including 51 homers) on the farm. In 1958, he replaced Whitey Lockman as starting first baseman in San Francisco.

Cepeda homered in his first major-league game and went on to capture Rookie of the Year honors. He also finished among the top 10 in MVP balloting. He was in good company, as Ernie Banks, Hank Aaron, and Willie Mays were also on that list.

Cepeda quickly established himself as one of the premier first basemen in the National League. His best season with San Francisco came in 1961, when he led the circuit in homers (46) and RBIs (142). He finished second in MVP voting to Frank Robinson that year and received the third of six consecutive All-Star selections. Braves hurler Lew Burdette once said that Cepeda was the toughest batter he ever faced. Teammate Willie Mays remarked that Cepeda "annoyed" almost every pitcher in the league.

In 1963, Cepeda opted not to play in the Puerto Rican Winter League, focusing on personal fitness instead. While working out, he dropped an 80-pound weight on the knee he had injured several years earlier, causing serious damage. Afraid to tell manager Alvin Dark about it, he played for two full seasons in sporadic pain. He opted for surgery in 1965, and was out for most of the year. Accused of being a malingerer, he was traded to the Cardinals partway through the 1966 campaign.

Cepeda made an immediate impression in St. Louis with his vibrant personality. Nicknamed "Cha Cha" for the Latin music he played in the clubhouse, the spirited slugger recalled, "We were one of the loosest teams ever. We would play around until five minutes before the game." Hall of Fame teammate Lou Brock said of Cepeda's cheerfulness, "You can get [upset] in this game, you know. But Cepeda is always there, very energetic, full of fire, and it's catching."

It certainly was.

With Cepeda acting as clubhouse cheerleader, the Cardinals made back-to-back World Series appearances in 1967 and 1968. In the former campaign, he was named NL MVP on the strength of his .325 batting average and league-leading 111 RBIs. After disposing of the Red Sox in the 1967 Fall Classic, the Cards had trouble with Tigers southpaw Mickey Lolich the following October. Lolich was masterful in his three starts, walking away with three victories and Series MVP honors.

Traded to the Braves before the 1969 campaign, Cepeda had a handful of good seasons left in him. His last stellar effort came with the Red Sox in 1973, when he drove in 86 runs and hit .289. He finished his career with Kansas City the following season.

Shortly after his retirement, Cepeda was arrested at the San Juan airport with more than 150 pounds of marijuana in his car. He served 10 months in prison. "The isolation, the disgrace, the feelings of numbness, they were horrible," he later said of his experience. In 1980, he was hired as a coach for the White Sox. Off the field, he donated his time to various charitable causes. Elected to Cooperstown in 1999, he stated his intention of being a "role model to the people of [his] country."

Roberto Clemente

Right Fielder

In his prime, Roberto Clemente was the gauge by which future greatness would be measured. A beloved and tragic figure, few players have made such an indelible mark on the sport. Perhaps former commissioner Bowie Kuhn said it best when he remarked, "[Clemente] gave the term 'complete' a new meaning. He made the word 'superstar' seem inadequate. He had about him the air of royalty." Indeed, Clemente's influence extended far beyond the shores of his native country. And in the years following his death, his persona attained an almost mythic quality.

Roberto was the youngest of seven children. Raised in Carolina, he helped his parents by doing odd jobs for neighbors. A devoted fan of outfielder Monte Irvin, he attended many ballgames while growing up. Years later, Irvin remembered local kids hanging around the ballpark while he was playing in Puerto Rico. He was in the habit of letting them carry his bags so they could gain free admission. He had no idea that Clemente was among those children until the Pirates icon told him long after the fact.

At a young age, Clemente began drawing comments about his powerful hands and remarkable throwing ability. He participated in track-and-field events at Vizcarrondo High School and was particularly adept at the javelin throw. Although many believed he could have represented his country in the Olympics, he chose to focus on baseball instead.

In 1952, Clemente attended a tryout camp presided over by Dodgers scout Al Campanis. While he was not signed, Campanis made a note to keep an eye on the budding outfielder. That same year, Clemente was offered a contract to play with the Santurce Cangrejeros. It was Roberto's first taste of real competition. In 1953, he made the All-Star Team.

The Dodgers scouted Clemente again before the 1954 slate. Impressed with his progress, Clyde Sukeforth recommended signing him. "I said to myself, there's a boy who can do two things as well as any man who ever lived," Sukeforth remarked. "Nobody could throw any better that that, and nobody could run better than that." Turning down offers from the Giants and Braves, Clemente entered the Dodgers system. Assigned to Montreal of the International League, he sat on the bench for a good portion of the 1954 campaign and sulked about it. Since he had been left unprotected, the last-place Pirates claimed him in the November draft. Dodgers vice president Buzzie Bavasi later admitted that Clemente had been signed solely to keep the rival Giants from getting their hands on him.

Clemente got off to a hot start in his 1955 big-league debut. He carried a .305 average into June before a second-half slump reduced that mark by 50 points. He was not even in the running for Rookie of the Year. Still, he showed great promise in the outfield, finishing second in the league with 18 assists. Clemente had one of the strongest arms in modern history. His 27 assists in 1961 were the highest total since the World War II era. Broadcaster Vin Scully once quipped, "Clemente could field the ball in New York and throw out a guy in Pennsylvania."

Despite his wondrous talents, Clemente's development as a player was rather slow. A car accident early in his career left him with lingering back problems. Although some of his complaints were very real, he was a borderline hypochondriac who griped incessantly about a wide variety of ailments. Convinced that he would die young, he missed ample playing time throughout the course of his career.

Clemente's intensity both on and off the field could be disconcerting to the people around him. He once commented, "If I [were] happy, I would be a bad ballplayer. With me, when I get mad, it puts energy into my body." Recognizing his unparalleled drive to succeed, renowned baseball writer Roger Angell wrote of Clemente, "He played a kind of baseball that none of us had ever seen before. . . . As if it were a form of punishment for everyone else on the field."

There were a host of other quirks that made Clemente unique. A chronic insomniac, he rarely slept for more than three or four hours at a time. He once joked that he could hit .400 if he could get sufficient rest. Highly sensitive, he worried about being misunderstood and underappreciated. He had arguments with multiple sportswriters throughout the years and tended to avoid the ones he felt were misrepresenting him. At the same time, he could be welcoming and abundantly generous to virtual strangers who recognized his talents. He was especially friendly to Spanish-speaking fans.

Clemente's first big season came in 1960, when he topped the .300 mark for the first time and exceeded his cumulative home-run total from the previous three campaigns. The dimensions of Forbes Field were infamously deep, but Clemente was more of a line-drive hitter who hammered balls into the gaps. While he had a keen batting eye, he never drew more than 56 walks in any season. He liked to swing the bat and didn't let too many pitches go by. Hall of Famer Juan Marichal once observed, "The big thing about Clemente is that he can hit any pitch. I don't mean only strikes. He can hit a ball off his ankles or off his ear."

From 1960 to 1967, Clemente maintained a .300 average each year. He won four batting titles in that span, reaching a career-high .357 in 1967. Most often appearing third in the batting order, he hit .327 with runners in scoring position during his career. He scored and drove in no fewer than 82 runs in the same season seven times.

Clemente was showered with accolades from 1960 until his untimely passing in 1972. A 12-time All-Star, he was named NL MVP in 1966. He captured World Series MVP honors in 1971. The most decorated outfielder in history, his 12 Gold Gloves were equaled only by Willie Mays. Clemente's efforts propelled the Pirates to four postseason appearances. He logged a .318 average in 26 October contests. The Pirates won three of the five series he appeared in.

As Clemente began to age, he became more relaxed and developed a sense of humor about himself. He served as a role model to younger players, who admired him for his hustle and determination. He once said, "I want to be remembered as a ballplayer who gave all he had to give." Hundreds of posthumous books and articles written about him concur that he is the greatest Hispanic outfielder in major-league history.

In the wake of a devastating earthquake in Nicaragua during the winter of 1972, Clemente busied himself organizing relief efforts. He worked tirelessly through the Christmas season, and when he learned that some of the care packages were being mishandled by profiteers, he opted to fly to Nicaragua to personally remedy the situation. The cargo plane he hastily chartered was old and in poor working condition. Around 9 p.m. on New Year's Eve—when most Puerto Ricans were celebrating—Clemente's plane took off. Overburdened with supplies, the aircraft experienced problems shortly after taking off. It crashed into the Atlantic Ocean about a mile off the coast. Despite a massive search and rescue effort, Clemente's body was never recovered.

Clemente's death left many shocked and bereaved. Before his passing, he had envisioned the establishment of a massive sports complex for Puerto Rican youths. Honoring his memory, Vera Clemente made her husband's dream a reality. The complex bearing his name helped produce many exceptional players throughout the years, including Juan Gonzalez, Bernie Williams, and Ivan Rodriguez. The Cooperstown Hall of Fame honored Clemente by waiving the standard five-year waiting period for induction. Fittingly, he was enshrined in 1973, along with his boyhood idol, Monte Irvin. Today, an annual award given to the player "who best exemplifies the game of baseball, sportsmanship, community involvement, and the individual's accomplishments to his team" is named after Clemente. It had previously been known as the Commissioner's Award.

Jose Cruz

Left Fielder

Jose Cruz came from a baseball family. His brothers Hector and Tommy both spent time in the majors. His son, Jose Jr., hit more than 200 homers in 12 big-league seasons. The most renowned of the bunch, Cruz might have become a household name in the United States had he spent his best years with a big-market club.

Born and raised in Arroyo, Cruz turned pro with the Cardinals at the age of 19. By then, he had already established himself as an exceptional player in his native land, where he carried the nickname "Cheo." He toiled in the Cardinals minor-league system for four seasons before getting a September call-up in 1970. He hit .353 in six appearances, but the Cardinals outfield was crowded, with Jose Cardenal in center, Lou Brock in left, and a right-field platoon of Leron Lee and Carl Taylor.

Taylor and Lee both slumped horribly in 1971, leaving an opening for Cruz. He was hitting .327 with the Tulsa Oilers when he was recalled to St. Louis. Inserted into the lineup in late June, he compiled a .274 average, with 46 runs scored, primarily out of the sixth or seventh slot in the batting order. When he failed to develop into a major star during the next three seasons, the Cardinals sold his contract to the Astros.

With St. Louis, Cruz had not been given an opportunity to show off his speed. In 1976, Houston manager Bill Virdon turned him loose on the basepaths. Between 1976 and 1980, Cruz averaged 36 steals per year, finishing among the top 10 in four straight seasons. He peaked at 44 thefts in 1977.

During Cruz's prime playing years, the Astros wore flamboyant orange and red rainbow uniforms. Cruz had his own unique style, sporting high socks and waving the bat high above his head. He had a dramatic leg kick before he swung. His arrival at the plate in Houston was

announced with a dramatic flair over the PA system: "Now batting . . .
Jose Cruuuuuuuuuuz!!!" It became a habit among fans to vocalize his
name as he was being introduced.

By the late 1970s, Cruz was the second most famous player from
Puerto Rico, behind Roberto Clemente. An excellent contact hitter, he
maintained a batting average of .267 or higher each year from 1976 to
1986. He topped the .300 mark six times during that span, reaching a
personal high of .318 in 1983, when he led the NL with 189 hits. Cruz
received MVP consideration five times during his career. He might
have generated a few more homers had he not played in the cavernous
Astrodome, where the foul poles were 360 feet from home plate. A
reliable run producer, the lefty-swinging outfielder drove in at least 70
runs in eight seasons and led the league twice in sacrifice flies.

If Cruz had a weakness, it was defense. He finished among the top
five in errors on six occasions. But his ample speed allowed him to cover
a lot of ground. By 1986, he had sufficiently polished his craft, leading
NL left fielders with a .984 fielding percentage. His range factor per
nine innings is among the top 40 marks of all time.

Cruz helped the Astros to three postseason appearances, reaching
base by hit or walk 30 times in 16 playoff games. The Astros never
advanced to the World Series during his playing days. By 1988, he was
40 years old and slowing down. Traded to the Yankees before the season began, he managed a feeble .200 average in 38 games and retired.
After that, he appeared in the short-lived Senior Professional Baseball
Association. From 1997 to 2009, he served as a first-base coach for the
Astros. He is still quite popular in Houston and remains a highly respected figure in Puerto Rico. His number (25) was retired by the
Astros.

Carlos Delgado

First Baseman

Born in Aguadilla, Carlos Delgado grew up with three siblings. His
father, "Don Cao," and grandfather, Asdrubal "Pingolo" Delgado, were
respected men in the community. Carlos said that it made him feel
"protected." It also inspired him to stay out of trouble. By 1988, he had
drawn the interest of five major-league teams. He was convinced by

veteran scout Epy Guerrero to sign with the Blue Jays. He finished high school before his pro career began.

Although Delgado's development in the minors was rather slow, the players around him knew he would eventually become a major star. "I remember when we signed him, he was 16," said former Cy Young Award winner Pat Hentgen. "You could turn your back on the field at the minor-league complex and you could tell it was him because of the sound. He had special hands and he had special bat speed from the time he was a teenager." Blue Jays announcer Buck Martinez agreed with that assessment, remarking, "He had power that you don't see very often." Despite his ability to crush the ball, Delgado spent portions of seven seasons in the minors before finding a permanent home in the big leagues. Originally a catcher, he was eventually reassigned to first base.

From 1996 to 2008, Delgado was among the most productive players in the majors. He drove in 90 or more runs 12 times, including a run of 11 consecutive seasons. He led the league with 145 RBIs in 2003. His 57 doubles in 2000 represent the seventh-highest single-season total in major-league history. Aside from Todd Helton, the players ahead of Delgado on the all-time list played in the 1920s or 1930s. In 2003, Delgado joined an elite group of players to smash four homers in a single game. His efforts lifted the Jays to a 10–8 win over the Devil Rays.

Delgado's exceptional power at the plate often overshadowed his other abilities. He was more than competent at first base, leading the AL in putouts each year from 1999 to 2003. He also paced the circuit in double plays four times, while finishing among the top five in assists on six occasions. While he committed a fair share of errors, the Blue Jays were never terribly concerned about it. He was used only sporadically as a designated hitter.

Outspoken and politically active, Delgado was not shy about sharing his personal convictions with others. He spent two years campaigning against the use of Vieques—a small island off the Puerto Rican coast—for target practice by the U.S. Navy. When the bombing was halted in 2003, Delgado joined a movement to compel the U.S. government to deal with the lingering environmental hazards caused by 60 years of military use. "It's still in the ground, it's still in the water," Delgado told reporters. "That's why we've got the highest cancer rate of any place in Puerto Rico."

Delgado was also fundamentally opposed to the U.S. occupation of Iraq. In 2004, he refused to stand for the singing of "God Bless America" during ballgames. "I'm not trying to get anyone mad," he said. "If I make the last out of the seventh inning, I'll stand there. But I'd rather be in the dugout." A *Sports Illustrated* writer came to the slugger's defense, remarking, "Good for him. In the world of mainstream sports, where cookie-cutter athletes rarely take a stand on any issue, let alone one as highly charged as a war, Delgado is a rarity." The Mets didn't care how unique Delgado's personal protest was. When they acquired him in November 2005, they ordered him to stop. Throughout the years, Delgado was actively involved in a variety of charities and community events. In 2006, he received the prestigious Roberto Clemente Award.

A serious hip injury in 2009 effectively ended Delgado's career. He underwent three surgeries before announcing his retirement in 2011. Through the 2016 campaign, he was one of only six players to collect 30 or more homers in 10 consecutive seasons. He still holds more than a dozen Blue Jays franchise records and is the all-time leader among Puerto Rican-born players in home runs and RBIs (although Carlos Beltran was poised to surpass him in the latter category at the time of this writing). Despite those lofty credentials, he was eliminated from the Cooperstown ballot in 2015. ESPN writer Jayson Stark remarked that Delgado was the "best player in history to get booted after his first year" and referred to him as a victim of the Hall's "messed up voting system."

Juan Gonzalez

Outfielder

Juan Gonzalez was born in Arecibo, a municipality on Puerto Rico's northern coastal plain. He grew up in a poor neighborhood, learning to hit bottle caps with a broom handle as a boy. In the youth leagues, he played alongside Bernie Williams and competed against Ivan Rodriguez. At the age of nine, he became an avid fan of Spanish wrestler Igor the Magnificent. At some point, he adopted the nickname "Igor." Gonzalez's father, a math teacher, tried to steer his son and two daughters away from the crime that was rampant in their barrio. Young Juan avoided trouble and ended up being signed by the Rangers at the age of 16.

Gonzalez's debut in the Gulf Coast League was not spectacular. Sharing a dugout with future stars Sammy Sosa and Dean Palmer, he hit .240 in 60 games. Despite the presence of so many budding sluggers, the team combined for just five homers that season. It's interesting to note that Gonzalez and Sosa later slugged more than 1,000 home runs in major-league play.

Gonzalez's first big season came in 1990, at Oklahoma City, where he went deep 29 times and drove in more than 100 runs. He received his second major-league call-up that year and won a permanent roster spot in Texas. For the next 11 seasons, he was one of the most prolific run producers in the majors.

Gonzalez was oddly proportioned with a muscular upper body and long, skinny legs. The nickname "Igor" seemed to suit him, as he appeared to many like a cartoon character. Unnaturally powerful, he was known for his ability to hit scorching line drives. Quite a few of his homers left the park in a relatively straight line.

Defensively, Gonzalez appeared most often in right field, although he patrolled every outfield station during his 14 full seasons in the majors. He was least effective in center field, where he led players at his position with eight errors during the 1992 slate. As a right fielder, he appeared among the top five in fielding percentage three times. He had a strong arm, finishing with double-digit assist totals twice.

Gonzalez gained wide acclaim for his ability to chase teammates across the plate. He once remarked, "I concentrate better when I see runners on base." His lifetime statistics bear witness to this fact, as he hit .301 with men on during his career and 30 points higher with the bases loaded. He launched eight homers and 14 doubles in the latter scenario.

Between 1992 and 2001, Gonzalez averaged 37 homers and 116 RBIs per year. He led the league twice in homers and once apiece in doubles and RBIs. A three-time All-Star, he captured a pair of MVP Awards, while finishing among the top 10 in voting on three other occasions.

Gonzalez generated controversy more than once during his career. During a game against the Yankees in 1998, he sulked when the official scorer failed to credit him with a pair of RBIs. He gestured angrily toward the press box while his team was in the midst of a dramatic rally. Gonzalez was so immersed in his tantrum that he failed to congratulate his teammate for hitting a two-run homer.

It wasn't the last unfortunate incident Gonzalez was involved in. Shortly before the 1999 All-Star Game, he announced he would refuse an invitation to join the AL squad if he was not elected by popular vote. As a result of that pronouncement, he was not invited. A few weeks later, he refused to play in the annual Hall of Fame exhibition game, stating that his wrist was sore and the pants he was provided with were too large. In Gonzalez's words, they were "clown pants."

The most serious blow to Gonzalez's reputation came in 2007, when he was mentioned in the infamous Mitchell Report. He had been fingered as a steroid user in *Juiced*, Jose Canseco's tell-all book, two years earlier. The evidence against Gonzalez was circumstantial, and the slugger unequivocally denied the claim, stating he had "nothing to hide." No official charges were ever brought against him.

Shy around reporters because of the language barrier, Gonzalez was never terribly popular in Texas. Even after he tied a record with five home runs in the 1996 American League Division Series against the Yankees, he failed to endear himself to fans. Teammate Rafael Palmeiro referred to Gonzalez as a "misunderstood" player. "He's a great person," said Palmeiro, "but he's not one to express a lot of emotion to the media. . . . He doesn't let people provoke him into a reaction. Most people don't like that, and they end up trying to trample him or make him look like a bad guy. Really, he is just a quiet, simple guy."

Near the end of his career, Gonzalez contended with back spasms and leg problems. A torn muscle in his hand slowed him down for the better part of two seasons as well. He made his last major-league appearance with Cleveland in 2005. He played for the Long Island Ducks of the independent Atlantic League the following year.

Despite a slew of injuries, Gonzalez ranked among the top 40 in slugging percentage and homers at the time of his retirement. He was equally successful in the annual Caribbean Series, posting the sixth-highest batting average and seventh-highest slugging percentage in history. He reached the 300-homer threshold faster than any other major-league player.

When Gonzalez made it big in the majors, he offered financial support to many of his less fortunate friends back home. After his retirement, he became involved in numerous charitable causes, although he insisted on remaining anonymous. "What value is it to help someone and then publicize it in newspapers?" he said. "That is not giving." Gonzalez was elected to the Caribbean Baseball Hall of Fame in 2015. He was eliminated from the Cooperstown ballot in 2012.

Javy Lopez

Catcher

Javy Lopez was one of five children born to Jacinto Lopez and Evelia Torres. He grew up in Ponce, describing his neighborhood as having "good people" and "good friends," adding, "Most were blue-collar working-class families." He learned the game of baseball from a pair of neighbors who organized a church team. He had no idea what he was doing at first and remembered accidentally running straight to second base during his first at-bat. By the age of 13, he was hitting for power and appearing on all-star teams.

As a boy, Lopez idolized Jose Cruz. At the age of 11, he had an opportunity to meet his hero and get some advice. Cruz told him that baseball was a "passion" he would have to "eat and sleep with" if he wanted to succeed. Although Lopez played with gusto after that, he never envisioned himself as a major leaguer. "I didn't start thinking about the big leagues until I was 15 or 16 years old," he recalled. "Before that, I just played for fun and because I loved it."

Lopez attended Academia Cristo Rey and was signed by the Braves as an amateur free agent in 1987. He had a stellar season in the South Atlantic League in 1992, hitting .321. After posting a cumulative .375 average in two trials with Atlanta, he was promoted for good in 1994. The Braves were in second place behind the Expos when the season was preempted due to a players strike. Lopez would remain the number-one catcher in Atlanta for more than a decade.

A sure-handed target behind the plate, Lopez finished among the top five in fielding percentage on five occasions. He had the benefit of working with Atlanta's "Big Three"—Greg Maddux, Tom Glavine, and John Smoltz—who formed the greatest pitching tandem of the 1990s (and perhaps of all time). With Lopez behind the plate, Atlanta's Hall of Fame trio collected no fewer than 47 wins per year from 1995 to 1999.

While Lopez never won a Gold Glove, he was a major contender in 1996, when he posted the highest range factor in the league and also led in assists.

In his prime, Lopez was one of the best offensive catchers in the majors. A three-time All-Star, he enjoyed his finest season at the plate in 2003, when he hit .328 and launched 43 homers (all but one as a catcher), setting a single-season record for players at his position. "I'm very proud to have the record—very proud to be in the book," he said. "It was a big accomplishment for me, a kid from Ponce, Puerto Rico, who learned how to play baseball on a concrete basketball court in my neighborhood." Lopez's 34 homers in 1998 are the seventh-highest mark in history.

Most often hitting out of the sixth or seventh spot in the order, the right-handed Lopez topped the .300 mark four times as a full-time player and drove in no fewer than 68 runs during six campaigns. The job of a catcher is a demanding one, and Lopez succumbed to injuries multiple times. The most serious one occurred in 1999, when he sustained a ligament tear in his right knee. Although he recovered, an ankle injury in 2006 ended his major-league career.

Lopez made 60 postseason appearances—all with Atlanta—and was one of the Braves' most reliable October performers. His finest showing came in the 1996 National League Championship Series against the Cardinals, when he captured MVP honors with 13 hits in seven games. He batted .278, with 10 homers and 28 RBIs, winning his only World Series ring in 1995.

Traded to the Orioles in 2004, Lopez finished his career with the Red Sox two years later. He made a comeback attempt with the Braves in 2008, but didn't make the cut in spring training. "I don't blame them," he said upon hearing the news, continuing, "The hitting wasn't there, and unfortunately I didn't throw the guy out on the stealing attempts. That's a concern." Lopez officially announced his retirement that year. His autobiography, *Behind the Plate: A Catcher's View of the Braves Dynasty*, was released in 2012.

Mike Lowell

Third Baseman

Mike Lowell's father Carl was a member of the Puerto Rican national team and played on a squad that defeated Cuba in the Pan American Games. Born in San Juan, Lowell moved to Miami with his family when he was four years old. Since his parents were both from Cuba, he has always identified himself as Cuban.

Lowell grew up rooting for the Philadelphia Phillies. His favorite player was Mike Schmidt, but he also took an interest in the career of Jose Canseco. Lowell excelled at math in school and once said he would have pursued accounting or investment banking as a career if baseball had not worked out for him. At Christopher Columbus High School, Lowell was too small to be a starter on the baseball team. He begged his parents to transfer him to Coral Gables High, where he became one of the school's star players. He later earned All-Conference honors at Florida International University as a second baseman and ended up being drafted by the Yankees.

In the minors, Lowell was moved to third base. He hit well at every stop, but the Yankees were well-stocked with talent and traded him to the Marlins after promoting him briefly in 1998. During the offseason, Lowell was diagnosed with testicular cancer. He underwent surgery and radiation therapy, making his debut with Florida on May 29. His numbers were fair considering what he had been through.

Beginning in 2000, Lowell enjoyed five consecutive seasons as one of the Marlins' top run producers. He averaged 25 homers and 95 RBIs per year between 2000 and 2004. He was on pace for a monster season in 2003, when a hand injury limited him to 130 games. He ended up with 60 extra-base hits and 105 ribbies.

After earning his third straight All-Star selection in 2004, Lowell captured a Gold Glove the following year. He led NL third basemen in double plays and fielding percentage. A fine defensive player, his .974 lifetime fielding percentage was the highest mark among retired third basemen entering the 2016 campaign.

Lowell was a major contributor to Florida's successful World Series run in 2003. Traded to the Red Sox in 2006, he got another chance at October glory. With David Ortiz and Manny Ramirez ahead of him in the lineup, Lowell saw a lot of pitches in the strike zone. He enjoyed one of his most industrious seasons at the plate in 2007, with 37 doubles, 21 homers, and 120 RBIs. He also posted a career-high batting average of .324, earning his fourth All-Star nod. During the postseason that year, he was among Boston's hottest hitters, collecting 18 hits and 15 RBIs in 14 games. He was named MVP of the World Series and later received consideration for AL MVP, finishing fifth in voting.

Lowell struggled with a torn hip labrum in 2008 and 2009. He missed more than 40 games in each season but still managed respectable offensive numbers with a cumulative total of 34 homers and 148 RBIs. Before the 2010 campaign, the Red Sox attempted to trade him to the Rangers, but the deal was nixed when it was discovered that Lowell was in need of thumb surgery. He entered the Red Sox camp that spring and won a roster spot. Serving as a reserve infielder, he hit .239 in 73 games and then retired. The Red Sox honored him that October with an on-field ceremony.

Eligible for the Hall of Fame in 2016, Lowell was eliminated from the ballot after failing to receive the minimum number of votes. Since his retirement, he has worked as an analyst for the MLB Network.

Felix Millan

Second Baseman

Born in the barrio of El Cerro del Calvario, Felix Millan had 10 siblings, two of whom did not survive beyond childhood. Millan grew up in sugarcane fields and used improvised materials to play ball. He often prayed that he would make it to the big leagues so he could help his parents out. His father worked at a sugarcane processing plant, and his mother washed clothes for a living. Together, they didn't make enough money to send Felix to school with a pair of shoes. When he was 10, he was sent to live with his grandparents.

A shy kid, Millan answered to the nickname "Nacho" from an early age. He honed his skills with local amateur teams and became known as "El Gatito" (which translates to "the Cat") for his style of play. "He's the type of player you never realize is around until the game is over," said one contemporary. "Then you look up and he's got two hits, an RBI, a stolen base, and he's been in two double plays."

After graduating from high school, Millan joined the U.S. Army and played military ball. In 1964, he was spotted by an A's scout in Puerto Rico's Double-A professional league. He was signed for the modest sum of $2,500. In November of that year, the Braves acquired him in the first-year draft.

Millan performed well in the minors and got his first call-up in 1966. He started the 1967 campaign in the majors but was sent back down in late May to improve his swing. He returned in September, elevating his average by 41 points. Millan had a unique batting style, choking almost halfway up on the bat—a method seldom used in the modern era. The practice afforded him superior bat control. He never struck out more than 35 times in any season, averaging just one whiff per every 26 plate appearances. He finished among the top 10 in sacrifice hits six times, leading the league in 1974. More than 80 percent of his hits were singles, but he did peak at 37 doubles in 1975.

Millan was the first Braves player with six hits in a game. He accomplished the feat in 1970. Five years later, he played a role in another record when he gathered four hits, but he ended up being erased each time by a double play. Joe Torre, who had the dubious distinction of grounding into all four double plays, said after the game, "I'd like to thank Felix Millan for making all of this possible"

Millan gained wide acclaim for his glove work, appearing among the league leaders in multiple defensive categories year after year. He captured two Gold Gloves and was named to three All-Star Teams. Traded to the Mets before the 1973 slate, he helped the Mets to a World Series appearance that year. He batted .316 against the Reds in the NLCS and added six hits (including a double and a triple) in the Fall Classic as the Mets bowed to the A's in seven games.

Millan had a few more decent seasons in New York after that, hitting .278 in a five-year span. On August 12, 1977, Ed Ott of the Pirates slid hard into Millan at second while breaking up a double play. Millan took exception to Ott's excessive use of force and punched him in the face with the baseball still in his hand. The Pirates catcher slammed Millan to the turf at Three Rivers Stadium, breaking Millan's collarbone. He never returned to the majors.

Millan continued to play in the Japanese Central League, winning a batting title in 1979. He also appeared in the Puerto Rican Winter League and the Senior Professional Baseball Association. Putting his instructional skills to use, he coached in the Mets minor-league system and worked with kids at Roberto Clemente's Sports City complex. Later still, he made international trips for Major League Baseball, tutoring young prospects. "I love it," he said in 2011. "From Africa, from the Netherlands, kids from different countries come in. There's a lot of good baseball players in the world."

Bengie Molina

Catcher

Bengie Molina's father "Pai" was a factory worker for 30 years. As a young man, he established himself as one of the best players around, drawing comparisons to a "scorpion" at second base. The Brewers invited him to a tryout in 1973, but his wife was expecting their first child (Bengie), and he didn't attend. He never complained about the decision. When his playing days were behind him, he spent the rest of his life coaching local youths. He was eventually elected to the Puerto Rican Baseball Hall of Fame.

Pai's three sons were among his star pupils. Before his untimely death from a massive heart attack at the age of 58, he taught them the value of humility, integrity, and hard work. Bengie honored his father's memory by upgrading the field Pai had presided over for so many years in the barrio of Espinosa. Bengie's memoirs (released in 2015) recount the profound impact his father had on the community. "I want people to know how much he valued respect and wanted to raise good human beings and wanted kids to behave," said Molina.

Bengie and his brother Jose were both chosen in the 1993 Amateur Draft. Bengie was the first to appear in the majors, during the 1998 campaign. Jose would make his debut the following year, while Yadier, the youngest of the brood, would get his big break in 2004. After graduating from Vega Alta High School, Bengie attended Arizona Western College. By the time he became the Angels' full-time catcher in 2000, he had spent portions of nine seasons in the minors.

Molina held the starting job in Anaheim and Los Angeles for six years. During his last few campaigns with the club, his brother Jose served as a backup. The Angels were in the habit of employing a platoon, and Bengie never appeared in more than 127 games behind the plate in any season. Although it took a few years for him to emerge as a power hitter, his defensive skills were evident early on.

Equipped with a strong, accurate arm, Molina finished first or second in runners caught stealing on five occasions. He foiled 31 percent of all stolen base attempts during his career, which is several points above the league average. Steady with a glove, he placed among the top five in fielding percentage in seven seasons. His lifetime mark of .994 is among the top 20 totals of all time. His brother Yadier is slightly ahead of him on the list. Molina was recognized for his defensive excellence with a pair of Gold Gloves.

In 2000, Molina put up double-digit home-run totals for the first time in his major-league career. He duplicated the feat for seven straight seasons beginning in 2003. He averaged 20 doubles and 14 homers per year between 2000 and 2009. Most often hitting near the bottom third of the order, he drove in no fewer than 70 runs on five occasions. His best offensive effort came with the Giants in 2008, when he reached career highs in doubles (33) and RBIs (95), while fashioning a highly respectable .292 batting average.

Molina was comically slow afoot, stealing just three bases during his career (all of which may have been due to defensive indifference). While playing for Toronto in 2006, he lined a ball into the gap and ended up going for a triple. After he slid safely into third, the entire Blue Jays dugout erupted in laughter. When Molina noticed this, he started laughing, too. It was his first triple in nearly six years. He would add three more to his lifetime totals before he retired.

Molina was involved in an unusual play late in the 2008 season. After hitting a ball over the fence that was initially ruled a single, he was replaced with a pinch-runner. Upon further review, the umpires changed their ruling and credited Molina with a home run. Since he had been removed from the game, Emmanuel Burriss rounded the bases for him. Molina got credit for the homer and a pair of ribbies, but the run was added to Burriss's totals. And so, Molina's lifetime run output should have been 458.

During his 13 seasons in the majors, Molina helped two different clubs to four postseason appearances. He won a World Series ring with the Angels in 2002. In 2010, he started the season with the Giants but ended up being traded to the Rangers shortly before the All-Star break. Molina's reassuring presence behind the plate was instrumental down the stretch, as the Rangers clinched the first pennant in franchise history. Facing the club that had traded him just months before, Molina slumped mightily at the plate. His Texas teammates didn't fare much better, as the Giants breezed to a championship. Since Molina had spent a significant portion of the season in San Francisco, he was guaranteed a World Series ring.

Molina announced his retirement after the 2010 campaign. Three years later, he took a job as a hitting instructor for the St. Louis Cardinals. In 2014, he joined the Rangers coaching staff, serving as a catching instructor and first-base coach. Entering the 2016 campaign, the Molina brothers had a combined total of six World Series rings in their possession.

Jorge Posada

Catcher

Born in Santurce, neither of Jorge Posada's parents were of Puerto Rican descent. His mother was Dominican and his father Cuban. Posada grew up in San Juan and played several sports in high school, including volleyball and track. Excelling at baseball, he made the school's all-star team as a shortstop.

Baseball was a Posada family legacy. Jorge's father and his uncle Leo were both star players in Puerto Rico during the 1950s. Jorge Sr. spent a few seasons in the minors, while Leo became a first-string player for the A's in 1961. When their careers were over, they remained in the game—Leo as a batting instructor and Jorge Sr. as a scout.

Following in their footsteps, Jorge learned to switch hit at the age of 13. He was scouted by the Yankees in 1989, but his father wanted him to get a college education first. Unfortunately, Jorge's SAT scores prevented him from attending a four-year school. He enrolled at Calhoun Community College in Decatur, Alabama, on a baseball scholarship.

Jorge had difficulty adjusting to life in the United States. Speaking only broken English, he encountered racism and ended up in quite a few fistfights. In the end, he persevered, getting drafted by the Yankees in 1990.

During his first year in the minors at Oneonta, Posada played mostly second base, but he also began to learn the basics of catching. His bat

developed quicker than his defense. In 1993, he led the Carolina
League in passed balls. The following year, he paced the International
League in errors. He was out for six weeks in 1994 with a broken leg
sustained in a violent collision at the plate. While catchers were allowed
to block the plate in Posada's day, he was hesitant about doing so for-
ever after.

Beginning in 1995, the Yankees began promoting members of the
so-called Core Four to New York. Andy Pettitte, Derek Jeter, and Mariano Rivera made their debuts before Posada, who appeared in one
September game that year. He spent most of the 1996 campaign at
Columbus before getting another call to the majors. In 1997, Posada
played backup to Joe Girardi. By 1998, he had won the starting job. He
held onto it for more than a decade.

Posada's name sometimes surfaces in discussions of the all-time
greatest Yankees catchers. Although he may not measure up to Yogi
Berra or Bill Dickey in the final analysis, he certainly gained enough
postseason experience to figure into the mix. Between 1998 and 2011,
Posada was a key figure in 27 postseason series. He helped the Yankees
to six pennants and four World Series titles in that span—totals exceeded by few Yankees backstops. Extremely comfortable on the October stage, Posada collected 79 walks and 103 hits in playoff action.

By 2000, Posada had emerged as one of the AL's best offensive
catchers, capturing five Silver Slugger Awards. He received serious
MVP consideration twice—in 2003 and 2007. The latter campaign was
one of his best at the plate, as he drove in 90 runs and posted a career-
high batting average of .338—fourth best in the league. He had a sharp
batting eye, drawing no fewer than 62 walks in eight consecutive seasons. His on-base percentage exceeded the .400 mark during four campaigns.

Injured in 2008, Posada played in only 51 games. He made a successful comeback the following year but began spending increasing
amounts of time as a designated hitter. He retired after the 2011 slate
with five All-Star selections to his credit.

Sabermetric scores put Posada on the cusp of the Hall of Fame. At
least two of his teammates—Jeter and Rivera—are a lock for the Hall.
Few catchers have been able to put up the consistent numbers that
Posada generated year after year. He is among the franchise leaders in
doubles and home runs. Only Bill Dickey and Yogi Berra played in

more games for the Yankees as catchers. In 2015, the Yankees retired Posada's number (20) and installed a plaque in Monument Park to honor him.

Vic Power

First Baseman

Vic Power's birth name was Victor Pellot. Born in Arecibo, he was the second of six children. He took an interest in baseball at an early age but was forbidden to play it by his father. When his father died of tetanus in the wake of an industrial accident, Power vowed to become a lawyer so he could bring a lawsuit against the company he believed was responsible. He changed his mind when the Criollas de Caguas offered him a contract. He played well and ended up being noticed by a Yankees scout.

In 1949, Power (still known by his birth name) was invited to play for Drummondville of Quebec's outlaw Provincial League. Several players in the circuit had been suspended by Commissioner Happy Chandler for jumping to the Mexican League in 1946. When Power's presence at the plate was announced, he noticed that the French-speaking fans began to laugh. Although he initially believed they were laughing because he was black, it turned out that his name was remarkably similar to the French word *pelote*, which means, "he who paws or pets women." From that point onward, Victor Pellot became "Vic Power."

With a pseudonym in place, Power began to show off his skills. The Provincial League affiliated itself with organized baseball in 1950, and Power drew interest from the Yankees again with a .334 batting average. The Yankees scout purchased Power for $7,500, but Power was given $500 by the team's general manager, only to later discover that he was entitled to receive the full $7,500.

Power's early experiences in baseball were vexing. Assigned to Syracuse of the International League in 1951, he sat down to eat at a restaurant one day and was promptly informed by a waiter that the establishment did not serve colored people. "That's okay," Power quipped comically. "I don't eat colored people." Power was not allowed to stay in white hotels. He was sometimes obligated to sleep in funeral parlors. "I slept with dead people at night," he later recalled. "Or let's say I tried to sleep. I was too scared most of the time. Puerto Ricans are a very superstitious people. Yet, the worst part about all this was that I had to compete with well-rested guys. Maybe that's why I didn't make the Yankees."

It wasn't the reason.

Promoted to Kansas City of the American Association in 1952, Power hit .331, with a league-leading 40 doubles and 17 triples. But the Yankees had Johnny Mize and Joe Collins at first base that year. They also had Moose Skowron playing alongside Power in the minors. Entering the 1953 campaign, the Yankees had yet to break the color barrier and felt that Power was too outspoken. The fact that he regularly dated white women didn't sit well with the Yankees organization either. While Power led the American Association with a .349 batting average in 1953, it was Skowron who ended up getting the call to New York. Power was packaged in a transaction involving 11 players and shipped to Philadelphia. At 26 years of age, he was relatively old for a rookie. The A's were going nowhere in 1954, and neither was Power, assembling a mediocre .255 batting average as his new team lost 103 games. Better days lay just ahead.

It didn't take long for Power to establish himself as one of the best defensive players in the league. He had unparalleled range and often dove for balls halfway to second base. He gathered in throws from teammates with dramatic flourish, prompting the following words from a *Baseball Digest* writer:

> Ask any player in the American League who's the biggest showboat, and chances are you'll get the lightning answer, "Vic Power." The rollicking Puerto Rican is upstage most of the time for the Kansas City A's, hamming up the most elementary situation at first base. He baits the crowd by making one-hand circus catches of easy bull's eye pegs and sometimes succeeds in nauseating his teammates.

While it's true that Power played with a mildly exaggerated flair, his glove work failed to nauseate the people responsible for handing out Gold Gloves. He captured seven in a row beginning in 1958.

One writer described Power as an "emotional player, great sense of humor, laughing, joking, cutting up, playing practical jokes, but he was also a sensitive man with a hair-trigger temper. Bigots couldn't stand him. In the vernacular of the 1950s, Power was one of 'them' who

'didn't know his place.'" When opposing pitchers threw at his head—
and they sometimes did—Power developed a knack for hammering the
high, inside ones to the deep recesses of the ballpark. Although his
offensive numbers don't exactly leap off the page, he compiled a highly
competent .284 lifetime batting average. His best year at the plate came
in 1955, when he reached personal highs in hits (190), triples (10), and
homers (19), while accruing a solid .319 batting mark. He finished ninth
in MVP voting that year.

A four-time All-Star, Power was the starting first baseman in five
different cities. He played for both Philadelphia clubs (the A's and
Phillies). In addition to his five-year stint in Kansas City, he spent four
seasons in Cleveland and three in Minnesota. He finished his career
with the California Angels in 1965.

Power appeared in his last major-league game during the 1965 slate.
In retirement, he lived in Guaynabo, Puerto Rico. He became active in
youth sports programs in San Pedro de Macoris and reportedly played a
major role in transforming the village into a hotbed of talent. Roberto
Alomar, Jose Cruz, and Willie Montanez were among his students.
Power died of cancer in 2005, at the age of 78.

Ivan Rodriguez

Catcher

Born in Manati, Ivan Rodriguez came of age in Vega Baja. His father
worked for a U.S.-based construction company, and his mother taught
elementary school. He took an interest in baseball early on. Originally a
pitcher, he was moved behind the plate by his father (who was his Little
League coach) due to the alarming velocity of his pitches. Rodriguez
played against Bernie Williams and Juan Gonzalez as a youth. He considered Gonzalez an archrival. At Lino Padron High School, Rodriguez
was scouted by Luis Rosa, a veteran birddog who was responsible for
signing Roberto Alomar, Benito Santiago, and Ozzie Guillen, among
others. Rosa was impressed with Rodriguez, commenting, "[H]e
showed leadership at 16 that I'd seen in few kids." In 1988, Rodriguez
signed with the Rangers, officially beginning his professional career.

Short and somewhat stout, at 5-foot-9, 205 pounds, Rodriguez
picked up the nickname "Pudge." Confident and poised, he worked his

way quickly through the Rangers farm system, attaining the rank of seventh among major-league prospects. By 1991, the Rangers felt he was ready for "The Show," calling him up in June. He quickly established himself as a first-stringer.

Rodriguez was aware of his value to the team, remarking, "I'm an everyday player. I hate sitting on the bench." Fiercely competitive, he described himself as an "aggressive" catcher who hated to lose. "It's hard for me to be on a team that's losing every day. That's not me," he once said. He endured a fair share of losses in Texas, as the Rangers finished below .500 six times during his tenure. It was hardly Rodriguez's fault, however, as he made 10 consecutive All-Star appearances and won the same number of Gold Gloves in that span.

Asked to evaluate Rodriguez, Hall of Famer Johnny Bench once remarked, "Well, you know, Pudge Rodriguez is as good as it gets." Considered one of the greatest catchers in history, even Bench couldn't match Rodriguez's lifetime total of 13 Gold Gloves. "I-Rod's" right arm was often likened to a "rifle," "cannon," or "Howitzer." He led the league in caught stealing percentage nine times, foiling 661 attempts during his career. His totals would undoubtedly have been higher had his reputation not preceded him. After a while, few runners were brave enough to challenge him.

A well-rounded player, Rodriguez held his own with a bat as well. He captured seven Silver Slugger Awards between 1994 and 2004, topping the .300 mark at the plate nine times in that span. His best season came in 1999, when he slugged 35 homers and drove in 113 runs (both career highs). His handsome .332 batting average helped elevate him to AL MVP status.

Traded to the Marlins before the 2003 slate, Rodriguez wore six different uniforms during his career. A master strategist behind the plate, he guided Kevin Brown, Rick Helling, and Mike Mussina to 20-win campaigns. Three of the teams Rodriguez played for made postseason appearances. He was a key ingredient in the Marlins' 2003 World Series title, hitting .313 in three playoff rounds, with three homers and 17 RBIs. He was named MVP of the NLCS that year.

Rodriguez spent his last major-league season with the Nationals in 2011. He announced his retirement the following year. On April 23, the Rangers signed him to a one-day contract so he could end his career as a member of the team. In a pregame ceremony, he threw from behind the plate to second base, where Michael Young tagged out an imaginary baserunner.

Rodriguez gained entry into the Hall of Fame in 2017, earning 76 percent of the vote. Among the catchers enshrined at Cooperstown, he ranks first in hits and third in RBIs. No catcher has ever received as many Gold Gloves—not even Johnny Bench, who more or less set the standard for defensive excellence behind the plate.

Benito Santiago

Catcher

Benito Santiago was born in Ponce and attended high school in Santa Isabel. He is the only John F. Kennedy High alumnus to reach the majors to date. Signed by the Padres at the age of 17, he ascended quickly through the minors and made his big-league debut during his fourth professional season. When he first arrived in San Diego, the Padres had a platoon of catchers that included Terry Kennedy and Bruce Bochy. Kennedy was traded to make room for Santiago, while Bochy spent a majority of the 1987 season on the bench.

Few rookies have made such a dramatic impact. After hitting .290 during his 1986 September call-up, Santiago collected 53 extra-base hits and 79 RBIs the following year, while assembling a 34-game hitting streak—the longest by a rookie. It was also the longest by a catcher. He had 12 multihit games during the skein, which lasted from August 25 to October 2. In light of his remarkable accomplishment, he was a unanimous choice for Rookie of the Year. He also earned the first of four Silver Slugger Awards.

Although Santiago never came close to duplicating the success of his rookie campaign, he remained a reliable offensive presence throughout his career. During seasons in which he appeared in at least 100 games, he averaged 20 doubles and 14 home runs per year. He was on pace to reach career-high marks in every slugging category during the 1995 slate, but an elbow injury kept him out of 81 games. Hitting from the right side, Santiago was a free-swinger who was fundamentally opposed to walks. Teammate John Kruk once quipped, "Benny's only rule is 'Thou Shalt Not Draw a Pass.'" Most often appearing sixth or seventh in the batting order, Santiago collected 920 RBIs—among the highest lifetime totals for catchers. He currently resides among the top five in triples and stolen bases as well.

Despite Santiago's contributions, the Padres came close to making a postseason appearance just once during his seven years with the team. That happened in 1989, when a 19–8 run in September left Santiago's squad three games behind the division-leading Giants. Santiago would make three playoff appearances elsewhere before he retired.

Defensively, Santiago was known for his powerful arm, which he used to not only foil stolen-base attempts, but also prevent runners from taking generous leads. He avoided having to spring to his feet by making snap throws from his knees. He picked off 50 runners during his career, while compiling a caught stealing percentage well above the league average. Howard Johnson of the Mets once told a reporter un-abashedly that he had made a personal decision never to run on Santia-go. Marveling at Santiago's extraordinary arm strength, a writer from *Inside Sports* magazine remarked, "This guy could be a pitcher—that's how hard he throws . . . and he's at his best throwing from the kneeling position." Santiago was the first Padres catcher to win a Gold Glove and only the fifth NL backstop to claim the honor in at least three consecu-tive seasons. He turned the trick from 1988 through 1990, joining John-ny Bench, Gary Carter, Tony Pena, and Del Crandall.

After leaving San Diego in 1992, Santiago traveled extensively. He hung around Florida until the Marlins promoted their top catching prospect (Charles Johnson) in 1995. His next 10 seasons included stops in Cincinnati, Philadelphia, Toronto, Chicago, San Francisco, and Kan-sas City. He finished his career with the Pirates in 2005. A five-time All-Star, Santiago made playoff appearances with the Reds and Giants. He was MVP of the 2002 NLCS, helping San Francisco to a five-game win over the Cardinals. He had six hits and five RBIs in the World Series that year. He seemed to improve with age, compiling a .277 regular-season batting average from the age of 38 onward.

After Santiago's resurgence in the 2002 postseason, he was cited by FBI investigators as a steroid user. A Giants clubhouse attendant claimed to have discovered a sealed package of syringes in his locker. As a result, Santiago's name appears in the *Game of Shadows* book, as well as in the Mitchell Report. He later came clean in front of a grand jury, admitting to his use of PEDs near the end of his career.

While Santiago's confession likely destroyed his chances of being elected to Cooperstown, it did not prevent the Padres of inducting him into their own Hall of Fame in 2015. After his retirement, Santiago settled in Fort Lauderdale. His son, Benito Jr., was a multisport star in college, excelling at both baseball and basketball. He was drafted in the 38th round by the Giants.

Ruben Sierra

Right Fielder

One researcher remarks, "Sierra was a shooting star, not a superstar." Like so many players before and after him, injuries prevented Ruben Sierra from realizing his full potential. But for the better part of a decade, he was among the most successful right fielders in the majors.

Sierra was born and raised in Rio Piedras, which was an independent municipality until 1951, when it was consolidated with San Juan. Sierra's father died when he was four years old, leaving his mother to raise five kids. Sierra's mother told him that to be successful, he needed to find his passion and do everything he could to keep it alive. Sierra developed a passion for baseball early on. As a boy, he idolized Roberto Clemente. He attended the same high school as fellow major leaguer Luis Alicea. Signed by the Rangers in 1982, he entered their minor-league system at the age of 17 and improved at every level. By the time he made his big-league debut in June 1986, he was drawing comparisons to his boyhood hero.

Although he committed a fair share of errors, Sierra had above-average speed, which allowed him to catch up to balls hit into the gap. He was known for his exceptional throwing arm, posting double-digit assist totals in four seasons. As the years wore on, his skills eroded somewhat, and he became an ordinary defensive player.

A switch-hitter, Sierra employed a high leg kick, positioning himself deep in the batter's box and well off the plate. Historian Bill James notes of Sierra, "As a right-handed hitter, [he] was reminiscent of Clemente, bailing out and flinging the head of the bat wildly with strong wrists." Sierra's home-run trot sometimes included a funny little hop followed by a series of shoulder waggles resembling dance moves.

Immediately upon arriving in the majors, Sierra became an everyday player. In his first full season with the Rangers, he drilled 30 homers and drove in 109 runs. He put up consistent numbers during the next eight seasons, averaging 22 home runs and 99 RBIs between 1988 and 1995. He reached the century mark in ribbies three times in that span.

Traded to the A's in 1992, Sierra joined the Yankees midway through the 1995 campaign. He arrived just in time, as the Bombers made their first postseason appearance in more than a decade. Sierra didn't assemble a stellar batting average in the 1995 ALDS against Seattle, but he made his hits count. In the first two meetings, he slammed a pair of homers and drove in four runs. He added an RBI double in game four. Although he left the Bronx in July 1996, he returned for a spell in 2003. He developed a reputation as a clutch October performer, with 16 hits (nine for extra bases) and 14 RBIs in seven postseason series with the Yankees.

Hampered by leg problems in the latter portion of his career, Sierra never appeared in more than 122 games in any season after his 31st birthday. He did capture Comeback Player of the Year honors in 2001, hitting .291, with 23 homers, after sitting out a majority of the 2000 campaign. A four-time All-Star, Sierra's best season at the plate came in 1989, when he led the AL in triples (14), RBIs (119), and total bases (344). He finished second to Robin Yount in MVP voting that year.

Sierra appeared in his last major-league game with the Twins in 2006. By the time he retired, he had played for nine different teams. Among Puerto Rican-born players, he is in elite company. Only five of his countrymen exceeded his home run and RBI totals. Although he was eliminated from the Cooperstown ballot after his first year of eligibility, he was elected to the Texas Rangers Hall of Fame in 2009. In an emotional speech, he said he "couldn't be more proud." After his retirement, Sierra assembled a fine collection of show horses. He also recorded several salsa-style musical CDs.

Danny Tartabull

Right Fielder

Danny Tartabull was born to Cuban parents in San Juan. His father Jose spent portions of nine seasons as an outfielder for the A's and Red

Sox. While Jose managed just two homers in his big-league career, Danny established himself as one of the most powerful right fielders in the AL during the late 1980s and early 1990s.

In 1961, Tartabull's father made a decision to continue playing in the United States rather than returning to Cuba, ruled by Fidel Castro. Although Tartabull spent a portion of his childhood in Puerto Rico, he attended high school in Opa-locka, Florida. Jose Canseco was also an alumnus. Signed by the Reds in the third round of the 1980 MLB Draft, Tartabull began his pro career as an infielder, spending time at second, third, and short. He was error prone at each position, warranting a switch to the outfield after he reached the majors.

Before the 1983 season, Tartabull entered the Mariners minor-league system. With the Calgary Cannons in 1985, he became the first shortstop at any level to hit 40 home runs since Ernie Banks turned the trick in 1960. He was named MVP of the Pacific Coast League that year. Tartabull was a September call-up in 1984 and 1985. When he showed little aptitude for performing infield duties, he was shifted to right field, where he remained for the majority of his career. He had a breakout season in 1986, collecting 25 homers and 96 RBIs. It was a bountiful freshman crop that year, and Tartabull finished fifth in Rookie of the Year voting, behind Jose Canseco, Wally Joyner, Mark Eichhorn, and Cory Snyder. Recognizing his value on the open market, the Mariners traded him to Kansas City with a pitcher of little note in exchange for three players. During the next several seasons, Tartabull made the Mariners regret the move.

In 1987, Tartabull enjoyed one of his finest slugging seasons, blasting 34 long balls and driving in 101 runs. He also compiled a .309 batting average—second best among KC regulars and the second highest of his career. He spent five seasons with the Royals, reaching the 100-RBI plateau during each season in which he was healthy. He missed significant amounts of playing time due to various ailments throughout the years. In 1990, a nagging leg injury kept him out of action for most of July and September.

After he led the AL with a .593 slugging percentage in 1991, the Yankees sought Tartabull's services. He signed a blockbuster deal, making him the highest-paid player in the game. Slowed again by injuries, he finally lived up to his hype in 1993, when he hammered 66 extra-base hits and drove in more than 100 runs. Tartabull swung for the fences often, and as a result, he piled up lofty strikeout totals. He drew a fair amount of walks as well, peaking at 103 in 1992. His on-base percentage was above the .360 mark in seven seasons as a full-time player.

Never a patient man, Yankees owner George Steinbrenner grew increasingly irritated with Tartabull's inability to remain healthy, making some uncharitable remarks to the press. Before long, the boo-birds began razzing Tartabull at Yankee Stadium. He became extremely unhappy in New York, escaping via a trade in 1995. He told the press afterward that it was like "being released from jail." Tartabull had one more excellent season left in him, collecting 27 home runs and 101 RBIs for the White Sox in 1996. The following year, he broke his foot and never successfully rehabbed.

During his heyday, Tartabull appeared in two episodes of the *Seinfeld* show and also did an episode of *Married . . . with Children*. Had he not missed so much playing time with various maladies during his prime, he undoubtedly would have ended up with more than 300 homers and 1,000 RBIs. In 2013, ABC News reported that Tartabull owed more than $275,000 in back child support and had skipped out on a court appearance. He made more than $33 million during his major-league career.

Bernie Williams

Center Fielder

Born Bernabe Williams Figueroa Jr., the longtime Yankees center fielder was the son of a merchant marine dispatcher and a college professor. His mother delivered him in San Juan, but the family lived in the Bronx until Bernie was a year old. During his formative years, Bernie mastered classical guitar and excelled at track and field. In the 1984 Central American and Caribbean Junior Championships, he captured four gold medals. While playing alongside budding slugger Juan Gonzalez, he got noticed by a Yankees scout. He was sent to a Connecticut training camp and offered a contract on his 17th birthday.

Bernie considered enrolling in a pre-med program at the University of Puerto Rico but felt that he would not be able to keep up with his studies while pursuing a major-league career. His progress in the minors was gradual, but he worked his way up to a *Baseball America* rating of number 11 by 1991. An injury to Roberto Kelly that year left an opening for Williams in New York. He appeared in 85 games as a center fielder, hitting .238.

Williams displayed exceptional defensive skills early on. Using long, loping strides, he covered a lot of ground and was not afraid to take chances. His sliding catches and over-the-shoulder grabs became regular occurrences. George Steinbrenner was displeased with his offensive development, however, and sought to trade him in 1993, and again in 1995. Had manager Buck Showalter yielded to the "Boss's" impulsive nature, the Yankees might have fewer World Series titles to their credit.

A switch-hitter, Williams kept his batting average above the .300 mark for eight consecutive seasons. He won a batting title in 1998, with a .339 effort. During his 16 years with the Yankees, he appeared in 121 playoff games, collecting 128 hits and 82 walks. He drove in 80 runs, several of which were of the game-winning variety. His most memorable hit was an 11th inning walk-off homer in game one of the 1996 ALCS against Baltimore. Through the 2016 slate, Williams ranked second during the postseason in doubles, homers, total bases, and runs scored. He is the all-time RBI leader in postseason play.

Completing the package, Williams won four consecutive Gold Gloves from 1997 to 2000. He resides among the top 20 of all time in putouts. Recurrent shoulder issues later in his career hampered his throwing ability somewhat. But he never had the strongest arm to begin with, finishing with double-digit assist totals just once.

Off the field, the five-time All-Star was soft-spoken, humble, and kindhearted. An annual benefit for the Hillside Food Outreach programs of New York and Connecticut bore his name for more than a decade. He was always more comfortable giving credit to the players around him as opposed to basking in the spotlight. "Don't let your job define who you are," he once said. "Your relationships will define who you are. No matter what you do in life . . . you are going to be in a position to make an impact on somebody's life."

Williams certainly had a profound effect on the Yankees' fortunes, scoring no fewer than 100 runs during eight seasons, while reaching the century mark in RBIs on five occasions. Used increasingly as a designated hitter and a corner outfielder in 2006, he turned down an invitation to spring training the following year. He preferred to end his stellar major-league career before it went into serious decline.

In 2008, Williams played in Puerto Rico with the intent to compete in the 2009 World Baseball Classic. Despite a quadriceps injury sustained with the Gigantes de Carolina, he participated in the tournament, going 0-for-5 with a pair of walks. He waited until 2015 to officially announce his retirement from the majors. That same year, the Yankees retired his number and honored him with a plaque in Monument Park at Yankee Stadium.

In 2003, Williams released his debut musical CD, entitled *The Journey Within*. The tracks reflect Bernie's love of jazz and Latin rhythms. Playing both lead and rhythm guitar, he composed seven of the album's songs. In 2009, his follow-up album was nominated for a Latin Grammy. Two years later, his book *Rhythms of the Game: The Link between Musical and Athletic Performance* was published. Eliminated from the Cooperstown ballot in 2013, Williams was subsequently inducted into the Caribbean Baseball Hall of Fame.

NOTABLE ACTIVE PLAYERS

Carlos Beltran

Outfielder

Carlos Beltran was born and raised in Manati. His mother was a stay-at-home mom, while his father worked in a pharmaceutical warehouse. According to Beltran, his father valued honesty above other personality traits. Beltran played Little League as a kid, and his team won the Puerto Rican championship. As a teenager, he became an avid follower of Bernie Williams, who signed with the Yankees in 1986, and played for Aricebo of the Puerto Rican League. Beltran was particularly impressed with Williams's switch-hitting abilities and taught himself to do the same.

In high school, it became clear that Beltran was a special player. He was moved to center field at the age of 15 and began attracting scouts to his games soon thereafter. Selected by the Royals in the second round of the 1995 Amateur Draft, he suffered from adjustment problems, mainly due to his limited grasp of English. Feeling lonely and homesick, he subsisted almost entirely on fast food during his first two seasons.

By the time he reached the majors, Beltran was swinging effectively from both sides of the plate. He used his exceptional speed to cover a lot of ground in the outfield. Called to Kansas City in September 1998, he earned a starting spot the following year. His first full season was spectacular, as he hit .293, with 22 homers and 108 RBIs, capturing Rookie of the Year honors.

Struck by injuries in 2000, Beltran was limited to 98 games. He recovered fully, stringing together four consecutive 100-RBI seasons. The Royals were a miserable club in 2004, and looking to trim costs, they sent Beltran to Houston in a three-team swap. Beltran helped the Astros to the NLCS and began a highly successful postseason career, hitting .435, with eight homers and 14 RBIs in 12 playoff games that year. The Astros failed to advance to the World Series despite his efforts.

Granted free agency, Beltran signed with the Mets in 2005. For three straight seasons, he was among their most reliable run producers, averaging 29 homers and 105 ribbies per year between 2005 and 2008. He added 10 hits (four for extra bases) in the postseason during that span. Hampered by knee problems, Beltran opted for surgery in the winter of 2010. He appeared in just 64 games that season and slumped at the plate. He got back on track in 2011, but the Mets dealt him to San Francisco in July. He hit .323 down the stretch as the Giants finished second in the NL West.

In 2012, Beltran ended up in St. Louis. During his two seasons there, he averaged 58 extra-base hits per year, while fashioning a .282 regular-season average. He turned it up a notch in the postseason, gathering 30 hits and 21 RBIs in 29 playoff games. He scored 14 runs in that same span. The Cardinals made it to the World Series in 2013, but the St. Louis pitching staff could not hold off the rampaging Red Sox, who averaged close to five runs per game.

In December 2013, Beltran returned to the Big Apple—this time as a Yankee. After a disappointing debut, he had a highly productive season in 2015. Through the first half of 2016, he led the team in homers and RBIs. He was traded to the Rangers in early August. Beltran is one of only five switch-hitters to amass 400 homers in his career—a list that includes Mickey Mantle, Eddie Murray, Chipper Jones, and Mark Teixeira. In 2016, Beltran became the all time leader in RBIs among Puerto Rican–born players.

Carlos Correa

Shortstop

Carlos Correa was born in Ponce, Puerto Rico's second most populated city. He grew up in the fishing village of Barrio Velazquez. His parents were not wealthy but had enough money to get by. Correa's father worked diligently with him during his formative years to help polish his baseball skills. Even after the family's home sustained heavy damage in a hurricane and Carlos Sr. was forced to take on extra jobs to pay for repairs, he still found time to play ball with his son.

Recurrent flooding eventually drove the Correas out of Barrio Velazquez. Carlos earned a scholarship to the Puerto Rico Baseball Academy and High School. In 2010 and 2011, he competed in various high-profile tournaments and earned glowing praise. In the latter season, he was named Rawlings Defensive Player of the Year. In addition to his fine performances on the diamond, he was an excellent student, graduating with a 4.0 average. After posting an SAT score of 1560, he signed a letter of commitment with the University of Miami.

When the Astros chose Correa in the first round of the 2012 MLB Draft, he was elated, commenting that he must be dreaming. He was honored with a parade in Santa Isabel upon returning home from the draft ceremony. A few days later, the details of his contract were finalized. He received a signing bonus of $4.8 million. In his pro debut season, he played for three different minor-league clubs, attaining a *Baseball America* ranking of number 13.

From 2013 to 2015, Correa kept his batting average well above .300, earning a call to Houston. He arrived in the majors as the number-three overall prospect. Proving he was deserving of that ranking, he captured Rookie of the Year honors with 45 extra-base hits and 68 RBIs in 99 games. His efforts propelled the Astros to a postseason berth. In the ALDS against the Royals, he hit .350, with a pair of homers. But it wasn't enough, as Houston dropped the series in five games.

Upon receiving baseball's top rookie honor in 2015, Correa was flabbergasted. "If you told me before the season started this was going to happen, I would not believe you," he said. "I was not supposed to be the first pick and was not the best player, but [my] hard work came through."

Correa was Houston's primary shortstop in 2016. He set personal high offensive marks with 76 runs scored, 36 doubles, and 96 RBIs. Defensively, he is among the best in the business, with a strong arm, sure hands, and a wide range. Astros manager A. J. Hinch believes Correa has a bright future. "He has good makeup. He has tremendous drive. I think he can be as good as anyone expects," commented Hinch.

Modest and unassuming, Correa often takes time to greet fans and sign autographs. He has aspirations of making a mark on the community in the tradition of Roberto Clemente. "I want to be able to be a great ballplayer, but an even better human being," he told a writer from *USA Today*. "I've got to show my face out there and get people to know me in order to be able to do great things for different foundations and different people, especially the kids."

Francisco Lindor

Shortstop

Francisco Lindor was born in Caguas, which lies about 20 miles from San Juan through a towering mountain range. He grew up with three siblings and took an interest in baseball at an early age. His father would stand on top of a steep slope and hit grounders swiftly downhill to him for practice. At the age of 12, Lindor moved with his father, stepmother, and youngest sibling to Florida. When he arrived in Orlando, he didn't understand English and was terrified. "I had some long days and long nights," he told a writer from *USA Today*. "It helped me grow up, become more independent, and appreciate my family."

Lindor first caught the eye of scouts while playing for the Montverde Academy baseball team. He was named to the All-USA high school squad. Chosen by the Indians in the first round of the 2011 MLB Draft, he could have attended Florida State on a full scholarship. A $2.9 million signing bonus steered him away from college.

Lindor made his pro debut in the New York–Pennsylvania League. Prior to the 2015 slate, he was ranked fourth by MLB.com and Baseball Prospectus. He was called to Cleveland that June and had a promising debut, hitting .313, with a league-leading 13 sacrifice hits. His first game included a highly embarrassing moment. After collecting his first major-league hit, he tripped and fell flat on his face while rounding first. He was able to return to the bag without being tagged out. Voting for Rookie of the Year was tight, and Lindor finished slightly behind fellow countryman Carlos Correa.

Lindor is considered to be one of the best young shortstops in the majors. In 2016, he finished among the top ten in assists, putouts, double plays, and fielding percentage. His productive bat helped guide the Indians to a World Series berth. He hit .310 in the postseason with 5 runs scored and 6 RBIs. It wasn't enough as Cleveland's championship bid fell short.

Lindor has a warm smile, and his enthusiasm is contagious. "He's got a natural spark," said teammate Trevor Bauer. "It helps keep things lively in the clubhouse. . . . He has a lot of fun."

Javier Lopez

Pitcher

Players like Javier Lopez tend to get buried in the mix. But he has held the thankless job of a situational reliever for more than a decade. Rarely called upon to face more than two or three batters at a time, his statistics appear ordinary on the surface. While closers get all the glory, Lopez has been content to do his job quietly and with minimal fanfare.

Born in San Juan, Lopez came of age in Fairfax, Virginia. As a kid, he dreamed of becoming an FBI agent like his dad. He attended the University of Virginia and played for the Cavaliers—a Division I team with 16 NCAA postseason appearances to its credit (through 2016). The school has sent dozens of players to the majors throughout the years. In 1998, Lopez was drafted by the Diamondbacks in the fourth round and began his pro career. Fulfilling a promise to his father-in-law, he eventually earned a degree in psychology.

Sturdily built, at 6-foot-4, 220 pounds, the left-handed Lopez relies heavily on a two-seam fastball. It isn't terribly swift by major-league standards, topping out in the high 80s. Using a sidearm delivery, Lopez offsets his not-so-fastball with a slider in the high 70s. He has been known to mix in a curveball or two as well. Originally groomed as a starter, he was moved to the bullpen in 2001. Struggling with his control, he compiled a dreadful 7.42 ERA in 22 Texas League games that year.

In 2002, the Red Sox claimed Lopez in the Rule 5 Draft. He was traded to the Rockies before the 2003 slate. Despite playing regularly in hitter-friendly Coors Field, he registered a 3.70 ERA in 75 appearances during his big-league debut. He was less effective during the next two seasons and wound up in Arizona.

In 2006, Lopez joined the Red Sox. He was highly effective during a three-year span, entering 158 games and posting a 2.70 cumulative ERA. After a horrendous season in 2009, he was shipped to Pittsburgh. He pitched effectively through July, when the Pirates traded him to the Giants. He has been with San Francisco ever since.

Lopez was an important member of three World Series–winning squads. In 2010, left-handers hit .162 against him during the regular season—the lowest mark among NL southpaws. He made nine postseason appearances that year, allowing no runs in eight of them. In the 2012 playoffs, he held opponents scoreless in three innings of work and allowed just two baserunners. He was at it again in 2014, yielding no runs in nine appearances. As of 2017, World Series opponents had yet to record an earned run off of him.

A late bloomer, Lopez was 25 years old when he reached the majors. He enjoyed his finest statistical campaign in 2015, at the age of 37, accruing a stingy 1.60 ERA in 77 appearances. He recorded 20 holds—an unofficial statistic invented in 1986, to measure the effectiveness of middle relievers and setup men. He also stranded 86 percent of his inherited runners—the best ratio in the league.

Lopez's warm-up music is "Coastin'" by hip-hop group Zion I. He claims that the key to his success has been to "slow the game down," which he insists "isn't as easy as it sounds." He is proud of his long-term success. "When you can show consistency in an inconsistent game, it's a source of pride," he said. "It's a reassurance that I'm still effective and relevant." As of 2016, he was still a mainstay in the Giants bullpen. He has averaged six strikeouts per nine frames throughout the course of his 14-year career.

Yadier Molina

Catcher

Some would argue that Yadier Molina is the most talented of the famous catching trio. At the end of the 2016 campaign, he already had more All-Star selections and Gold Gloves than his brothers (Bengie and Jose) combined. He was also superior in the categories that count most for catchers—fielding percentage and caught stealing percentage.

The youngest of the Molinas, Yadier grew up in Bayamon. His father "Pai" played amateur baseball and worked 10-hour shifts in a Westinghouse factory. When he finished work for the day, he would accompany his sons to Jesus Mambe Kuilan Park, located across the street from the family's home, to teach them the basics of the game. Pai must have known a thing or two about baseball because all three of his sons forged major-league careers.

When Yadier was 15, his father arranged a workout with the Hatillo Tigers—an amateur team. Molina passed the audition and immediately became a starting catcher in a league filled with players much older than him. He got noticed by a Twins scout while playing high-school ball in Vega Alta. He also attended a workout with the Reds at Riverfront Stadium before being drafted by the Cardinals.

Yadier began his pro career in 2001. Proving scouts wrong, he developed quickly with the bat, hitting .280 in the Midwest League during the 2002 slate. In 2004, his .302 average in the PCL alerted the Cardinals that he was ready for prime time. He appeared in 51 games with the Cardinals, throwing out would-be basestealers at a rate of 47 percent—nearly twice the league average.

In the next 11 seasons, Molina retained the starting catcher's position in St. Louis. Aside from one dismal season at the plate in 2006, his batting averages ranged from .252 to .319. He was a .300 hitter on four occasions. Typically hitting in the bottom third of the order, he averaged 57 RBIs per year between 2005 and 2015. A power surge in 2012 gave him a career-high 22 homers. He peaked at 44 doubles the following year.

Popular among fans, Molina made seven consecutive All-Star appearances from 2009 to 2015. Showing poise and leadership behind the plate, he has helped the Cardinals to nine playoff appearances and captured two World Series rings. He is a lifetime .328 hitter in the Fall Classic.

Defensively, Molina is among the most accomplished catchers in history. Only Johnny Bench and Ivan Rodriguez have more Gold Gloves. Molina ranks first among active players in caught stealing percentage. He is second in putouts, assists, and double plays behind 19-year veteran A. J. Pierzynski. "I feel good catching, and that's what I want," he once said. "I feel good when I make a swing, but catching is the most important thing." Frequent batterymate Adam Wainwright offered glowing praise for Molina. "You don't ever have to worry about bouncing a ball to Yadier. He's a human vacuum behind the plate. The only thing you have to think about is making the pitch because you know Yadier's going to catch whatever you throw."

At 33 years of age, Molina presumably has a few good seasons left in him. His sabermetric similarity scores compare to Thurman Munson and Tim McCarver—two of the top backstops of the 1970s. Molina keeps moving up the ladder statistically each year, and his name has begun to surface in Hall of Fame discussions.

3

VENEZUELA

ORIGINS OF BASEBALL IN VENEZUELA

Baseball was introduced to Venezuelans by students who had studied at American universities. In May 1895, the Franklin brothers (Amenodoro, Augusto, Emilio, and Gustavo) founded the first organized team in Caracas. The first official game pitted members of the club against one another in a split-squad match. Within a few weeks, the city was enamored with the "new" sport.

In 1912, entrepreneur William H. Phelps opened a baseball shop in Maracaibo. He later formed a league composed of three teams, known as "The Red," "The Blue," and "The Black." By the beginning of the 1920s, there were nearly a dozen ballparks in Maracaibo with 30 clubs using them. In 1917, the Magellanes team was founded. Known today as the Navegantes del Magallanes, it is the country's oldest existing ballclub.

Pro baseball came to Venezuela with the establishment of the Federacion Venezolana de Beisbol in 1927. A championship tournament was held that summer, with four teams—Maracay, Royal Criollas, San Martin, and Santa Maria—competing for top honors. In 1930, the Association of Professional Baseball became the governing body of the sport in Venezuela.

The Venezuelan national squad made its first tournament appearance at the Central American and Caribbean Games in 1938. The following year, pitcher Alejandro Carrasquel became the first Venezuelan-born player in the majors, making his debut with the Washington Senators. Since then, more than 200 Venezuelans have found their way to the big leagues.

Founded in 1945, the Venezuelan Professional Baseball League houses eight of the highest-level teams in the country. The regular season consists of a 63-game schedule played in a round-robin format. The postseason features two semifinal rounds and a best-of-seven final. The champions move on to the Caribbean Series to face teams from the Dominican Republic, Puerto Rico, Mexico, and Cuba. Through 2016, Venezuelan clubs had won seven Caribbean Series titles.

Recognizing the depth of the talent pool, major-league teams began establishing camps in Venezuela during the 1990s. At one point, 23 of 30 major-league clubs had set up operations there. By 2016, only the Tigers, Rays, Phillies, and Cubs remained. Economic troubles, political unrest, food shortages, and rising crime rates have made it difficult for the surviving camps to stay in business. It is uncertain how long they will continue to operate. Despite Venezuela's current hardships, the country continues to export a steady stream of talented players to the majors, the most notable of whom are profiled on the pages that follow.

MAJOR STARS OF THE PAST

Bobby Abreu

Right Fielder

Bobby Abreu was born in Maracay, a populous city in the northern state of Aragua. While the city is a busy commercial center, the surrounding areas produce sugarcane, tobacco, coffee, and cocoa. Abreu attended the same high school as Dave Concepcion and Carlos Guillen. He was signed by the Astros as an amateur free agent and came to the United States at the age of 17. The Astros had Steve Finley, Luis Gonzalez, and Eric Anthony in the outfield while Abreu was moving up the ladder. He was somewhat undervalued, never attaining a ranking higher than 29th as a prospect.

After several productive seasons in the minors, Abreu was invited to Houston. Sent back down in 1997, he was mediocre in a second trial.

The Devil Rays claimed him in the expansion draft and then traded him to Philadelphia for Kevin Stocker. Stocker would last just three more seasons in the majors. Abreu's career put him on a possible trajectory to Cooperstown.

Abreu was among the era's best five-tool players, although many people don't realize it. He had impeccable plate discipline, drawing more than 100 walks in eight consecutive seasons. A lifetime .291 hitter, he exceeded the .300 mark on six occasions. He had ample power, averaging more than 60 extra-base hits per year between 1998 and 2011. On the bases, he was a threat to steal, peaking at 40 thefts in 2004, and retiring with 400. He was a member of baseball's 30/30 club twice. Abreu's defense went unrecognized until 2005, when he finally captured a Gold Glove. His powerful arm landed him among the top five in assists in seven campaigns. He led the league twice in that category.

Despite his accomplishments, Abreu flew under the radar for most of his career, mostly because of the teams he played for. He spent portions of 11 seasons in the relatively small-market cities of Houston and Philadelphia. He made just one postseason appearance during that span. By the time he arrived in the media hotbed of New York, he was 32 years old and entering the final productive stretch of his career. Surrounded by players with tackier numbers, he was overlooked for the All-Star Team year after year. The notoriously fickle fan base in Philly never fully embraced Abreu, complaining that he took a lot of called third strikes and refused to play aggressively in right field like some of his predecessors. Abreu answered the latter charge with the claim that he was looking to avoid injury. He certainly did, appearing in more than 150 games for 13 straight seasons.

In an era riddled with steroids, Abreu did not escape scrutiny. During a 2005 interview, he admitted to using creatine—a bodybuilding supplement that was not on the list of banned substances at the time. He also admitted that he was tempted to try androstenedione—the drug that tarnished slugger Mark McGwire's image. "Sometimes it crossed my mind," Abreu confessed, "but I said 'That's okay,' I'll stay with creatine . . . I want to go to GNC and take stuff that will build my muscles that is safe." Although his name appeared on a list of suspected steroid users, no charges were ever brought against him.

Abreu received Most Valuable Player consideration seven times during his career, but his finest all-around season came in 2004, when he hit .301, hammered 78 extra-base hits, and drove in 105 runs. He also drew a career-high 127 walks, running his on-base percentage up to .428. He made the first of two consecutive All-Star appearances that year. In 2005, he participated in the annual Home Run Derby and pounded a ball 517 feet—among the longest shots in the history of the competition.

After reaching the 100-RBI mark in back-to-back campaigns with the Yankees, Abreu signed with the Angels, enjoying one great season with the club. His career began to wind down after that. Out of the majors in 2013, he played in the Venezuelan Winter League, hitting .320 in 172 at-bats. He joined the Mets organization the following year, but his numbers were not impressive enough to warrant another season in the big leagues. He announced his retirement at the end of September. Abreu's sabermetric similarity scores compare favorably to Bernie Williams, Dwight Evans, and Luis Gonzalez—three exceptional players who have all been overlooked for the Hall of Fame.

Abreu has given back to the community at large throughout the years, affiliating himself with blood drives and various youth programs. During the 2003 and 2004 campaigns, he bought $10,000 worth of tickets to Friday night games for children in his "Abreu's Amigos" program. Kids received jerseys and refreshments, and were allowed to meet Abreu during batting practice. In 2004, the slugger received Major League Baseball's Roberto Clemente Award, which is given to the player who "best exemplifies the game of baseball, sportsmanship, community involvement, and the individual's contribution to his team."

Edgardo Alfonzo

Third Baseman/Second Baseman

Edgardo Alfonzo attended high school in Caracas, the largest city in Venezuela and one of the most violent in the world. A 2016 survey placed the murder rate at 119.87 per 100,000 residents. Most homicides in Caracas go unsolved. Alfonzo managed to escape serious harm, signing with the Mets organization at the age of 17. He hit .332 in his Gulf Coast League debut and followed with a .350 mark in 1992.

By 1995, the Mets felt that Alfonzo was ready for big-league action. He appeared mostly at third base but also subbed at second and short. Playing sparkling defense, he held his own at the plate as well, hitting .278 in 101 games. He might have received some Rookie of the Year consideration had he not been sidelined for two months with a herniated disc in his back.

During his eight seasons in New York, Alfonzo alternated at second and third base. He fielded both positions significantly above the league average. He finished among the top five in fielding percentage three times at each position and led National League second basemen in that category during the 1999 slate. Somehow, he never won a Gold Glove.

Nicknamed "Fonzie," Alfonzo wore the number 13 for most of his career, in honor of fellow Venezuelan Dave Concepcion, whom he idolized as a kid. The Mets were a team on the rise, and Alfonzo was a major part of it. The 1999 Mets infield has been rated by Bill James as one of the best of all time, with John Olerud at first, Alfonzo at second, Rey Ordonez at short, and Robin Ventura at third. Alfonzo enjoyed his best all-around season that year, reaching personal highs in doubles (41), homers (27), and RBIs (108). His 123 runs scored remain the second highest single-season total in franchise history. As good as the 1999 Mets were, the Braves were even better, winning the National League Championship Series in six games.

Alfonzo got back to business the following year, accruing a career-best .324 batting average and a handsome on-base percentage of .425— fifth best in the league. He remained a patient hitter throughout his career, averaging 54 walks during seasons in which he played in at least 100 games. His strikeout totals were fairly low for a guy with moderate power. In the 2000 postseason, Alfonzo gathered 16 hits and six walks as the Mets made it all the way to the World Series, facing their intercity rivals—the Yankees. Three of the five games were decided by a single run as the Mets' championship bid fell short.

In 2001, Alfonzo missed a month with another back injury. He strained an oblique muscle the following year and was forced out of action for three weeks. Although he hit .308, with 16 homers, the Mets granted him free agency at season's end. He spent three years with the Giants as their primary third baseman. In the 2003 National League Division Series, he hit .529 against the Marlins, with five RBIs in four games; however, his efforts could not propel the Giants to the next round.

By 2005, Alfonzo's numbers had begun to taper off. In December of that year, he was traded to the Angels for Steve Finley. Released by the Angels and Blue Jays in 2006, he signed a minor-league contract with the Mets but never reappeared in the majors. He continued in the Venezuelan Winter League through 2012, also spending one unsuccessful season with the Yomiuri Giants of the Japanese Central League. He began coaching for the Brooklyn Cyclones—a Mets affiliate—in 2014, and was still a member of the staff as of 2016. He ranks among the Mets franchise leaders in multiple categories, including runs scored, hits, and batting average.

Luis Aparicio

Shortstop

Born in Maracaibo—a baseball-obsessed city in the northwestern state of Zulia—Luis Aparicio grew up around the sport. His father, Luis Sr., was an exceptional shortstop who had turned down an offer from the Washington Senators in 1939. He later became coowner of the Maracaibo Gavilanes—a Venezuelan Winter League team. In 1953, Caracas hosted the Amateur World Series, and young Luis was chosen to play for Venezuela. Although Cuba won the tournament, Aparicio dazzled fans with his blazing speed and slick glove work. After the tournament, he informed his parents that he was quitting school to become a professional player. His mother wasn't pleased, but his father offered him a spot on the Maracaibo roster. On November 18, 1953, Luis Sr. officially passed the torch to his son in a ceremony held at the Gavilanes home stadium.

It didn't take long for Aparicio to get noticed by major-league scouts. Recognizing the young shortstop's potential, Gavilanes manager Red Kress—a former major leaguer—contacted Indians general manager Hank Greenberg. After seeing him play, scout Cy Slapnicka offered Aparicio a $10,500 bonus. Greenberg felt that Slapnicka was being too generous, cutting the bonus in half and making it contingent upon an official tryout. Insulted, Aparicio walked away from the deal. The White Sox had heard about Aparicio from Chico Carrasquel—a superb defensive shortstop who made his big-league debut in 1950. Spotting a golden opportunity, the White Sox swooped in and made Aparicio an offer he could not refuse. Carrasquel had no idea he would later be traded to make room for Aparicio on the roster.

Aparicio joined the Waterloo Whitehawks of the Three-I League in 1954, and began a meteoric rise to the majors. By 1956, he was Chicago's starting shortstop. He hit .266, while leading the league in stolen bases and sacrifice hits, capturing Rookie of the Year honors. Appearing most often at the top of the order, the speedy Aparicio was the American League's reigning stolen base king for nine straight seasons. A spray hitter with little power, 79 percent of his lifetime hits were singles. He exceeded the .300 mark just once, and his averages typically hovered in the .260 range. Although his offensive numbers don't exactly leap off the page, he earned respect from opposing pitchers for his focus at the plate. "He doesn't hit a ball long enough to kill you," griped Whitey Ford, "but believe me there is nothing more aggravating than to get past good hitters and then have a weak hitter come up and brush across a couple of runs. . . . Every time I faced him, he seemed to hit me a little better."

Aparicio's peers were equally in awe of his defensive skills. Using his wide range and strong, accurate arm, he robbed opposing batsmen of hits with regularity. "He's the best I've ever seen," said ChiSox owner Bill Veeck. "He makes plays I know can't possibly be made, yet he makes them almost every day." By the time he retired, Aparicio had captured nine Gold Gloves and set an all-time record for assists and double plays (since broken by Ozzie Smith). He was also named to 10 All-Star Teams.

In 1959, Aparicio helped his "Go-Go Sox" (nicknamed for their ability to get on base and steal) to their first World Series appearance since the dreaded fix of 1919. Playing alongside fellow Hall of Famers Nellie Fox and Early Wynn, Aparicio hit .308 in the Series. After an 11–0 blowout over the Dodgers in the opener, the Chicago bats cooled off as Los Angeles rolled to a six-game victory.

In 1962, Aparicio put on an inordinate amount of weight and showed up for spring training out of shape. He had an off season at the plate, hitting just .241. Manager Al Lopez felt that he wasn't giving 100 percent, and when GM Ed Short suggested a salary cut for the following year, Aparicio requested a trade. He ended up being packaged in a six-player deal that landed him in Baltimore.

While playing for the O's, Aparicio won two Gold Gloves and led the league twice in steals. In 1965, Cuban sensation Bert Campaneris replaced Aparicio as the AL's premier base rustler, pacing the circuit for four straight seasons. Aparicio's last productive year for thefts came in 1969, when he finished ninth, with 24. As he began to age out, he became more selective about when to run. During his last four major-league seasons, he was successful in 73 percent of his attempts.

In 1966, Aparicio had a chance to avenge the 1959 Series loss at the hands of the Dodgers. He played in all four games of Baltimore's sweep of LA. After an off year in 1967, he began a second stint with the White Sox. He enjoyed his last great offensive season in 1970, compiling a career-high .313 average in 146 games. Even when his skills declined, he remained immensely popular with fans. He made the All-Star Team as a member of the Red Sox in 1971 and 1972, despite sitting out 89 games. In his farewell season, he drove in 49 runs, primarily out of the second spot in the order, while hitting at a respectable .271 pace.

Aparicio was elected to Cooperstown in 1984. It was his sixth appearance on the ballot. He was enshrined with two other luminaries from his generation—Harmon Killebrew and Don Drysdale. The White Sox retired his number that same year. In 2003, Aparicio was inducted into the Venezuelan Baseball Hall of Fame. Four years later, he was honored yet again with entry into the Hispanic Heritage Baseball Museum Hall of Fame. An annual award given to the top Venezuelan player in the majors bears his name. A bronze statue of Aparicio stands outside U.S Cellular Field in Chicago next to a bronze likeness of his former double-play partner, Nellie Fox.

Tony Armas

Outfielder

Tony Armas grew up with 13 siblings in Puerto Piritu. His younger brother Marcos would play briefly for the Oakland A's. His son Tony Jr.—a pitcher—would win 53 big-league games in 10 seasons. The most successful of them all, Tony Sr. was signed by the Pirates at the age of 17. He languished in their farm system during one of the team's most fruitful periods, missing three NLCS appearances and a World Series title. When he began to show off his power on the farm in 1976, manager Danny Murtaugh invited him to Pittsburgh. He appeared in four games before being shipped to Oakland in a nine-player trade. He would establish himself with the A's.

Armas was by no means a well-rounded player. He had virtually no speed and hit for moderately low averages. While he was competent in the field, he was prone to injury, ending up on the disabled list a dozen times. During his 13 full seasons in the majors, he sat out almost 700 games for various reasons. He was a consistent power threat and reliable RBI man when he was in the lineup.

Armas had four healthy seasons during his career, the first one coming in 1980, when he played in 158 games and clubbed 35 homers—fourth best in the league. He also finished among the top 10 in RBIs that year, with 109. Proving this was no fluke, he led the AL in long balls during the strike-shortened 1981 campaign. With fiery manager Billy Martin at the helm, the A's swept the Royals in the American League Division Series but were annihilated by the Yankees in the American League Championship Series. Armas hit .545 in the first round and then managed just two hits—a pair of singles—against New York pitching. Hurt during the 1982 campaign, he was on pace for a 30-homer/100-RBI season before sitting out 24 games. Alarmed by his fragility, the A's packaged him in a multiplayer deal with the Red Sox that included Carney Lansford. Oakland got the better end of the transaction, as Lansford became one of the most popular and productive third baseman in A's history.

Although he didn't stay healthy for long, Armas enjoyed two fabulous seasons in Boston. He swung for the fences every chance he got and struck out with reckless abandon. Despite hitting .218 in 1983, he clubbed 36 homers and drove in 107 runs. He was even better the following year. In a career-high 679 plate appearances, he led the league in homers (43), RBIs (123), and total bases (339). He also topped the circuit with 156 strikeouts. Injured often during the next two seasons, he struggled in Boston's ALCS showdown against the Angels in 1986. Demoted to the bench in the World Series that year, he made just one pinch-hit appearance in the seventh inning of the Series finale. Having been out of action for more than two weeks, he looked rusty at the plate, striking out on three pitches. He was released after

Boston's disheartening seven-game loss. He spent the last three years of his career with the Angels, remaining productive in a limited role. He retired after the 1989 slate.

Due to his many injuries, Armas's big-league career is a question of what might have been. Between 1980 and 1985, he hit more homers than any AL player (187). He finished among the top 10 in MVP voting twice and made two All-Star appearances in that span. He was on target to hit more than 350 home runs had he remained healthy. His power was equally prominent in the Venezuelan Professional Baseball League, where his 97 long balls stood as a record until 2007. Armas was inducted into the Caribbean Baseball Hall of Fame and Venezuelan Baseball Hall of Fame. As of this writing, he is serving as a batting instructor for the Leones de Caracas in his native country.

Chico Carrasquel

Shortstop

Born in Caracas, Chico Carrasquel had 10 siblings. His father was a laborer in a beer factory. His uncle, Alejandro "Alex" Carrasquel, was the first Venezuelan in the majors, making his debut with the Senators in 1939. Carrasquel quit school in his mid-teens to pursue a baseball career. He was tremendously successful in the junior leagues from the age of 17. Signed by the Dodgers in 1949, he was assigned to Montreal, where manager Clay Hopper refused to play him because he couldn't speak English. "I was very lonely that year," Carrasquel recalled long after the fact. "I would go to my hotel room and look at myself in the mirror and say, 'Buenos dias, Chico. Como estas?'" Transferred to the Texas League, he got ample playing time. He hit .315 and led the league in fielding, but his path to the majors was blocked by the presence of Hall of Famer Pee Wee Reese. The White Sox acquired him after the 1949 slate and inserted him into their starting lineup on Opening Day of the following year.

Carrasquel gradually learned to speak English with the help of Cuban teammate Luis Aloma. In his rookie year, he accrued a career-high .282 batting average. At one point, he assembled a hitting streak of 24 games. It was a competitive rookie class, and Carrasquel finished third behind Whitey Ford and slugger Walt Dropo, who drove in 144 runs for the Red Sox. Carrasquel had an excellent follow-up campaign, making the first of four All-Star appearances. He was the first Venezuelan to start in the Midsummer Classic.

In 10 major-league seasons, Carrasquel's batting averages ranged from .282 to .223. Although he was capable of hitting home runs, he packed more than half of them into a three-year span (1954–1956), during which he collected 30. Most of his lifetime hits were singles. He had speed but was not a great basestealer. After swiping 14 bags in 18 tries during the 1951 slate, he was successful in less than 50 percent of his future attempts. He was used as a leadoff man until it became evident that he didn't get on base often enough to reliably fill the role. Most often appearing seventh or eighth in the order, he was dependable in the clutch, driving in 50 or more runs four times. He racked up a handsome .360 average, with nine hits and six walks, in limited duty as a pinch-hitter. He didn't strike out much, averaging one per every 10 at-bats.

Carrasquel was noted mainly for his glove work, which earned him lasting acclaim. The first Venezuelan to be successful in the big leagues, he became a hero in his native country, where he was hailed as a defensive prodigy. Gold Gloves were not handed out until Carrasquel was at the tail end of his career, but it's likely he would have claimed at least one. He led AL shortstops in fielding percentage during three seasons and finished among the top five in putouts six times. Despite the brevity of his career, he ranks among the top 100 of all time in that category, along with double plays.

One researcher said of Carrasquel, "He may not have revolutionized the position like latter-day greats Ozzie Smith and Omar Vizquel, but he brought panache, born of his innate love of the sport and the excitement and joy he felt while on the baseball field." In Spanish-speaking territories outside of Venezuela, he was known as "El Gato de Venezuela," because of his cat-like reflexes.

None of the teams Carrasquel played for reached the World Series. Traded after the 1955 slate to make room for Luis Aparicio (whom he had selflessly promoted), Carrasquel ended up in Cleveland. When a reporter asked if the veteran shortstop was having difficulty with anyone in Chicago, former ChiSox GM Frank Lane quipped, "Yes—with American League pitching." It was not the first potshot that Lane would take at Carrasquel. In the late 1950s, Vice President Richard Nixon visited Venezuela, where an anti-American demonstration nearly erupted in violence. "If these Venezuelans can't hit any better than Chico Carrasquel, then Nixon hasn't got a thing to worry about," Lane jested.

It's true that Carrasquel's offensive numbers fell steadily as his career progressed. He was hitting .256 in June 1958 when the Indians traded him to Kansas City for slumping infielder Billy Hunter. He was traded again in October—this time to Baltimore. He was released twice, in 1959 and 1960.

When his playing days were over, Carrasquel returned to Venezuela, serving as a manager and a major-league scout for the Royals and Mets. He also had a long stint as a Spanish-language broadcaster for the White Sox. In addition, he served in their front office. Carrasquel died in May 2005, from a heart attack. He was a member of the Latino Baseball Hall of Fame inaugural class of 2010.

Dave Concepcion

Shortstop

Born David Ismael Benitez Concepcion, the future Reds star grew up in Ocumare de la Costa, located in the northern region of the country on the Caribbean Sea. Cocoa production and fishing are the town's main industries. Concepcion's ancestors were among the original settlers. The son of a truck driver, young David idolized Hall of Fame shortstop Luis Aparicio while growing up. He attended Agustin Codazzi High School and later worked as a bank teller. On the side, he played for a local team. His coach, Wilfredo Calvino, also happened to be a Reds scout. When Concepcion began to shine on the diamond, Calvino offered him a contract. He signed against his father's wishes.

Originally a second baseman, Concepcion was moved to short by manager George Scherger in the Florida State League. Explaining the transition, Scherger said, "He looked like a shortstop to me. He had a whip arm and the good, fluid motion of a shortstop." It was Concepcion's strong arm that later captured manager Sparky Anderson's attention and won him the starting job in Cincinnati. Invited to spring training in 1970, he took the number 13. "The players told me not to take 13, that it's a bad number," Concepcion chuckled. "But 13 is my lucky number." Standing 6-foot-2 and weighing only 155 pounds, Concepcion was injured early on and missed a handful of games. When Pete Rose inquired what was wrong, a teammate informed him that Concepcion had pulled a muscle. "He may have pulled a bone," Rose joked. "But there's no way that man could pull a muscle."

Concepcion made the team as a starter in 1970, but after accumulating 14 errors by mid-June, he was benched briefly. When he returned to the lineup, he made just eight more errors and elevated his batting average to a respectable .260. A badly sprained thumb curtailed his production during his sophomore year. He slumped again in 1972, and was limited to 119 appearances.

Concepcion could be hard on himself when he felt he wasn't producing. Realizing this, Sparky Anderson asked future Hall of Famer Tony Perez to room with the youngster. "He can't stand an 0–for-4 day," Perez once remarked. "It kills him. I try to tell him things like, 'don't get your head down' . . . I always try to pick him up." It must have worked to some extent, because Concepcion emerged as a top-flight shortstop in 1973, making his first All-Star appearance. Eight more selections would follow. Concepcion was a vital component of Cincinnati's "Big Red Machine," which also featured Perez, Rose, Johnny Bench, and Joe Morgan. Between 1970 and 1979, the Reds made five postseason appearances. Concepcion was a major producer, hitting .297 in 34 games, with 13 runs scored and 13 runs driven in (lending credence to his theory about the number 13 being lucky). The Reds won two World Series titles in four tries during Concepcion's career.

In his prime, Concepcion often occupied the third spot in the batting order. He enjoyed his best regular-season effort in 1979, when he reached career highs in homers (16), RBIs (84), and runs scored (91). He not only made the All-Star Team that year, but also claimed a Gold Glove and finished ninth in MVP voting. He placed even higher in 1981, capturing 32 percent of the vote. By then, the Machine had been partially disassembled with the departure of Rose, Perez, Morgan, and Sparky Anderson. Concepcion was the longest-tenured member of the 1975–1976 championship squads, spending his entire career in Cincinnati. He retired after the 1988 campaign, when his numbers went into serious decline.

Concepcion had good speed, stealing 321 bases in 19 seasons. He peaked at 41 thefts in 1974. Recognized as one of the best defensive shortstops of the era, his lifetime total for assists has him ranked 11th on the all-time list at the time of this writing. He led the league twice in that category and won five Gold Gloves. Catcher Tim McCarver summed it up nicely in 1983, when he referred to Concepcion as "one of the best shortstops ever to play baseball. He's a good RBI man, hits for average, and is a Gold Glove fielder. He has good speed and can steal bases. There's not much left."

Despite that ringing endorsement, Concepcion was eliminated from the primary Cooperstown ballot in 2008, after 15 years of eligibility. In his first appearance on the Veterans Committee ballot, he received more votes than any other player but still fell short. He is a member of the Caribbean Series Hall of Fame and Latino Baseball Hall of Fame. His number—the dreaded 13—has been retired by the Reds.

Andres Galarraga

First Baseman

Andres Galarraga was one of those big players who looked like he couldn't get out of his own way. Listed at 6-foot-3, 235 pounds, he began his pro career in Venezuela at the age of 16. His teammates on the Leones del Caracas club included future major leaguers Tony Armas, Manny Trillo, and Bo Diaz. Originally a catcher and third baseman, Galarraga was shifted to first, where he earned the nickname "El Gato" (literally, "the Cat") for his quickness. Some of the big-league scouts who watched him play felt he was too heavy for the majors. Leones manager Felipe Alou disagreed, recommending him to the Expos, who signed him in 1979.

It took Galarraga several minor-league seasons to establish himself as a power hitter. He had a breakthrough year in 1984, when he collected 27 homers in the South Atlantic League. He added 25 more for the Indianapolis Indians the following season, earning an invitation to Montreal. It wasn't much of a debut, as he hit just .187 in 24 appearances, but he slowly emerged as one of the better first basemen in the NL.

Galarraga enjoyed his first great offensive season in 1988, when he led the NL in hits (184) and doubles (42). He made his All-Star debut that year, going 0-for-2, with a strikeout, in a 2–1 pitching duel that was

won by the AL. Galarraga piled up strikeouts at an alarming rate, averaging one per every four at-bats. He certainly knew how to crush the
ball when he connected, however, gathering more than 400 doubles
and 300 homers during his prime slugging years, which stretched from
1987 to 2001.

Galarraga was far from one-dimensional. He was a highly dependable, if not outright exceptional, first baseman, leading the league in
putouts four times and double plays on three occasions. Despite his
considerable bulk, he earned his feline nickname with a career range
factor of 9.94 per game (among the best all-time marks). Gold Glove
Awards were dominated by Will Clark and J. T. Snow of the Giants
during Galarraga's career, but he did manage to claim a pair for himself—in 1989 and 1990.

The big first baseman was slowed by injuries in 1991. After suffering
a hamstring injury early on, he ended up having arthroscopic surgery on
his knee. His glove and bat were sorely missed as the Expos tumbled to
sixth place—19 games under .500. Uncertain about the slugger's future,
the Expos traded him to the Cardinals and filled the empty defensive
slot with a platoon of players.

Galarraga was a big target and had a tendency to crowd the plate. As
a result, he was hit by pitches often—178 times during his major-league
career. In 1992, he sustained a broken wrist after being plunked and
missed more than 60 games. Believing him to be injury prone, the
Cards dished him to Colorado, where he began a career revival.

In the hitter-friendly confines of Coors Field, Galarraga became one
of the game's premier home-run threats, clubbing 30 or more long balls
in five consecutive seasons. He reached the peak of his slugging abilities
in 1996, cranking 47 circuit blasts, while driving in 150 runs—tops in
the majors. He led the NL in ribbies the following year as well. By
1998, the Rockies could no longer afford him, and he signed with the
Braves for a significant pay increase. He remained highly productive,
drilling 44 homers and driving in 121 runs.

In 1999, Galarraga had a major health scare. He developed a sore
back in spring training that persisted despite the efforts of trainers and
team doctors. Sent for an MRI, the diagnosis was grim—a lymphatic
tumor on one of the vertebra in his lower back. He sat out the entire
1999 campaign while undergoing chemotherapy. At 37 years of age,
doctors didn't know whether he would return to the game.

In 2000, Galarraga reported to spring training in prime playing shape with high hopes and a characteristically bright smile. It was a feel-good story, as he hit .302, with 28 homers and 100 RBIs—excellent numbers for any 39-year-old, let alone one who had survived cancer. *Sporting News* recognized him as the NL Comeback Player of the Year. His career began to wind down after that.

In 2004, Galarraga's cancer returned, and he underwent extensive periods of chemotherapy. Remarkably, he beat it a second time and played at the Triple-A level for the Angels. In September, he was called to Anaheim, hitting the 399th homer of his career—a record for Venezuelans that stood until 2015. He told a correspondent from *USA Today* he hoped his experience would "help many people like me overcome this battle. For those who are suffering this, keep fighting and don't lose faith in God."

In 2005, Galarraga tried out for the Mets. Despite hitting well in spring training, he decided to retire. He was elected to the Latino Baseball Hall of Fame in 2011. He settled in West Palm Beach, Florida, after leaving the game behind. According to one source, he is fairly talented at painting landscapes.

Freddy Garcia

Pitcher

Freddy Garcia was born in Caracas and attended high school in Baruta. Signed by the Astros as an amateur free agent, he spent portions of four seasons in Houston's farm system before a trade sent him to Seattle. The Mariners received Garcia and Carlos Guillen in exchange for future Hall of Famer Randy Johnson. Garcia made the Mariners roster out of spring training in 1999, and had a spectacular debut, posting a 17–8 record, with 170 strikeouts. He finished second in Rookie of the Year voting to Royals sensation Carlos Beltran. Moreover, he placed among the top 10 candidates for the Cy Young Award.

Manager Lou Piniella had difficulty with the headstrong Garcia during his big-league debut. When Piniella removed him from a game early one day, Garcia yelled loudly before storming back to the dugout. Later in the season, when Garcia was getting hammered in one of his starts, Piniella sat calmly in the dugout, relaxing. He waited until 10 runs had scored before replacing Garcia, who never complained about being removed from a game again that year.

Garcia earned the nickname of the "Chief" for his commanding presence. A big man, he was listed at 6-foot-4, 235 pounds during his prime playing years. A fierce competitor, he prided himself for putting forth his best effort during every start. Teammate Kenny Williams said, "[Garcia's] heart is something that comes out when he is on the mound."

Garcia had a diverse repertoire that featured a standard fastball that topped out in the mid-90s before injuries decreased its velocity. He also employed a variety of other pitches, including a split-fingered fastball, a hard slider, a curve, and a changeup. A frequent flyer on the disabled list, he won more than 130 games during seasons in which he was healthy.

Between 1999 and 2002, Garcia was considered one of the best starters in the majors. He won an ERA title and was named to two All-Star Teams in that span. The Mariners were heavily criticized for trading him to the White Sox midway through the 2004 slate. He was a vital component of Chicago's championship run in 2005, winning 14 regular-season games. In the postseason, he yielded just five earned runs in 21 innings of work, winning all three of his starts. He was the pitcher of record when the ChiSox clinched the ALDS and the World Series.

After 2005, Garcia posted an ERA below 4.00 just once. Suffering from various ailments, he made limited appearances with three different clubs between 2007 and 2009. He got back on track with the Yankees in 2011, posting a 12–8 record, with a 3.62 ERA—his lowest since 2001. The Yankees used him as a swingman in 2012, but he flopped in the role, averaging 5.2 earned runs per nine frames. The Orioles signed him for the 2013 slate but dished him to Atlanta in August. He made one quality start against the Dodgers in the NLDS, ending up with a no-decision. It was his last season in the majors. In all, Garcia won 59 percent of his major-league decisions.

In 2014, Garcia signed with the EDA Rhinos of Taiwan's Chinese Professional Baseball League. He pitched six shutout innings in his debut. He has remained active in the Venezuelan Winter League and Mexican League. In 2016, he made five appearances for the first-place Sultanes de Monterey, based in Nuevo Leon, Mexico.

Ozzie Guillen

Shortstop

Ozzie Guillen was born in Ocumare del Tuy, located in the northern state of Miranda. Noted for its warm, clear weather, most inhabitants make their living farming or raising livestock. Guillen grew up admiring Venezuelan shortstops Chico Carrasquel, Luis Aparicio, and Dave Concepcion. Following in their footsteps, he was signed by the Padres before he had finished high school. His alma mater—Caracas High School—has sent more than a dozen players to the majors. Guillen taught himself to switch hit but gradually became a left-handed hitter as he began to move up the ladder.

In four minor-league seasons, Guillen hit below .290 just once—in his Gulf Coast League debut. A .347 performance at Reno in 1982 put him on the team's radar. In December 1984, the Padres were looking for a reliable starting pitcher. They ended up trading Guillen and three other players to the White Sox for right-hander LaMarr Hoyt. Of the players included in the transaction, Guillen proved to be the most useful.

As starting shortstop for the ChiSox in 1985, the 21-year-old Guillen hit .273 and fielded his position impeccably, capturing Rookie of the Year honors. During his 13 seasons in Chicago, Guillen would rank among the top players at his position, earning three All-Star selections. His finest season came in 1990, when he drove in a career-high 58 runs and captured a Gold Glove. It was the only time he would claim the honor, as Cal Ripken Jr. and Omar Vizquel ran away with it for the next 11 seasons.

Guillen had little power at the plate, collecting just 28 homers in 16 seasons. He never accumulated more than 36 extra-base hits in any campaign. He had exceptional speed early in his career, averaging 24 steals per year between 1987 and 1991. He legged out seven or more triples five times. But in April 1992, he severely injured his knee in a collision with outfielder Tim Raines. This curtailed his stolen-base production and limited his range at short.

Guillen remained a first-stringer in Chicago until 1998, when he signed with the Orioles as a free agent. When he got off to a slow start at the plate, he was released. He finished the season with the Braves. Before then, Guillen had played in just one postseason series—an

ALCS loss to the Blue Jays. With Atlanta, Guillen reached the postseason twice, making it all the way to the World Series against the Yankees in 1999. He appeared in three of the four games as New York executed a sweep. Released by the Braves in April 2000, he played his last major-league season with Tampa Bay.

Following his retirement as a player, Guillen coached for the Expos in 2001 and 2002. He was a member of the world champion Marlins staff the following year. In the offseason, he was hired to replace Jerry Manuel as manager of the White Sox. During Guillen's debut, the team remained in first place until late July, when a sudden swoon left them chasing the Twins for the rest of the season. In 2005, Guillen led the ChiSox to their first pennant since 1959 and their first World Series title since 1917. He was the first manager born outside the United States to pilot a world championship club. He was named Manager of the Year by the Baseball Writers' Association of America.

During his eight seasons at the Chicago helm, Guillen generated controversy repeatedly with his bold and inappropriate remarks. In 2010, he described illegal immigrants as "workaholics" and complained that many Americans are "lazy." In 2012, he received a five-game suspension for making an outrageous comment about Fidel Castro. "I respect Fidel Castro," he said bluntly. "You know why? A lot of people have wanted to kill Fidel Castro for years, but that mofo is still here." Guillen's lack of a filter led to difficulties with White Sox executive Ken Williams and resulted in his eventual dismissal. He took over the Marlins in 2012, leading the club to a dismal 69–93 finish. He was released at season's end with three years to go on his contract.

Despite Guillen's problems with Williams, the Chicago VP said of Guillen in 2015, "I feel like baseball is missing something. I think it misses personalities and characters. A guy who has had as much success as he has and has as much baseball knowledge as he has and has a desire to be in uniform should be in uniform somewhere. Hopefully, he gets another chance to show it." Guillen was flattered when he heard the remark. Perhaps inspired by it, he signed a contract with the Tiburones de La Guaira of the Venezuelan Professional Baseball League for the 2016–2017 season.

Magglio Ordonez

Right Fielder

Born in the baseball breeding ground of Caracas, Magglio Ordonez attended high school in Coro—the oldest city in western Venezuela. He was signed by the White Sox at the age of 17 and came to the United States in 1992. His first two minor-league seasons were rough, as he hit at a combined .206 clip. By 1994, he was still hovering at the A level. He gradually matured as a hitter, compiling a .329 average for the Nashville Sounds in 1997. Called to Chicago that year, he entered 21 games and batted .319. The following season, he was part of a complete outfield overhaul, starting alongside newcomers Mike Cameron and Albert Belle. Ordonez hit .282 in 145 games, finishing fifth in Rookie of the Year voting.

For the next five seasons, Ordonez was Chicago's primary right fielder, averaging 32 homers and 118 RBIs. He was named to four All-Star Teams in that span, while receiving two Silver Slugger Awards. A right-handed hitter, the powerful Ordonez had a quick, compact swing and was able to spray the ball to all fields. He was also an exceptional defensive player, finishing among the top five in assists and fielding percentage eight times apiece. He led the league once in each category.

Injuries in 2004 severely limited Ordonez's playing time. Granted free agency at season's end, he signed a lucrative contract with the Tigers. As a result, he missed out on the 2005 championship run made by the White Sox. He was of limited use to Detroit that year, sitting out close to three months while recovering from a hernia operation. Healthy in 2006, he gathered 57 extra-base hits and 104 RBIs.

Ordonez enjoyed his signature campaign in 2007, when he finished second in MVP voting to Alex Rodriguez of the Yankees. His .363 average earned him a batting crown—the first Tiger to win it since Norm Cash in 1961. His league-leading 54 doubles were the highest total in Detroit since George Kell's 1950 season. In addition, his 139 RBIs were the most since Rocky Colavito drove in 140 in 1961.

Ordonez became immensely popular in Tigertown, especially within the Hispanic community, where he kept a tangible presence. Recognized by President George W. Bush for his work, he said, "I want to spend time with my fans. This team made a big commitment to sign me here. I have to return to that, I have to be here." Prior to 2009, Ordonez had long, curly hair. Many fans at Comerica Park took to wearing wigs under their caps in honor of the player they affectionately called "Maggs."

Ordonez's 2007 season was a tough act to follow. His .317 average and 103 RBIs in 2008 looked somewhat ordinary in comparison. Although he hit at a highly respectable .310 clip the following year, he managed to drive in just 50 runs as the Tigers finished sixth in the wild-card race. In July 2010, Ordonez injured his ankle sliding into home. X-rays revealed a fracture, and he was lost for the season. He was off to a hot start in the 2011 playoffs before reinjuring the ankle that had plagued him the previous year. Without him, Detroit lost the ALCS to Texas in six games. During the course of his career, Ordonez played in six postseason series, collecting 17 hits, 9 walks, and 9 RBIs in 21 appearances.

Unable to return to the sport, Ordonez announced his retirement in June 2012. A ceremony was held at Comerica Park to honor him. A member of the United Socialist Party of Venezuela, Ordonez was elected mayor of Sotillo the following year. Located in eastern Venezuela, the city has a population of 250,000. In addition to his mayoral duties, Ordonez has stayed close to baseball as part-owner of the Venezuelan Winter League club the Caribes de Anzoategui.

Johan Santana

Pitcher

On June 1, 2012, Mets manager Terry Collins left Johan Santana on the mound to complete the first no-hitter in Mets history. Working with a surgically repaired shoulder, Santana walked five batters and used 134 pitches to polish off the Cardinals. Questions remain as to whether this was a good decision on Collins's part. During Santana's next 10 starts, he posted an 8.27 ERA. Injured in spring training the following year, he hasn't appeared in a regular-season game since.

The decision to leave Santana in that fateful game still haunts Collins. He described Santana's triumph as the "worst night [he] ever spent in baseball." Santana himself holds no grudges. "You can't say it was the right decision or the wrong decision because you don't know. No doctor ever told me. Maybe if I would have gotten knocked out in the fourth inning everything would have been different or nothing would have been different." With Santana's career derailed at the age of 33, no one will ever know just how good he could have been.

Santana was born in the geographically isolated town of Tovar. Before him, the town had never produced a major leaguer. Santana's father Jesus was a star shortstop at the semipro level, and young Johan sought to emulate him. When a coach told Santana that left-handers don't normally play shortstop, he learned to relay the ball to first with his right hand. As a teenager, he played in the outfield but did not stand out offensively. According to multiple reports, he was somewhat of a ham who enjoyed eliciting responses from the crowd. His throwing arm eventually elicited a response from the Houston Astros.

The local Chiquilines team competed annually in Venezuela's national baseball tournament and exceeded expectations each year. Having heard about the young Santana, Astros scout Andres Reiner drove 10 hours through the Andes Mountains to Santana's home. Santana had previously failed a tryout with the Rockies at their Venezuelan camp. He wasn't about to let a second opportunity pass him by.

With the Astros' Dominican Summer League team in 1996, Santana worked mostly in relief, limiting opponents to a .178 batting average. After a rough follow-up season, he got back on track in 1998. Chosen by the Marlins in the 1999 Rule 5 Draft, he was traded to Minnesota before the 2000 campaign. The Twins were required to keep him on the roster for the entire year, and he appeared ill-equipped, getting hammered for a 6.49 ERA. He spent the next two seasons bouncing between the majors and the minors. Santana began the 2003 slate in the Minnesota bullpen. By mid-July, he had been inserted into the rotation. From August 3 to September 20, he won eight consecutive decisions. A scoreless outing in his regular-season finale lowered his ERA to 3.07. His fine performance as a swingman earned him Cy Young consideration that year.

From 2004 to 2008, Santana was arguably the best starter in the majors. He averaged 238 strikeouts per year and led the league three times. He also claimed three ERA titles, two Cy Young Awards, and a Gold Glove. Although he was a Triple Crown winner in 2006, he actually had a better season in 2004, with 20 wins, a 2.61 ERA, and 265 strikeouts. He was unbeaten after the All-Star break that year, winning 13 straight decisions.

Santana's efforts propelled the Twins to four playoff appearances. In the 2004 ALDS against the Yankees, he surrendered just one run in 12 innings of work. In the 2006 ALDS versus Oakland, he tossed a five-hitter and lost. He never made it to the ALCS.

In 2008, Santana signed a contract with the Mets that made him the highest-paid pitcher in baseball history. His first season was a great success, as he compiled a 16–7 record, with a league-leading 2.53 ERA. Moreover, he finished among NL front-runners in strikeouts, shutouts, and complete games. Unfortunately, he had been pitching on a bad knee that required surgery. Injuries would plague him for the remainder of his career.

In 2009, Santana missed several starts due to bone chips in his elbow. In 2010, he tore his rotator cuff. He was out for the entire 2011 campaign. The following season was full of disappointment, as he sprained his right ankle and strained a muscle in his back. He finished his last big-league season with a 6–9 record and a 4.85 ERA. Granted free agency in November 2013, various comeback attempts were disastrous. In spring training with the Orioles in 2014, he tore his Achilles tendon. Signed by the Blue Jays the following year, he ended up with an infected toe and didn't throw a single pitch.

In his prime, Santana had supreme command of a two-seam fastball, a slider, and a changeup. With a 20-mile-per-hour difference between his fastball and change, he averaged close to nine strikeouts per nine innings during his 12-year career. As of this writing, the four-time All-Star has yet to officially announce plans for his retirement. Approaching the age of 40, his return appears highly unlikely.

Manny Trillo

Second Baseman

Manny Trillo was born in Caripito, in the state of Monagas. He later attended high school in the busy city of Maturin—Venezuela's hub for petroleum development. Signed as an amateur free agent in 1968, he would travel extensively throughout his career. After two seasons in the minors, the A's scooped him up in the Rule 5 Draft. Prior to 1975, he was traded, along with two other players, in exchange for future Hall of Famer Billy Williams. Trillo entered one of his most productive stretches with the Cubs but didn't stop there, becoming a fixture in the Phillies infield for four seasons. He played for two clubs in 1983 and had a layover in San Francisco before returning to the city that had put him on the map (Chicago). He finished his career with the Reds in 1989.

Trillo once said, "The best thing about baseball is that you can do something about yesterday tomorrow." There were plenty of tomorrows for Trillo, and he often made the most of them. Originally a catcher, he was converted to a third baseman in the Phillies farm system. When the A's brought him up in 1973, they used him at second base. He was unwittingly involved in a bit of controversy during the 1973 World Series, when A's owner Charlie Finley tried to deactivate second baseman Mike Andrews after two crucial errors in the 12th inning of Game Two. Finley fraudulently placed Andrews on the disabled list and attempted to insert Trillo into the lineup, but Commissioner Bowie Kuhn saw through the ruse, forcing the flamboyant Oakland executive to reactivate Andrews. Trillo entered one World Series game with the A's in 1974. Inserted as a pinch-runner, he scored on a sacrifice fly by Bert Campaneris. It was his last taste of the postseason until 1980.

In 1975, Trillo's career finally took off. Although he had appeared briefly in the majors the previous two seasons, he failed to meet rookie qualifications. In his official debut, he finished third in Rookie of the Year voting, behind Gary Carter and John Montefusco. With a throwing arm that has been described as "whip-like," he led the NL in assists each year from 1975 to 1978. His seemingly effortless movements around second base led some to believe he was loafing. "They always ask me 'Why do I play so smooth?' 'Why do I always look like I don't want to play,'" Trillo once said. "That's just the way I play. You never see me go slow for a ball."

The 1977 Cubs suffered one of the worst second-half collapses in modern history. After posting a 51–30 record before the midsummer break, they finished at .500—20 games behind the Phillies. Trillo was hitting .340 through June and made the All-Star Team, but he "slumped" to .280 by season's end. Between 1979 and 1982, he captured three Gold Gloves and a pair of Silver Slugger Awards with the Phillies while making two more All-Star appearances. In 1980, he was MVP of the NLCS, tagging Houston pitchers for a .381 average. He drove in the winning run in Game Five of the World Series as the Phillies disposed of the Royals in six games.

Among the best defensive second basemen in history, Trillo set a record (since broken) for consecutive errorless chances, with 479. During the skein, he narrowly missed the record for errorless games (91), which had been set by Hall of Famer Joe Morgan. Trillo ranks among the top 50 in putouts and assists. His range factor per nine innings is the fourth best in history at his position.

At 6-foot-1, 150 pounds, Trillo wasn't breaking down fences with his bat, but he did accrue a competent .263 lifetime average. His best offensive effort came in 1980, when he hit .292, with 41 extra-base hits and 43 RBIs. Swinging from the right side of the plate, he most often appeared in the bottom third of the batting order. He compiled a .282 average with the bases loaded.

Used as a utility man after 1987, Trillo was finished in the majors after the 1989 slate. He moved on to a long coaching career in the majors and minors, working for the Cubs, Phillies, Yankees, and Brewers. In 2007, he was inducted into the Venezuelan Baseball Hall of Fame.

Omar Vizquel

Shortstop

Described by one writer as a "unique defensive strategist whose range and dramatic flair reminded many of Ozzie Smith," Omar Vizquel began polishing his skills on the fields of Venezuela's capital city—Caracas. He learned to get the ball to first quickly by barehanding grounders. The Mariners felt he would develop into a fine player and signed him straight out of high school.

After five seasons on the farm, Vizquel began making sporadic major-league appearances. He struggled with the bat in the early part of his career. Discounting the 1992 slate, when he hit .294 in 136 games, he managed a weak .239 average during his career with Seattle. The Mariners sent him back to the minors multiple times between 1989 and 1994. He was traded to the Indians before the latter campaign.

Vizquel's wife, who was originally from Seattle, was extremely unhappy about the trade, bursting into tears when she heard the news.

Vizquel himself was skeptical at first, but he quickly changed his mind. "I got over the trade in a hurry once spring training started and I saw all the great players we had. There was really a good vibe about the team," he said.

Vizquel came into his own in Cleveland, establishing himself as one of the most capable shortstops in the majors. From 1999 to 2001, he had the benefit of working with Hall of Famer Roberto Alomar around second base. "We clicked right away," Vizquel recalled years after the fact. "Robbie was so gifted and so smart. He knew where the ball was going to be hit." Vizquel had a pretty good idea himself, setting the all-time mark for double plays by a shortstop. His 11 Gold Gloves are second only to Ozzie Smith. Speaking of Vizquel's defensive excellence, sportswriter Bob August proclaims, "Vizquel makes a specialty of his magical art. Average players sometimes make great plays, but most of these plays are performed by the artists of their craft. As a shortstop, Vizquel has provided me with more exciting moments than any other baseball player."

Vizquel's offense steadily improved over time. He was approaching the 3,000-hit mark when age finally caught up with him. He had little power, averaging just 26 extra-base hits per year in 24 seasons, but he had superb bat control, leading the league in sacrifice hits four times. The players ahead of him on the all-time list for sacrifices played in bygone eras. On the basepaths, Vizquel was gifted with speed. Only a handful of shortstops surpassed his lifetime total of 404 steals. His best offensive season came with Cleveland in 1999, when he reached career-high totals in runs scored (112), hits (191), RBIs (66), and batting average (.333). He reached the postseason five times—all with the Indians. In 57 games, he reached base by hit or walk on 82 occasions.

Vizquel played for six different teams and was the oldest player in the majors during his last season in 2012. During his career, he donated his time to various charitable organizations. In the wake of a devastating mudslide that killed 25,000 in Venezuela, Vizquel helped raise more than $500,000 for the relief effort. He served as honorary spokesperson for an arts program in Cleveland known as "Young Audiences." He was also involved in "Schools Now," a program that secures educational funds through the sale of entertainment booklets.

Vizquel's 2003 autobiography *Omar! My Life on and off the Field* spent four weeks on the *New York Times* Bestseller List. It also touched off a feud with former teammate Jose Mesa. Vizquel's criticism of the relief pitcher's performance in the 1997 World Series made Mesa furious. Vowing to hit Vizquel every time the two squared off, Mesa kept that promise twice. In three other showdowns, Vizquel produced two groundouts and an RBI single.

When his playing days were over, Vizquel took a job as an infield coach for the Angels. In November 2013, the Tigers hired him as a first-base coach. In addition, he served as an infield and baserunning instructor. Although he has more hits than any Venezuelan-born player in history, he remains humble about his chances of being elected to Cooperstown. "I never pictured myself as a Hall of Famer," he once said. "I know I've got some great numbers, but I never compare myself to the shortstops in the Hall of Fame." Vizquel is set to appear on Cooperstown ballots in 2017. He has already been enshrined in the Cleveland Indians Hall of Fame and the Hispanic Heritage Baseball Museum Hall of Fame.

Carlos Zambrano

Pitcher

Carlos Zambrano was born in Puerto Cabello. His father was a trucker who struggled to make ends meet. Zambrano's family members were devout Christians, and he remains a deeply spiritual man. By the time young Carlos was a teenager, he was more than six feet tall and weighed more than 200 pounds. He started out as a switch-hitting outfielder but had aspirations of becoming a pitcher. He made the switch under the tutelage of Julio Figueroa, a former moundsman for the Venezuelan Olympic team. Zambrano's fastball had dramatic downward movement, and he learned to use that to his advantage.

Even as a boy, Zambrano was highly competitive and hated to lose. He had difficulty controlling his emotions at times—a trait that would follow him into adulthood. Nevertheless, he was spotted by Cubs scout Alberto Rondon, who accompanied him to Arizona for a tryout. He ended up with a $5,000 contract.

Zambrano began his pro career in 1998. He had a breakout season in the Pacific Coast League during the 2001 slate, earning a call to Chicago in August. He fared rather poorly in six appearances, warranting a demotion to the farm. By July of the following year, he was a full-time starter for the Cubs. He held opponents to a .235 batting average but suffered in the won–loss column with a 4–8 record. Things began to turn around for him in 2003.

In his prime, Zambrano employed six pitches, relying most heavily on his sinker, which peaked in the low 90s. He also resorted to his cutter quite often. In addition, he sprinkled in a mix of splitters, sliders, curves, and four-seam fastballs. Highly emotional on the mound, he was known to antagonize opponents and teammates. When things went poorly, he sometimes pinned the blame on others. He received two lengthy team suspensions, one in 2010 and another in 2011. He was also suspended by MLB after arguing with umpire Mark Carlson and firing a ball angrily into the outfield.

When he was on his game, Zambrano was one of the best right-handers in the NL. He enjoyed his most productive stretch from 2003 to 2008, making three All-Star appearances and receiving Cy Young consideration the same number of times. He averaged 15 wins per year in that span, peaking at 18 in 2007.

When Zambrano made the All-Star Team in 2004, he was the youngest Chicago player to do so. Although his career ended on a down note, he is known as one of the best offensive pitchers of his generation. He holds the major-league record for most home runs in a season without a double or triple, with six. He accomplished the unusual feat in 2006. A switch-hitter, he won three Silver Slugger Awards, exceeding the .300 mark at the plate on three occasions. His 24 homers are seventh on the all-time list for pitchers.

Zambrano authored his personal masterpiece in 2008—a no-hitter over the Astros. It was the first by a Cubs pitcher since Milt Pappas's gem in 1972. The Cubs eventually grew tired of Zambrano's volatile temperament and traded him to the Marlins before the 2012 slate. He fared poorly and never reappeared in the majors. In 2013, he played in the Venezuelan Winter League, compiling a 1–2 record, with a 4.85 ERA. He announced his retirement in 2014. He won 168 games at the professional level.

NOTABLE ACTIVE PLAYERS

Jose Altuve

Second Baseman

Jose Altuve was born in Maracay, a city in the north-central region of Venezuela, near the Caribbean coast. To some, it is known as the "Garden City." Altuve grew up playing ball alongside future major leaguer Salvador Perez. The two remained friends throughout childhood. Perez was not surprised when Altuve made it to the majors a month before he did. "[Jose] always believed in himself," said the Royals All-Star catcher. "I always knew he'd make it all the way to the majors. He works hard. He plays hard."

Altuve is small in stature, at 5-foot-6, 165 pounds. His height became an issue early in his career when the Astros dismissed him from their Venezuelan training facility because he was allegedly too short. Altuve's father insisted he try again, and Jose followed through. The second time was a charm, as the Astros offered him a contract before the 2007 campaign.

Altuve's pro career began in the Venezuelan Summer League, where he hit .343. He was summoned to the United States in 2008, playing for the Tennessee-based Greenville Astros. By 2011, he had moved up to the Double-A level. He hit .389 in the California and Texas leagues that year, earning a call to Houston in July. He has been with the club ever since.

Defense is a vital aspect of Altuve's game. Through the 2016 campaign, he had finished among the top five in putouts and assists four times. In 2015, he posted the highest fielding percentage in the AL, capturing his first Gold Glove. He has also led the league in double plays twice.

Altuve swings from the right side of the plate. He is primarily a pull hitter, sometimes prompting defensive shifts. His exceptional speed allows him to beat out balls hit deep in the hole. He doesn't have much home-run power but has a knack for finding the outfield gaps. He has gathered no fewer than 31 doubles in five consecutive seasons.

An imminent threat to steal, Altuve makes pitchers uncomfortable. Entering the 2017 campaign, he had swiped 30 or more bases five times. His finest all around season came in 2016, when he captured his second batting title and collected a career-high total of 71 extra-base hits. He drove in 96 runs that year. His appearance in the 2016 All-Star Game was the fourth of his career.

In a memorable moment of unintentional comic relief, Altuve faced Mets reliever Jon Rauch on May 1, 2012. At 6-foot-11, Rauch is the tallest pitcher in the majors. The 18-inch height difference between he and Altuve is believed to be the largest since St. Louis Browns owner Bill Veeck sent a 3-foot-7 circus performer named Eddie Gaedel to the plate against Tigers hurler Bob Cain. The towering Rauch got the best of the diminutive Altuve that day, inducing a lineout to first.

Elvis Andrus

Shortstop

Elvis Andrus was born in Maracay, in the state of Aragua. His father was a university professor who died when he was young. Andrus's mother has never been forthcoming about whether she named him after the iconic rock star. Nowadays, Andrus is a hero to many native Venezuelans, some of whom openly name their children after him.

Signed as an amateur free agent in 2005, Andrus was one of the hottest properties in baseball. After his first pro season, he was considered Atlanta's number-two prospect. In July 2007, the Braves were looking to add some power to their lineup. They traded Andrus to the Rangers in a seven-player deal that included slugger Mark Teixeira. Andrus made his major-league debut two seasons later.

Impressed with his skills, manager Ron Washington made the 20-year-old Andrus a starting shortstop in 2009. Andrus didn't disappoint, finishing second in Rookie of the Year voting. He has held onto that starting job ever since. Andrus often resides at the top of the betting order, typically hitting second. A consistent performer, his averages ranged from .258 to .286 between 2009 and 2015. A free swinger, he has never drawn more than 64 walks in a season. He averages one strikeout per eight plate appearances. He is an excellent bunter, leading the league in sacrifice hits three times and placing among the top five on four other occasions. Most of his hits are singles, but he has a knack for delivering in the clutch. Entering the 2016 campaign, he had a .355 batting average with the bases loaded. His above-average speed has allowed him to swipe at least 21 bags in eight straight seasons.

Defensively, Andrus is one of the most dependable shortstops in the majors. There are few balls he can't get to, and when he does, he uses his powerful arm to erase potential hits. As of 2016, he had placed among the top five in assists and double plays seven times apiece. His lifetime fielding percentage is in the top 20 among active players. Despite his prowess at short, he has never won a Gold Glove.

Andrus helped the Rangers to five postseason berths (including a pair of World Series appearances) during his first eight seasons in the majors. He hit .294 in the 2010 playoffs, scoring eight runs and driving in four more. He added eight hits and five runs in the 2011 World Series.

Miguel Cabrera

Third Baseman/First Baseman

Miguel Cabrera is yet another player hailing from the baseball hotbed of Maracay. His parents were both highly regarded amateur players who literally met on a baseball diamond. Cabrera lived close to Maracay Stadium, and to attend games, all he had to do was hop the fence that separated his backyard from the right-field foul line.

Cabrera's father cautioned him to focus on his studies in the event that a baseball career failed to materialize. It wasn't an issue. During his teen years, Cabrera received personal instruction from Venezuelan great Dave Concepcion. He was already being scouted by the Twins, Yankees, and Dodgers. In the end, it was the Marlins who signed him before the 2000 slate. According to popular legend, Yankees owner George Steinbrenner fired three of his Venezuelan scouts for missing the boat.

Cabrera began his career at shortstop, but his sizeable frame left him with limited range. With a rifle-like arm, he made the switch to third base easily in the South Atlantic League. By 2003, he was too talented to keep in the minors any longer. He made his debut in late June, driving in 62 runs in 87 games. He would reach the century mark in RBIs for the next 11 seasons.

During his major-league career, Cabrera has spent significant time at both first and third base. He is competent at both. He led the league in putouts at third base in 2012. At first base, he paced the circuit in assists on three occasions.

Cabrera is believed by many to be the best pure hitter in baseball. He not only hits for power and average, but also walks a lot and generates relatively low strikeout totals for a modern-era slugger. After guiding the Marlins to an improbable World Series victory over the heavily favored Yankees during his rookie season, he led the team in RBIs for the next several campaigns. The Marlins have never been good about retaining their top players, and in 2007 Cabrera was traded to the Tigers, along with pitching mainstay Dontrelle Willis. It proved to be a colossal blunder on the part of the Marlins.

Assuming he stays healthy, Cabrera is on a trajectory to Cooperstown. Entering the 2017 slate, he had four batting titles to his credit. In 2012, he became the first AL player to win a Triple Crown since Carl Yastrzemski in 1967. With 44 homers, 139 RBIs, and a .330 batting mark, he was an obvious choice for MVP. His follow-up season was nearly identical, netting him a second MVP nod.

Cabrera's hitting exploits have dazzled teammates and opponents for more than a decade. Coach Bill Robinson dubbed him "baseball's version of LeBron James." Hall of Famer Frank Robinson once griped, "We haven't found a weakness in him yet. There are ways of getting him out, but if you do it too much, he'll burn you." Cabrera doesn't let strikeouts or slumps get him down. "When I was coming up, I just wanted to play baseball, and I'm doing what I love to do most," he said. "How can I feel pressure doing what I love to do?" Former Marlins manager Jack McKeon observed, "The thing you like about Cabrera is when he strikes out, he comes back and just puts his helmet away. He says, 'Hey, I'll get them next time.'"

At the end of the 2016 campaign, Cabrera had seven Silver Slugger Awards to his credit. Including the two seasons in which he claimed the honor, he has received MVP consideration 13 times. His All-Star selection in 2016 was the 11th of his career. Signed through 2023, he shows no immediate signs of slowing down. His sabermetric similarity scores compare to the all-time greats, including Hank Aaron, Frank Robinson, and Joe DiMaggio.

Alcides Escobar

Shortstop

Alcides Escobar's uncle Jose made a brief appearance with the Indians in 1991. His cousin Kelvim had several excellent seasons as a pitcher for the Blue Jays and Angels. Born in La Sabana, Escobar started playing ball at the age of four. He idolized fellow Venezuelan Omar Vizquel while growing up. At the age of 16, he was noticed by Milwaukee scout Epy Guerrero. Guerrero, who was responsible for discovering Tony Fernandez and Carlos Delgado, felt that Escobar would mature into a fine player someday. Escobar signed with the Brewers for $35,000.

Escobar began his minor-league career in 2004, with the Montana-based Helena Brewers. Although he hit and fielded well, the parent club already had J. J. Hardy at shortstop. When Escobar compiled a .304 batting average in limited action during the 2009 slate, the Brewers were inspired to traded Hardy to the Twins in exchange for center fielder Carlos Gomez. Escobar played his first full season in 2010. Proving he had some wrinkles to iron out, he slumped to .235 at the plate while finishing third among NL shortstops in errors. Before the 2011 slate, he was dealt to the Royals in a six-player deal.

When Escobar first arrived in Kansas City, the Royals were a young team with a lot of growing to do. As Escobar began to mature as a player, the Royals slowly rose to contention. After a third-place showing in 2013, the team made consecutive World Series appearances in 2014 and 2015. Escobar played a major role in bringing a world championship back to Kansas City after a drought of more than 30 years.

A fine defensive player, Escobar has led the league in putouts and assists once apiece. He has placed among the top five in fielding percentage on four occasions. He has remarkable range and makes highlight-reel plays with regularity. He won his first Gold Glove in 2015.

At the plate, Escobar has little power and likes to swing the bat. Entering the 2017 campaign, he had never walked more than 36 times in a season. A streaky hitter, his averages have ranged from .234 to .293 as a full-time player. On the bases, he has good speed, averaging 24 steals per year between 2010 and 2015.

Escobar has a knack for rising to the occasion. In seven postseason series, he has compiled a .311 batting average. He was especially effective against Toronto pitching in the 2015 ALCS, when he gathered 11 hits in six games and captured series MVP honors.

Carlos Gonzalez

Outfielder

Carlos Gonzalez was born and raised in Maracaibo—the capital city of Zulia, which is among the most populated states in the country. One of his distant cousins was a member of the Venezuelan national team and played in the 1953 Amateur World Series. Like many poor Venezuelan youths, Carlos used crude materials to play ball when he was young. His father had to work extra hours on the side to buy him a glove and cleats.

Gonzalez made a name for himself in his early teens, when he smashed a tape-measure homer off of future Mariners sensation Felix Hernandez. He fared well in overseas play and began attracting scouts to his games. Signed in 2002 by Diamondbacks scout Miguel Nava, Gonzalez changed teams twice before assuming full-time playing status. The A's brought him to the majors in 2008, but it was the Rockies who handed him a starting center-field position two seasons later.

Gonzalez has struggled with injuries throughout his career, some of them rather serious. In 2011, he hurt his wrist twice. In 2014, he suffered a torn labrum. He missed a combined total of 127 games in those seasons. When healthy, he shines offensively and defensively.

Gonzalez has spent significant time at each outfield station, compiling a fielding percentage above the league average at each. He has good speed and covers a lot of ground. He also has a strong arm, ranking high among active players in assists. His aptitude in the field is no secret, as he has captured three Gold Gloves.

The outfielder holds his own at the plate as well. His 162-game average includes 30 homers and 99 RBIs. He has exceeded the .300 mark at the plate three times. He won a batting title in 2010, with a .336 mark. Colorado has always had a profound effect on player stats, and Gonzalez is no exception. Through 2016, he has compiled a .330 batting average at Coors Field. His best all-around season came in 2010, when he led the NL with 197 hits and 351 total bases. In July of that year, he hit for the cycle against the Cubs. He finished third in MVP voting, behind Joey Votto and Albert Pujols.

In 2011, Gonzalez signed a seven-year contract worth $80.5 million—the largest ever offered to a two-year player. His selection to the All-Star Team in 2016 was the third of his career. Gonzalez's power appears to be on the rise. He played in 153 games in 2015—the highest total of his career—and reached the 40-homer plateau for the first time. He hit .298 the following year with 100 RBIs.

Felix Hernandez

Pitcher

Few Latino pitchers have been as precocious as Felix Hernandez. He had two ERA titles, a Cy Young Award, and six All-Star selections to his credit before his 30th birthday. During the last decade, he has lived up to his regal nickname of "King Felix." Hernandez was born in Valencia, a densely inhabited city in the state of Carabobo. His father owned a successful trucking company and had been an excellent pitcher in his youth. Felix closely followed the career of Freddy Garcia while growing up. By the age of 14, he was matching Garcia's velocity. During a tournament in Maracaibo, he was regularly hitting 94 on the radar gun, and scouts were practically tripping over one another to sign him. In the end, Hernandez decided that the Mariners were the best fit.

Hernandez entered the minor leagues at 17. His career on the farm was rather brief. After compiling a 30–10 record in portions of three seasons, he was called to Seattle. He was the youngest player in the majors when he made his debut. A sign of great things to come, he posted a 2.67 ERA in 12 starts, while averaging eight strikeouts per nine innings.

Hernandez has good command of four pitches—a two-seam fastball, slider, curve, and change. His fastball topped out at 100 miles per hour when he first came to the majors, but nowadays he relies more on strategy and finesse. Although his favorite two-strike pitch is a change-up, he often goes to his two-seamer, which has dramatic sinking action and induces a lot of groundball outs. Pitching coach Rick Adair said, "Almost every pitch Felix throws has unbelievable movement. If you grade his four pitches on a scale from two to eight, all four of them are seven or eight."

Hernandez undoubtedly would have accrued higher win totals had he spent his career with a different club. During his first 11 seasons in the majors, the Mariners finished last in the AL West six times. He has been a frequent victim of poor run support, getting staked to two runs or less in close to 40 percent of his appearances. He has consistently kept games close with a cumulative 3.16 ERA through 2016.

Hernandez's winningest season came in 2009, when he notched a 19–5 record. While he "slumped" to 13–12 the following year, he posted the lowest ERA in the league, at 2.27. Rewarded for his efforts, he received the AL Cy Young Award. In 2014, he finished second in Cy Young voting, behind Corey Kluber of the Indians.

Highly durable, Hernandez worked no fewer than 200 innings in eight consecutive seasons from 2008 through 2015. He has averaged 216 strikeouts per year in that span. Entering the 2016 campaign, he was third among active players in complete games. He is the Mariners' all-time leader in wins, strikeouts, and ERA. In June 2016, he suffered a severe calf strain while jumping to celebrate a home run. The bizarre injury landed him on the 15-day disabled list. He returned to action in late July.

Victor Martinez

Catcher/First Baseman/Designated Hitter

Victor Martinez was born in Ciudad Bolivar, a major river-port city in the southeastern region of the country. His father died unexpectedly of a heart attack when Victor was young, leaving his mother to raise four children. She worked as a nurse in two different hospitals to make sure her kids had what they needed. Martinez started out as a softball player and idolized Ozzie Guillen growing up. Most of the kids in his neighborhood could switch hit, and Victor taught himself to do the same.

Martinez reportedly got his first glove after his mother won a modest sum in a lottery. He sprouted to six feet tall in his mid-teens and fared well against older competition. He signed with the Indians in 1996.

Originally a shortstop, Martinez had limited range due to his size. When the Indians told him they intended to try him out as a catcher, he considered quitting. Fortunately, he persevered, becoming one of the best backstops in the Venezuelan Summer League. In 1999, he came to the United States. By the time the Indians promoted him for good in 2003, he had attained a *Baseball America* ranking of number 16.

Never known for his strong arm, Martinez placed first or second in stolen bases allowed four times during his years as a catcher. He made a reliable target behind the plate, however, averaging just three passed balls per season. His fielding percentage was among the top five on two occasions. He was an ideal batterymate, mixing tough love with strong encouragement.

Martinez established his offensive presence in 2004. Playing in his first season as a full-timer, he hit .283, with 62 extra-base hits and 108 RBIs. Entering the 2016 slate, he had driven in 80 or more runs eight times. His best season to date came in 2014, while playing for the Tigers. He hit .335 that year, with an on-base percentage of .409. His league-leading 28 intentional walks helped boost the latter number. Martinez has more power as a lefty, generating a majority of his 200-plus homers from that side of the plate.

A five-time All-Star, Martinez has played for three different clubs during his 14 seasons (Indians, Red Sox, and Tigers). He spent the longest stretch of time with Cleveland. During his prime years with the Tribe, he served as a team leader. Before each game, he would greet each starting player with a customized handshake—a ritual that came to be known as "Victor Time." His leadership has helped each of his teams to the playoffs. While he has never been to a World Series, he has fashioned a .315 postseason batting average.

Martinez was 37 years old at the start of the 2016 campaign. Catching has taken its toll on his knees, and he hasn't made an appearance behind the plate since 2014. In the past several seasons, he has been used increasingly as a designated hitter and a first baseman. He shows no signs of slowing down offensively. He hit .289 in 2016 with 27 homers and 86 RBIs. He is property of the Tigers through 2018.

Miguel Montero

Catcher

Miguel Montero hails from Caracas. He developed an aptitude for the game at an early age and entered the Diamondbacks minor-league system in 2002. After hitting .286 on the farm, with 75 RBIs in 2006, he was called to Arizona. He served as a backup to Chris Snyder for two full seasons. When Snyder went on the disabled list the following year, the situation was reversed. Montero excelled as an everyday player, hitting .294, with 46 extra-base hits, in 128 games.

Although Montero is a bit error-prone, he has fared well in other defensive categories. In 2011, he posted the highest caught stealing percentage in the NL. He has two no-hitters on his catching resume. The first came in 2010, while working with Edwin Jackson. Montero is a fierce competitor and doesn't mince words with his batterymates. "I hate to lose," he once said. "And I hate to give up a hit. Even though it's the pitcher's ERA, it hurts me when they give up a run because I take it personally."

Offensively, Montero has been among the most productive catchers in the majors for several years. Between 2009 and 2015, he averaged 14 homers and 63 RBIs. He received two All-Star selections in that span. His best season at the plate came in 2011, when he reached career highs in doubles (36), homers (18), and total bases (231). He was given a modest amount of MVP attention that year.

Montero's efforts boosted the Diamondbacks to a pair of playoff appearances, in 2007 and 2011. He hit .296 in nine postseason games. Traded to the Cubs before the 2015 slate, he has assumed full-time catching responsibilities in Chicago. His presence behind the plate has helped right-hander Jake Arrieta tremendously. Arrieta turned in his first 20-win effort during Montero's Chicago debut. "Some guys need a pat on the back, some guys need to be yelled at," Arrieta said. "And I'm one of the guys that likes to be yelled at. [Montero] recognizes things in situations that I need to do differently, and it's great to have a voice like that behind the plate." Montero used his voice to guide Arrieta to a no-hitter against the Dodgers in August 2015.

In 2016, Montero helped the Cubs to their first championship in over a hundred years. His grand slam in Game 1 of the NLCS lifted the Cubs to an 8-4 win over the Dodgers. He added a clutch RBI single in Game 7 of the World Series, pushing across the winning run in the tenth inning.

Salvador Perez

Catcher

Salvador Perez was born in Valencia, a major economic center in the state of Carabobo. At the age of four, he was abandoned by his father. He was raised by his mother, who enrolled him in a baseball academy at the age of six. Although he was competent as a pitcher and a shortstop, he preferred catching. By the time he reached his early teens, he had set his sights on a professional career. He attained that goal in 2006, when he signed with the Royals.

After a breakout season in the Texas League and the PCL in 2011, he was summoned to Kansas City. He was one of several catchers vying for playing time, but he outhit them all, posting a .331 average in 39 games. Before the 2012 campaign, he signed a five-year, $7 million extension with the club.

Perez's 2012 campaign started late. While catching a bullpen session before a spring-training game, he tore his left meniscus. Out of action until June, he picked up right where he had left off the previous year, finishing the season with a .301 average.

Beginning in 2013, Perez began a run of four consecutive All-Star appearances. In 2016, Perez led AL catchers in nearly every defensive category, including runners caught stealing and fielding percentage. He had captured three consecutive Gold Gloves prior to then.

Perez has averaged 18 homers and 71 RBIs during his seasons as a full-time player. He has no interest in drawing walks, reaching a career high of just 22 free passes in 2014. Just 25 years old, he has already appeared in seven postseason series. He was MVP of the 2015 World Series, which was won by the Royals.

Perez is a bit superstitious. Before a 2013 game, teammate Alcides Escobar sprayed Victoria's Secret perfume on him as a joke. Perez got four hits that day and has continued to wear perfume as a good-luck charm, although he reportedly switched to 212 Men cologne in 2014. Playful by nature, he is known for giving teammates Gatorade showers. He has also amused fans with his humorous postings on Instagram.

Martin Prado

Utility

Martin Prado hails from Maracay. He grew up with three siblings in a single-parent family. Compared to other Venezuelan major leaguers, his career started a little late. He didn't appear in his first minor-league game until he was 19. By the time he reached the majors to stay, he was approaching his mid-20s.

Highly versatile, Prado has played all over the diamond during his career. Since making his major-league debut with the Braves in 2006, he has appeared at every infield station except pitcher and catcher. He has spent the largest chunk of time at third base, where his fielding percentage is second among active players.

Since ending his seven-year tenure with the Braves in 2013, Prado has traveled extensively. He has worn four different uniforms in the past five seasons. His ability to fill multiple positions makes him a valuable commodity. And his offensive numbers certainly don't hurt his solvency when it comes time to negotiate a contract.

Prado has moderate speed and adequate power. He finished with double-digit home-run totals in six straight seasons. He has gathered no fewer than 36 doubles on five occasions. His batting average has never fallen below .260 during his time in the majors. He cracked the .300 mark in three consecutive seasons. To date, he has made just one post-season appearance, in the 2012 Wild Card Game with Atlanta.

In a bizarre snapshot from his career, Prado's bat once landed upright after he had tossed it aside and headed to first base in a game against the Mets. Broadcaster Keith Hernandez remarked that the incident "would never happen in a hundred years." Prado was Miami's primary third baseman in 2016. He hit .305 with 75 RBIs.

Francisco Rodriguez

Pitcher

Francisco Rodriguez has more than a dozen siblings. His parents split up shortly before he was born, and he ended up being raised by his grandparents. He grew up in a poor section of Caracas, making money on the side by break dancing and taking bets for bookies. He learned to play baseball using a broomstick and rolled-up newspaper. His earliest gloves were made of cardboard.

Graciano Ravelo, a former player who would later become a Rangers scout, ran a baseball school in El Valle. He kindly took Rodriguez under his wing. By the time Rodriguez had reached his mid-teens, he was one of the best young pitchers in the region. He turned down multiple offers from major-league teams to compete in a youth tournament in Mexico. After a 14-strikeout performance, he traveled to the United States for another round of competition. When he returned home, the Angels and Yankees offered him hefty signing bonuses. Realizing that he had a better chance of becoming a primary player in Anaheim, he signed with the Angels in 1998.

The man who would later be known as "K-Rod" began his minor-league career at the age of 17. Promoted to the majors in September 2002, he pitched 5.2 scoreless innings and struck out 13. The Angels liked what they saw, making him their setup man the following year. While he got off to a rocky start, he finished strong, at 8–3, with a 3.03 ERA. Rodriguez made his first All-Star appearance in 2004, becoming only the sixth pitcher in Angels history to strike out 100 batters in a season without starting a game. Converted to a closer in 2005, he became one of the most dominant forces in baseball during the next several seasons.

Rodriguez has a sizeable repertoire for a closer. He throws a two-seam and four-seam fastball. His slow curve and changeup keep hitters off balance. Entering the 2017 campaign, he was averaging 10.6 strike-outs per 9 innings. His best season in that regard came in 2004, when he fanned 123 batters in 84 innings (an average of 13.2 per nine frames).

In 2008, Rodriguez saved his 200th game, becoming the youngest player in history to reach that milestone. On September 13, he registered his 58th save, breaking the single-season mark set by Bobby Thigpen in 1990. He finished the season with 62 saves—a record that was still standing at the time of this writing.

Traded to the Mets in 2009, Rodriguez had a mediocre year and then tore a thumb ligament during an altercation with a family member in August 2010. The Mets eventually dealt him to the Brewers. After a couple of mediocre seasons, he returned to form in 2014, placing third in the NL with 44 saves. He had another great year in 2015, posting a

2.21 ERA, with 38 more saves. A six-time All-Star, he was property of the Tigers in 2016. His 44 saves were second in the AL.

Now in his mid-30s, Rodriguez presumably has a few good seasons left. There are currently only three players ahead of him on the all-time saves list. Assuming he remains healthy, he is poised to surpass Lee Smith's total of 478. From there, he will be setting his sights on Trevor Hoffman's career mark of 601.

4

CUBA

ORIGINS OF BASEBALL IN CUBA

Baseball was introduced to Cuba in the 1860s by college students returning from the United States. A student named Nemesio Guillot, who attended Spring Hill College in Mobile, Alabama, is said to have brought the first bat and ball to the island. In 1868, Nemesio and his brother Ernesto formed the Havana Baseball Club. A winning tradition was born when the newly formed squad defeated the crew of a U.S. ship docked in Matanzas.

Before long, baseball became the preferred sport on the island—even more popular than bullfighting, which was a cultural obligation. During the first Cuban War of Independence, baseball was temporarily banned, but it made a comeback in the 1870s. The first official game took place in Pueblo Nuevo on December 27, 1874. It wasn't much of a contest, as Habana defeated Matanzas, 51–9.

In 1878, the Cuban League was founded. Originally composed of three teams, the circuit began to grow during the Spanish–American War. When the league was desegregated at the turn of the century, the quality of play improved significantly, as many Negro League stars began spending their winters in Cuba.

By the 1930s, Cuba had become a baseball-obsessed country, and amateur teams had sprung up throughout the island. In particular, sugar mill baseball (composed of players who worked in the sugar industry) became a primary source of talent. Most amateur fields were in poor shape, with sparse accommodations for spectators. Many aspiring players sought to bypass the amateur level and head straight for the professional leagues.

After dictator Fulgencio Batista was ousted from power during the Cuban Revolution, the new government, headed by Fidel Castro, outlawed professional baseball and dramatically restructured the sport. A new system of amateur leagues was introduced—the most prominent being the Serie Nacional de Beisbol. Known to Americans as the Cuban National Series, it was founded in 1961. Today, it still fields 16 teams, stocked with the island's best and brightest players. The 90-game schedule begins in November and ends in March, when an eight-team tournament to determine the league championship takes place. When the season is complete, the most talented players are appointed to the Cuban national team, which competes in various international tournaments. The Cuban team is among the most decorated in the world, having won 25 World Cups.

Most players are not allowed to leave the country because the Communist government prohibits them from signing with Major League Baseball teams. But the allure of money and freedom is a powerful motive for many players and their families. Players habitually desert their teams during tournaments in foreign countries. Some even hire smugglers to sneak them out of Cuba. In 2016, baseball consultant Joe Kehoski estimated that 95 percent of players leaving the country are smuggled out. "There is always a profit motive," said Kehoski. "I can't remember the last time a decent player was smuggled out of Cuba and there wasn't a smuggler there who expected payment."

Beginning with Esteban Bellan, a Cuban-born infielder who joined the Troy Haymakers in 1871, Cuba has exported a steady stream of stars to the United States. Regrettably, baseball's color barrier prevented some of the nation's top players (for example, Hall of Famers Cristobal Torriente, Martin Dihigo, and Jose Mendez) from participating in big-league competition. But since the late 1940s, the major-league talent pool has been far more diverse. The following players are among the best Cuba has produced.

MAJOR STARS OF THE PAST

Bert Campaneris

Shortstop

Born Dagoberto Blanco Campaneris, the man who would later be called "Road Runner" grew up in Pueblo Nuevo—a small village in the Matanzas region of Cuba. Campaneris's father held a job making lariats. "Campy" began his baseball career as a catcher but easily made the switch to other infield stations. A bit undersized at 5-foot-10, 160 pounds, he was signed by A's scout Felix Delgado for the lowly sum of $500 in 1961. His younger cousin, Jose Cardenal, had been signed by the Giants the previous year.

Campaneris spent portions of three seasons in the minors, playing well at each level. He had a breakout year with the Birmingham Barons in 1964, earning a promotion to the big leagues. His major-league career got off to a promising start when he homered on the first pitch he saw from Minnesota's staff ace, Jim Kaat. Campaneris added a homer later in the game to become the first player to go deep twice in a debut.

Located in Kansas City, the A's were a woeful team in those days. After losing 105 games in 1964, they got off to another dismal start the following year. With attendance slumping dramatically, A's owner Charlie Finley tried to draw fans to the park with a wild promotional scheme he called "Campy Campaneris Night." More than 21,000 fans turned out to see Campaneris play all nine positions in a game against the Angels. Although Campy's first and only career pitching assignment was mediocre at best (he gave up a run on a hit and two walks), he landed on a short list of major-league hurlers to work ambidextrously.

The rest of Campaneris's career was equally eventful. With blazing speed, he stole 30 or more bases in 10 straight seasons. He led the league six times, peaking at 62 steals in 1968. To date, he still ranks among the top 20 of all time. Campy was a skilled bunter, leading the league in sacrifices on three occasions. His lifetime total of 199 is high for the modern era. To date, only three players with careers lasting beyond the 1970s have surpassed Campaneris's mark. In fact, Campy, with his superior speed and ability to put the ball in play, likely would have prospered in the Deadball Era.

While 79 percent of Campaneris's lifetime hits were singles, he could hit for power when he put his mind to it. He demonstrated this in 1970, when he suddenly blasted 22 homers after finishing in single digits in the previous six seasons. He had 54 extra-base hits that year—a career high.

Campaneris never won a Gold Glove, but he had a strong arm and wide range. Although he led American League shortstops in errors on three occasions, he paced the circuit in putouts the same number of times. He currently ranks among the top 25 in that category.

Campaneris developed a reputation for being feisty. In the second game of the 1972 American League Championship Series, he had already collected three hits and scored a pair of runs when Detroit manager Billy Martin ordered a knockdown pitch. Hit in the leg by Lerrin LaGrow, Campaneris threw his bat at the mound. The benches cleared, and in the scrum that followed, Martin went after Campaneris. After the game, the Detroit skipper said hypocritically, "The man's got no guts. There shouldn't be any place in baseball for a man to throw a bat. The man's an idiot. If he had come out and taken a punch at my pitcher I could respect him—but a bat?" Campaneris was fined and suspended for the rest of the ALCS. He was allowed to play in the World Series against the Reds but was ordered to sit out the first seven games of the following season.

Campaneris's fondest moment came in game three of the 1973 ALCS, when his 11th-inning homer lifted the A's to a win. "That was my MVP moment," he said. "If we [lost] that game, we would have been eliminated the next day." Campy had three homers during that postseason, which ended with a World Series title for the A's.

After a third consecutive world championship in 1974, Finley began selling off his best players. Campaneris ended up with the Rangers in 1977, but he held no grudges. "I got along with Charlie better than some of the other guys," he said. "I was with him a long time, and he was nice to me. He did me favors when I needed them." With his skills in decline, Campaneris was dealt to the Angels during the 1979 slate. He finished his major-league career with the Yankees in 1983. He went out with a bang, hitting .322 in 60 games.

Finished as a player, Campaneris coached for the Seibu Lions in 1987 and 1988. The team won the Japan Series both years. Campy has kept busy in his retirement, participating in many Old-Timers' Games and charity golf tournaments as a member of the Major League Baseball Players Alumni Association.

Jose Canseco

Outfielder

Jose and his twin brother Ozzie were born in Havana. Their father had prospered as a territory manager for the Esso Oil Company but became destitute in the wake of the Cuban Revolution. When the Castro government offered to relocate those who opposed the regime to Miami in 1965, the Cansecos immigrated. An avid fan of baseball, Jose Sr. introduced his sons to the game during their formative years. Both would have major-league careers, although Jose would prove to be far more successful. As a boy, Jose wasn't especially gifted and had to work hard to develop his skills. He remembered his father telling him he would amount to nothing.

Determined to prove his dad wrong, Jose stuck with baseball throughout high school, finally making the varsity squad during his senior year. He ended up being named team MVP. After graduating in 1982, he was signed by the A's in a late round of the MLB Amateur Draft. He began his pro career at Idaho Falls. By the time he made his major-league debut in 1985, he had grown from a scrawny teenager into a muscular hulk. It would later become common knowledge that he had used steroids to complete the transformation.

During the next several seasons, Canseco emerged as one of the premier sluggers in the AL. During a productive six-year span, he and teammate Mark McGwire combined for at least 50 homers and 150 RBIs per year. The media began referring to the powerful duo as the "Bash Brothers." Canseco reached the peak of his offensive prowess in 1988, becoming the first player to gather 40 home runs and 40 stolen bases in a single season. He was a unanimous choice for MVP that year.

Unusual incidents followed Canseco throughout his career. He once joked to a reporter, "If anything freakish is going to happen, it'll happen to me." Never known as a proficient fielder, he once allowed a ball to bounce off his head and over the outfield wall for a home run. In 1993, he convinced Rangers manager Kevin Kennedy to let him pitch in a blowout loss to the Red Sox. The resulting injury kept him out of action for the remainder of the season.

Away from the diamond, Canseco's life played out like a bad soap opera. In 1989, he was arrested for reckless driving. In 1992, he was charged with aggravated battery after he ran his Porsche into his first wife's BMW. He would later be sentenced to a year of probation for assaulting his second wife. Because of his personal troubles and frequent injuries, he changed teams seven times between 1992 and 2001.

Through it all, Canseco kept hitting when he was healthy. Some of his homers were of the tape-measure variety. In the 1989 ALCS, he drove a ball into the third deck of the SkyDome—an estimated 480 feet. Billy Beane, who witnessed the shot from the A's bench, commented, "That wasn't just a home run. It was a home run of biblical proportions." A's pitcher Matt Young remarked, "Mark McGwire hit one off the facing of that deck the last time we were here, but this one took one look at Mark's spot, spit on it, and kept going."

During his 17-year career, Canseco averaged 27 long balls per season despite sitting out more than 700 games with various maladies. More than 40 percent of his lifetime hits went for extra bases. A six-time All-Star, Canseco's last productive season came in 1998, when he blasted a career-high 46 homers, while driving in 107 runs for the Blue Jays. His final major-league appearance was with the White Sox in 2001. He played independent ball through the 2015 slate.

Even after he left the majors, Canseco continued to generate controversy. In his 2005 autobiography *Juiced*, he openly admits to using steroids, while accusing several former teammates of doing the same. The book was poorly received by critics and peers, many of whom considered it slanderous. But three years later, Canseco got to say "I told you so" with the release of his second book, *Vindicated*. By then, most of his earlier claims had been substantiated.

The drama continued for Canseco in subsequent years. While serving as player-coach for the Yuma Scorpions of the North American League in 2011, he was fined and suspended for his role in a bench-clearing brawl. In 2012, he filed for bankruptcy, and in 2013, he was falsely accused of sexual assault. The following year, he accidentally shot himself while cleaning his gun, badly injuring one of his fingers.

Jose Cardenal

Outfielder

Jose Cardenal was born in Matanzas—known to some as the "Venice of Cuba," for its numerous waterways and artsy culture. His cousin Bert Campaneris also enjoyed a distinguished major-league career. Cardenal attended Jose Marti High School and was signed by the Giants as an amateur free agent. He was sent to El Paso of the Texas League in 1961, shortly before the infamous Bay of Pigs incident. "A few weeks later, I would never have gotten out," he reminisced years after the fact. "Most of my family is still in Cuba."

Cardenal made the most of the opportunity, spending 18 seasons with nine different clubs. He helped two of those teams to postseason appearances. Although he never led the league in any major offensive category, he finished among the top 10 in stolen bases eight times. Renowned baseball historian Bill James created a statistical category known as "power speed number," which quantifies the combination of homers and stolen bases. While the statistic didn't officially exist in Cardenal's time, he placed among the league leaders in seven campaigns.

Cardenal enjoyed his peak seasons between 1965 and 1976. A line-drive hitter with exceptional bat speed, his batting averages ranged from .317 to .236 during that stretch. In 1973, he was named Cubs MVP by Chicago baseball writers. He was highly successful as a pinch-hitter, reaching base 73 times in 215 trips to the plate, excluding fielder's choices. Most often occupying the first or second spot in the batting order, he compiled a creditable .300 average as a cleanup man.

Cardenal developed a reputation for being temperamental. In 1974, he was at odds with Chicago management and refused to play in the season opener, claiming that one of his eyelids was stuck open. In another peculiar snapshot from his career, he was accused of cheating by leaving extra baseballs in the ivy at Wrigley Field. Cardenal recalled the game in question, saying, "During batting practice, guys were hitting balls over my head into the fence, and I had to go digging around in the ivy to find [them]. After awhile I got sick of it. There were rats in there. They hit a few more into the vines, but I just let them stay there." During the game that followed, a ball was hit by an opponent into the same area of the outfield, and a pair of neglected batting-practice balls dropped out of the ivy. Instead of rooting around for the one in play, Cardenal held the batting practice balls aloft—one in each hand—for the umpire to see. The batter was forced to stop at second base, and Cardenal later admitted the hit could easily have been stretched into a triple.

Cardenal's playing career ended after the 1980 slate. He went on to coach for several teams, most notably the Yankees during their championship run of the late 1990s. Having participated in more than 2,500 professional games, he developed strong opinions about the sport. "Hitting is concentration, discipline, and practice," he told a journalist. "A player may get by on raw ability in school or the low minors, but he must work hard on learning to hit if he wants to make it big." Cardenal believed that players earn too much money upon reaching the majors and (in his words) "they stop learning."

During his nomadic playing career, Cardenal's longest tenure came with the Cubs from 1972 to 1977. He was modest about his talents, remarking, "I did all right with a glove but didn't hit like I should." He did just fine through the years, retiring with a solid .275 lifetime average. From 2005 to 2009, he served as senior advisor to the general manager of the Washington Nationals. He was let go when the upper management was restructured.

Leo Cardenas

Shortstop

Born in Matanzas, Leo Cardenas reportedly had 14 siblings. He came to the United States as a teenager and lied about his age to meet the minimum major-league requirements. He was among the last players to make it out of Cuba before the borders were sealed. While playing for Savannah of the South Atlantic League in 1957, Cardenas became irritable and depressed. Apparently, none of his letters home were being answered. It was soon discovered by teammate Curt Flood that Cardenas—who barely knew English and was somewhat unfamiliar with American customs—was dropping his letters into a trash can that resembled a U.S. Post Office box. Flood directed Cardenas to the proper depository, and the issue was resolved.

Cardenas worked his way up to the Triple-A level in 1959, joining the Havana Sugar Kings of the International League. During one unforgettable game that year, he and a teammate were accidentally shot by a group of rowdy Fidel Castro supporters, who started firing rifles inside the stadium to celebrate the fall of dictator Fulgencio Batista. Cardenas fully recovered, making his major-league debut with the Reds the following season.

When Cincinnati's regular shortstop, Eddie Kasko, went down with an injury in 1961, Cardenas filled in, impressing manager Fred Hutchinson. By 1962, Cardenas was a first-stringer. A writer from *Sporting News* remarks, "Not only has [Cardenas] proved himself to be one of the Reds' better clutch hitters, but he's giving the club its best short-stopping since Roy McMillan's fancy capers were leaving Crosley Field fans spellbound." Comparing Cardenas to the National League's premier shortstop, Maury Wills, coach Reggie Otero commented, "Cardenas is 10 years younger than Wills. The only edge Wills has over Leo is speed. And he has that over just about every other player in the league."

Cardenas picked up several nicknames during his career, among them "Spider," which was a reference to his spindly frame (5-foot-11, 160 pounds). He was also known as "Mr. Automatic" for his defensive skills. Cardenas was one of the finest fielding shortstops of the era. He led the league in putouts four times, fielding percentage on three occasions, and double plays twice. He was recognized for his excellence in 1965, receiving a Gold Glove Award.

Offensively, Cardenas was a free-swinger who drew relatively few walks (although he led the league in intentional walks twice). He had some power, peaking at 20 homers in 1966. He clubbed 30 or more doubles three times and finished in double digits for triples during the 1965 campaign. Cardenas was named to five All-Star Teams and received Most Valuable Player consideration during three seasons. He gathered his highest percentage of votes in 1969, when he hit .280, with 70 RBIs, helping the Twins reach the ALCS. During his 16 years in the majors, Cardenas appeared in three postseason matchups. In 1961, his Reds lost to the Yankees in the World Series. In 1969 and 1970, his Twins bowed to the Orioles in the ALCS

Cardenas played for five teams during his big-league tour, spending nine seasons in Cincinnati and three in Minnesota. Later in his career, he played for the Angels, Indians, and Rangers. He ranks among the top

50 in multiple defensive categories. He was elected to the Cuban Baseball Hall of Fame in 1979, and the Cincinnati Reds Hall of Fame two years later. As of this writing, he was still making regular appearances at various team functions.

Mike Cuellar

Pitcher

Some pitchers rely on speed, while others get by on finesse. Mike Cuellar definitely resided in the latter category. With a repertoire full of slow junk, one sportswriter quipped that Cuellar's "swiftest offering could be caught barehanded." But the crafty left-hander was among the most dominant hurlers in the majors during a six-year period. "Mike always thinks two pitches ahead," said batterymate Elrod Hendricks. "When they make an out on one of his setup pitches, he looks like they've spoiled his fun."

Cuellar was born in the Las Villas province of Cuba, which was then known for its sugar production. His entire family worked in the sugar mills. Looking to escape a life of perceived drudgery, Cuellar joined the army under dictator Fulgencio Batista. While playing military ball, he tossed a no-hitter and was courted by both Cuban and American scouts. He began his professional career with the Havana Sugar Kings of the International League, helping the team to a championship in 1959. Things were chaotic in Cuba that year with Batista having been ousted from power by Fidel Castro's forces. During the Junior World Series, which pitted Cuellar's Sugar Kings against the Minneapolis Millers, thousands of soldiers surrounded Havana's Gran Stadium, and shots could be heard outside the ballpark. Cuellar made several appearances as the Sugar Kings won the Series.

Cuellar's minor-league career included failed trials with the Reds and Cardinals. He finally caught on with the Astros in 1965. In portions of four seasons with Houston, he notched a 37–36 record—fairly impressive considering that Houston was out of contention each year. Traded to Baltimore in a five-player deal before the 1968 campaign, he entered the prime of his major-league career.

From 1969 to 1974, Cuellar won no fewer than 18 games each year, reaching the 20-win threshold four times (including a run of three consecutive seasons). He led the AL in winning percentage twice, as his ERA ranged from 2.38 to 3.48. Recognized for his efforts, he shared Cy Young honors with Denny McLain in 1969.

A four-time All-Star, Cuellar was a clutch postseason performer, winning two of four World Series decisions, while posting a 2.61 ERA. In the 1969 Series opener, he turned in a complete-game effort, breezing to a 4–1 win over Tom Seaver and the Mets. His 10-inning gem in game three of the 1973 ALCS resulted in a tough-luck loss. Cuellar struck out 11 Oakland opponents in that game.

Cuellar was extremely superstitious. According to teammate Paul Blair, he used the same number of steps to walk to the mound and the dugout each time he entered or exited the field. He refused to begin his warm-ups until someone had kicked the rosin bag to the back of the mound for him. He wore a "lucky" gold medallion and continued to take batting practice even after the designated-hitter rule went into effect so he could maintain his daily routine. His bizarre sense of humor and ongoing rituals earned him the nickname "Crazy Horse."

Cuellar began to falter in 1976, posting a 4–13 record, with a suspect 4.96 ERA. When the season was over, he blamed his troubles on the management. "[Earl] Weaver buried me," Cuellar groused. "I have him to thank for a lousy season. I don't think he wants me to win." Having watched the fading southpaw get chased from the mound in more than a dozen consecutive starts, Weaver retorted, "I've given him more chances than I gave my first wife."

Released by the O's in December 1976, Cuellar signed with the Angels. He struggled in two appearances and finished his career in the minors. By the time he threw his last pitch, he had won 248 professional games. In 1984, he was inducted into the Cuban Baseball Hall of Fame. In later years, Cuellar served as a pitching instructor for the Orioles, rarely missing a reunion or team function. In 2010, he was unexpectedly diagnosed with stomach cancer. He died that year in Orlando, Florida.

Jose Fernandez

Pitcher

Perhaps Marlins owner Jeffrey Loria said it best when he remarked, "Sadly, the brightest lights are often the ones that extinguish the quickest." Loria was referring to Marlins pitching sensation Jose Fernandez, who died tragically on September 25, 2016. The 24-year-old phenom, described by many as having an effervescent personality, was in the midst of his greatest season to date when a boating accident cut his life short.

Fernandez grew up in Santa Clara, Cuba. One of his neighbors was future Cardinals shortstop Aledmys Diaz. The two played on the same youth league team. In 2005, Fernandez's stepfather, Ramon Jiminez, defected from Cuba and settled in Tampa, Florida. Fernandez was apprehended and jailed three times before successfully following suit. He left the island for good in 2007, with his mother and sister. In yet another chilling escape tale, he was forced to dive into turbulent waters to save his mother, who had fallen overboard. The three arrived safely in Mexico and later settled in Tampa.

Fernandez attended Braulio Alonso High School and trained under Orlando Chinea, who had worked with some of Cuba's top pitchers before defecting to the United States. Fernandez quickly established himself as one of the best young players, helping his school's team to a pair of state championships, in 2009 and 2011. In his senior year, he threw two no-hitters.

Selected in the first round of the 2011 MLB Draft, Fernandez excelled in the Marlins minor-league system, attaining a *Baseball America* rating of number five. After compiling a 14–1 record, with a 1.75 ERA, on the farm in 2012, he won a roster spot with Miami the following year. His debut was spectacular, as he made the All-Star Team and captured Rookie of the Year honors. After seeing the young right-hander pitch, Tampa Bay Rays manager Joe Maddon tweeted, "Jose Fernandez might be the best young pitcher I've ever seen at that age. I believe he will go far." There were many who agreed with that assessment before misfortune struck.

In 2014, Fernandez was the youngest pitcher since Doc Gooden to make an Opening Day start. Shortly into the season, the precocious right-hander tore his ulnar collateral ligament and underwent Tommy John surgery. He didn't return to big-league action until July 2 of the following season. He was used sparingly, averaging just 5.2 innings per start. In limited duty, he compiled a stellar 6–1 record, with a 2.92 ERA. The year held even more promise for him, as he officially became a U.S. citizen.

In 2016, Fernandez returned to top form. Cutting down on the use of his fastball to preserve his arm, he began working on his secondary pitches, which included a sinker, changeup, and slurve. He made the All-Star Team and grew even stronger as the season progressed. On September 9, he struck out 14 Dodgers. Less than two weeks later, he collected 12 strikeouts in an eight-inning stint against the division-leading Washington Nationals.

On the night of September 25, Fernandez and two of his friends were killed in Government Cut, a channel that separates Miami Beach from Fisher Island. The 32-foot boat the men were traveling in was moving along at a high speed when it crashed into a jetty and capsized. None of the boat's occupants were wearing life jackets.

In his rookie season of 2013, Fernandez captured the hearts of many during a tearful reunion with his grandmother, who he once referred to as the "love of his life." Fernandez walked her out to the mound and asked if she wanted to throw a ball to home plate. "It's far," he told her, to which she replied allegorically, "It's not far." With his zest for life and irrepressible enthusiasm, Fernandez endeared himself to legions of Latino fans. *Los Angeles Times* writer Angel Rodriguez commented, "He was part of many Cubans' extended family. It felt like he was that successful, talented cousin that would show up at your Nochebuena gathering with great stories and a bigger smile."

At the time of his passing, Fernandez was carrying a 16–8 record, with a 2.86 ERA. His average of 12.48 strikeouts per nine innings was tops in the NL. Immediately following his death, the Marlins cancelled their game against the Braves and announced that Fernandez's uniform number (16) would be retired. A public memorial and funeral procession was held in Miami. Sadly, Fernandez's girlfriend, Maria Arias, was carrying their first child—a daughter they had named Penelope.

Tony Gonzalez

Outfielder

Had he remained healthy and played on a successful team, Tony Gonzalez might have become a household name in the United States. But the Cuban-born outfielder spent nine of his 12 major-league seasons with the underachieving Phillies. The club finished in fourth place or lower in every season but one during Gonzalez's tenure, averaging more than 80 losses per year and dooming Gonzalez to a career of virtual anonymity.

Gonzalez was born in Central Cunagua. His parents labored in a massive sugar mill complex. The mill had its own ballpark, and Tony was exposed to baseball at an early age. During sugarcane season, he would help his father carry heavy sacks of product, strengthening his arms considerably. To some, he was known as "Little Dynamite," in reference to the way the ball exploded off his bat. As a teenager, Gonzalez played for Central Espana—a sugar mill team affiliated with an amateur league in Matanzas. It was there that he was noticed by a Reds scout, who offered him $10 and a ticket to Havana. According to Gonzalez, the Reds reimbursed themselves out of his first paycheck.

After touring Cuba with a team composed of Class C and Class D players, he was invited to Cincinnati's training camp in 1957. He failed to make the club and would spend three seasons in the minors. By 1959, he had become the most productive member of the Havana Sugar Kings, leading the team in numerous offensive categories. He joined the Reds the following spring and, after a slow start, was traded to the Phillies in a five-player deal. By the time the season ended, he had raised his batting average by more than 60 points.

In 1962, Gonzalez played errorless ball. According to his Society for American Baseball Research biography, it was the first errorless season by an everyday center fielder in the majors. During the course of his big-league career, Gonzalez spent ample portions of time in each outfield station, fielding all three positions above the league average. He posted the highest defensive percentage among NL outfielders three times yet somehow never captured a Gold Glove.

Another honor that eluded Gonzalez was an All-Star berth. This had a lot to do with the era in which he played. In Gonzalez's time, the All-Star selections were dominated by such luminaries as Willie Mays, Hank Aaron, Roberto Clemente, and Frank Robinson. Philly skipper Gene Mauch was fond of using a platoon system and often sat Gonzalez against lefties. While it's true that Gonzalez was less successful against left-handed pitching, his inclusion in a platoon made his statistics seem a bit ordinary on the surface. Gonzalez tolerated Mauch's practice but was not overly fond of it. "It's hard to stay loose," he once said to a reporter. "When you face lefties once in a while, you press up there."

Gonzalez was hit by pitches fairly often—71 times in the majors and 24 in the minors. On at least one occasion, he was carried off the field on a stretcher. He suffered from back and eye problems likely related to the number of beanings he received. Still, his batting average ranged from .339 to .264 between 1960 and 1970. In 1967, he finished second in the batting race to Roberto Clemente, who trumped Gonzalez by 18 points.

After the 1968 season, prospect Larry Hisle was set to become the everyday center fielder in Philadelphia. Gonzalez was left unprotected in the Expansion Draft, and the Padres picked him up. He stayed with them until June, when he was traded to Atlanta for three players. He got along well with his new comrades, especially the Spanish-speaking Felipe Alou and Rico Carty. A reporter remarked that he was a positive clubhouse presence, stating, "Quick with a smile and quicker with a needle, Gonzalez is well liked by his teammates." Atlanta won the division that year and advanced to the NL playoffs. Gonzalez swung the bat well in all three games, gathering five hits, while scoring four runs. In the first game, he doubled and homered off of Mets ace Tom Seaver. It was Gonzalez's only taste of the postseason.

The following August, Gonzalez was traded to the Angels. He hit .304 down the stretch for them. After completing his last major-league season in 1971, he migrated to the Mexican, Japanese, and Eastern leagues. In his last professional season, as a player-coach for the Reading Phillies, he compiled a handsome .345 batting average. He stayed on as a coach through the 1976 slate. He later worked for the Angels' minor-league chain. In 1984, he was inducted into the Cuban Baseball Hall of Fame.

Livan Hernandez

Pitcher

Livan Hernandez was born in the Villa Clara province, located in the central region of the island, with the Atlantic Ocean to the north and the Escambray Mountains to the south. His family was poor, and Hernandez sought to improve his situation by playing baseball. He became a star member of the Cuban national team, carrying the club to Junior World Championships in 1992 and 1993. In the 1994 World Cup, he struck out 14 in 9.2 innings as Cuba went unbeaten. Being part of the national team didn't pay much, and in 1995 Hernandez fled the country via Mexico with the help of recruiter Joe Cubas. The Marlins were looking to sign some Latin players to make their club marketable to South Florida's large Hispanic community. Hernandez was acquired as an amateur free agent in January 1996. He described his first year in the United States as a "lonely struggle."

A big right-hander, at 6-foot-2, 245 pounds, Hernandez was known for his slow curveball, which he often used as a strikeout pitch. He ascended quickly through the minors and was called to Florida in September 1996. His only appearance that year was a three-inning relief stint against the Braves. He spent the first several months of the 1997 slate on the farm, earning another call-up in June. He became an overnight sensation, jumping out to a 9–0 start as the Marlins captured their first postseason berth. After a successful relief outing against the Giants in the National League Division Series, Hernandez shut down the Braves in two National League Championship Series appearances. He was named MVP of the series.

With just 18 major-league appearances to his credit, Hernandez was the least experienced pitcher ever to start Game One of the World Series. He lasted 5.2 innings against Cleveland, picking up the win. In Game Five, he yielded three runs in the bottom of the third but held the Indians scoreless for the next five innings. Florida gained a 3–2 Series edge with a sloppy 8–7 win that day. After some delicate negotiations between the United States and Cuba, the Castro government allowed Hernandez's mother to attend Game Seven. Hernandez had not seen her in more than two years. "This is the happiest moment of my life," he said after the Marlins clinched the Series. "My mother's here and we're champions." The 22-year-old hurler was the second rookie ever to win a World Series MVP Award.

Hernandez's career lasted through portions of three decades. He was considered an excellent defensive pitcher, going errorless during seven seasons, while leading his peers in assists twice. He was also highly durable, logging more than 200 innings in eight consecutive campaigns. Between 2003 and 2005, no NL hurler spent more time on the mound. He once threw 150 pitches in a single game. An often-overlooked fact, Hernandez was a fair hitter, batting .230 or higher seven times. He collected 50 extra-base hits (10 of them homers), with 85 RBIs, throughout his big-league tenure.

Hernandez's defection to the United States was not the only drama he managed to create. After posting a 45–45 record in portions of four seasons with the Giants, he got into a violent altercation in a parking lot with an elderly man. He is said to have swung a golf club during the incident. Displeased with the negative publicity, the Giants traded him to the Expos.

Between 2005 and 2012, Hernandez wore seven different uniforms. By the age of 37, he was having difficulty getting batters out. He threw his last major-league pitch in 2012, retiring with 178 lifetime victories. Having spent seven seasons with the Washington Nationals, he participated in the club's winter Fan Fest in 2014. He also served as a pitching instructor that year. His half-brother Orlando was also a pitcher of note.

Orlando Hernandez

Pitcher

Orlando Hernandez was a major star in his homeland, earning the nickname "El Duque" for his status as Cuban baseball royalty. A two-time National Series champion, he went 4–0 in the Pan American Games and Intercontinental Cup in 1995. Against the Dutch national team, he struck out 13 batters in seven innings.

When Hernandez's half-brother Livan (who was 10 years younger) defected from Cuba in 1995, Hernandez was suspended from play. The following year, he allegedly accepted a cash gift from a scout with ties to Major League Baseball. He was subsequently "banned for life," taking a job as a manual laborer in a mental hospital. In December 1997, he defected from Cuba. His agent, Joe Cubas, released an embellished tale involving a leaky raft and stormy weather, but in reality Orlando had escaped in a large fishing vessel with a fully functional outboard motor. The enterprising right-hander was detained in the Bahamas while Cubas arranged for him to meet with New York Yankees officials. He was signed to a four-year contract.

Hernandez entered the Yankees rotation in June 1998. He was an instant success, winning his first two starts, while allowing just two earned runs in 16 innings. He finished the season at 12–4, with a 3.13

ERA—the lowest of his major-league career. He won two more games in the postseason as the Yankees captured their second World Series title in a three-year span.

Hernandez would prove to be one of the most successful October performers in Yankees history—a bold statement considering the overwhelming success of the franchise. From 1998 to 2001, El Duque posted a 2.48 ERA in 14 postseason appearances. He wasn't even charged with a loss until the Mets tagged him for four runs in Game Three of the 2000 World Series. The Yankees won 86 percent of the postseason games he appeared in during that span. Later in his career, Hernandez returned to the October stage with the White Sox, getting charged with no runs in two appearances.

On the mound, Hernandez was a painfully slow worker who always seemed to be fiddling with his cap and uniform. He would often shake off signs from his catcher before calling for a mound conference. This led to a few arguments with frequent batterymate Jorge Posada. Hernandez was renowned for his high leg kick and assortment of slow curves. He was an excellent fielder who was known to improvise. Against the Mets one afternoon, he had trouble getting the ball out of his glove on a slow roller back to the mound, so he threw his mitt with the ball still in it to first base.

Because he didn't reach the majors until the age of 32, El Duque's big-league career was rather brief. He was beset by injuries throughout and never appeared in more than 29 games after the 2000 campaign. In 2004, he didn't join the Yankees until July, spending time rehabbing in Tampa and Columbus. Although he posted an 8–2 record, with an economical 3.30 ERA in the Bronx that year, the Yankees were looking for someone more durable and granted him free agency. He pitched for three different clubs before ending his career in the Washington Nationals minor-league system in 2010. His cumulative record in the Cuban and U.S. leagues is 216–112. That winning percentage would have placed him among the top 20 of all time had he spent the entirety of his career in the majors. Since his retirement, he has appeared in multiple Yankees Old-Timers' Games.

Dolf Luque

Pitcher

Dolf Luque was not an intimidating physical presence at 5-foot-7, 160 pounds, but as the old saying goes, he had the heart of a lion. In portions of 20 major-league seasons, the spirited right-hander won 194 games and helped two different clubs reach the World Series. In 1923, he assembled one of the greatest seasons ever by a pitcher, going 27–8 for the Reds, with a 1.93 ERA. He finished second in strikeouts to Dazzy Vance that year, narrowly missing a Triple Crown. During his long playing career, which spanned three decades, he posted double-digit win totals in 11 seasons and finished among the top 10 in saves on six occasions. He was also a three-time shutout leader.

Luque was the only Cuban player to attain a level of big-league fame during the first half of the twentieth century. Baseball's color barrier prevented such Caribbean-born legends as Martin Dihigo, Cristobal Torriente, and Jose Mendez from playing in the majors. Luque, who was lighter-skinned, slipped though the barrier with the Braves in 1914, after posting a 22–5 record for the Long Branch Cubans of the New York–New Jersey League the previous year. He spent portions of the next four seasons on the farm before arriving in the majors to stay in July 1918.

Luque was 10–3 for the pennant-winning Reds in 1919. Although his statistics can only be regarded skeptically given that the World Series was fixed that year, Luque made two relief appearances and yielded just one hit in five innings of work. He returned to the Fall Classic with the Giants in 1933, getting a relief win in Game Five. His postseason portfolio included 9.1 scoreless frames and 11 strikeouts.

Luque's explosive temper became legendary. Exposed to racism continuously, he was sensitive about his origins. According to popular legend, he once stormed into the Giants dugout in the middle of a game and punched Casey Stengel (then a player) in the mouth, believing that Casey had made some racially charged remarks. On another occasion, he threw a ball into the Pittsburgh dugout in retaliation for some ethnic slurs made by players on the bench. A run scored during the incident, and a subsequent protest lodged by Cincinnati management resulted in the game being replayed from the point where it had been interrupted.

Luque's best seasons were unquestionably with the Reds. Between 1919 and 1927, his ERA never rose above 3.43—a remarkable accomplishment in the so-called Lively Ball Era. In 1922, when he paced the NL with 23 losses, he was supported by two runs or less in 17 of his starts. His ERA of 3.31 was sixth best in the league that year. Traded to Brooklyn before the 1930 slate, Luque went 21–14 in a two-year span. He turned 40 in 1931, and defied his age by becoming an effective reliever for three full seasons with the Giants. From 1932 to 1934, he entered 99 games—63 as a closer. He gathered 18 wins and 16 saves, while compiling a cumulative ERA in the mid-3s. He was 44 years old when he appeared in his last major-league game.

When his playing days were over, Luque managed and coached for numerous teams at various levels. His temper had not mellowed any, and stories of his epic run-ins with players abounded. In 1953 and 1954, his Tecolotes de Nuevo Laredo team won the Mexican League championship. A number of his players, including Sal Maglie, Bobby Avila, and Camilo Pascual, had distinguished major-league careers. Luque was inducted into the Cuban Baseball Hall of Fame in 1958.

Minnie Minoso

Outfielder

Born in Perico, Minnie Minoso grew up in the Matanzas province and left school at the age of 14 to work in the sugar fields. His semipro career began with a candy company team in Havana. Moving slowly up the ladder, he joined the Cuban Winter League in 1945, capturing Rookie of the Year honors.

In 1946, Minoso signed with Alex Pompez's New York Cubans for a reported salary of $150 a month. He spent several seasons in the Negro Leagues, playing third base and earning abundant praise from peers. "He was a great ballplayer," said pitcher Dave Barnhill. "When the ball was hit to him, the pitcher had to lie down on the ground because Minoso threw the ball all the way to first base about four feet off the ground."

Harlem Globetrotters owner Abe Saperstein noticed Minoso while serving as a part-time scout for the Indians. Cleveland purchased Minoso's contract and sent him to Dayton of the Central League. By the time

Minoso landed a permanent job in the majors, he was 25 years old. In April 1951, he was included in a three-team trade that landed him in Chicago with the White Sox. According to multiple sources, he had difficulty communicating. But Minoso didn't need a firm grasp of English to lead the league in triples and stolen bases during his rookie season. He made the first of seven All-Star appearances that year and finished fourth in MVP voting. He missed out on Rookie of the Year honors by a couple of votes.

For more than a decade, Minoso was among the most exciting players in the majors. White Sox owner Bill Veeck once remarked, "I don't believe there is a player in the game today who can give you the thrill he can. Without him in the lineup, it's just another game." Minoso was a five-tool player. From 1951 to 1961, his batting average ranged from .326 to .280. In that same span, he gathered no fewer than 43 extra-base hits per year. He led the league in triples and stolen bases three times apiece, while maintaining a minimum on-base percentage of .369. Minoso was not afraid to take one for the team, getting hit by more pitches than his AL peers on 10 occasions. In May 1955, he sustained a hairline skull fracture after being plunked by Yankees hurler Bob Grim. Remarkably, he returned to action in less than three weeks. Minoso loved telling the story about how he was hit by a pitch and homered in the same at-bat. It happened while he was playing in the minors. Denied first base when the umpire determined he had made no attempt to avoid the pitch, he dug in and drove a later offering into the seats.

Defensively, Minoso was among the best in the game, capturing three Gold Gloves in a four-year span. He had exceptional range and a strong arm, finishing with double-digit assist totals in nine seasons. His career mark in that category places him among the top 20 left fielders of all time.

According to multiple sources, Minoso was the superstitious type. In an amusing (and possibly apocryphal) anecdote, he allegedly showered in full uniform one day in an effort to break out of a batting slump. When he followed with a multihit game the next day, several of his teammates were observed doing the same.

Before the 1958 campaign, Minoso was traded to the Indians for Hall of Fame pitcher Early Wynn and outfielder Al Smith. Minoso was distraught. "I felt like the whole world was over for me," he said. "I felt like my city had put me out." Minoso hit .302, with 92 RBIs, for the Indians in 1959, while the White Sox captured their first pennant in several decades. Bill Veeck, who always had a soft spot for the charismatic outfielder, gave him a championship ring anyway and reacquired his contract. Minoso enjoyed his last two productive seasons in Chicago. His numbers dropped off sharply in 1962, and he was out of the majors by the end of the 1964 campaign.

Minoso continued in the Mexican Leagues into his late 40s. Veeck hired him as a coach in 1976, convincing him to appear in a game. He went 0-for-4 as a DH and singled as a pinch-hitter the following day. At 50 years old, he was among the oldest players to hit safely in the majors. In 1980, he rejoined the club for two plate appearances, becoming the second man to play in five different decades (Nick Altrock preceded him). Minoso's quest for the record books continued at the age of 68, when he suited up with the St. Paul Saints—an independent club. Although he grounded out in his only at-bat, he became the first six-decade player. Determined to push the envelope, he pinch hit for the Saints 10 years later, drawing a walk. He is the only seven-decade professional player in history.

While he received quite a bit of support throughout the years, Minoso remains outside the Hall of Fame at the time of this writing. "If it's meant to be, it's meant to be," he once said. "I've given my life to baseball, and the game has given me so much. That's all that matters." If Minoso does gain entry into Cooperstown, it will be posthumously. He died in 2015, at the age of 89.

Tony Oliva

Outfielder

Tony Oliva was born in the Pinar del Rio province, the island's western-most territory. It is a mountainous region with limestone hills and flat, fertile valleys. Oliva's father harvested tobacco and was said to be exceptionally skilled at rolling cigars. Tony played ball with his dad, brothers, and neighbors in a lot near the family's farm on weekends. He became one of the best hitters in the region and was eventually noticed by a Twins scout. Although Tony was hesitant to leave his parents and siblings behind, his father convinced him it was in his best interest.

Forged documents were presented upon his arrival in the United States, possibly to make him appear younger or perhaps to grant him access in the first place—Oliva and his wife both told different versions of the story. Whatever the case, he failed to make the cut during spring training due to shaky defense and was sent to Wytheville of the Appalachian League.

Oliva's defensive shortcomings wouldn't keep him down for long. He hit .370 during his first two minor-league seasons, earning a September call-up in 1962. The Twins weren't ready to promote him yet, so he spent another season on the farm. In his second September summons, he went 3-for-7 at the plate, giving him a cumulative .438 batting average in 16 major-league games. He became Minnesota's everyday right fielder in 1964.

Oliva was not a top prospect upon entering his first full season. A writer from *Baseball Digest* referred to him as a "fair hitter" who could "make a good utility outfielder." He proved that assessment wrong with a spectacular rookie campaign, leading the league in runs scored, hits, and doubles, while capturing a batting crown. His 374 total bases were a rookie record. He received 19 of 20 first-place votes for Rookie of the Year.

A scribe from the *Christian Science Monitor* waxed poetic about Oliva's offensive skills, writing, "Watching Oliva hit a baseball is like hearing Caruso sing." But in reality, Oliva didn't have much patience at the plate. His highest walk total in any given season was 55. By the same token, he seldom struck out, averaging one per every 10 at-bats. His philosophy on hitting was simple. "You pick out the pitches that appeal to you. It's the same as getting married. You pick out a girl that appeals to you."

Fans in Minnesota found him tremendously appealing in 1965, when he won his second consecutive batting crown, helping the franchise to its first postseason berth since leaving Washington. Facing the Dodgers in the World Series, Oliva's bat cooled off. His only big hit came in Game Four, when he clubbed a sixth-inning solo homer off of Don Drysdale. He ended up with a .192 average, just three points below the cumulative team mark. The Dodgers won the Series in seven games.

Upon his arrival in the majors, Oliva had a glaring weakness, which was noticed by Twins trainer "Doc" Lentz. "From the knee down, his right leg was bent at a 45-degree angle," Lentz recalled. "I remember thinking, 'Even if he makes it to the majors, he'll only last as long as those knees hold out.'" While they lasted well into the 1970s, Oliva's knees required constant attention. He endured a slew of surgeries, missing significant playing time. In spite of his ailments, he was among the best hitters in the majors for more than a decade. Between 1966 and 1971, he led the league in hits and doubles three times. He was named to the All-Star Team every year in that span and received serious MVP consideration twice. He was runner-up in 1970. His third and final batting crown came the following year, when he posted a .337 mark during an injury-plagued season in which he sat out 36 games. His efforts propelled the Twins to playoff berths in 1969 and 1970. Both were losing causes.

Although Oliva's defense was rough when he first arrived in the majors, he eventually mastered his craft. He had wide range at his position, leading AL right fielders in putouts six times. He finished among the top five in fielding percentage during seven campaigns and paced the circuit twice in assists. He captured a Gold Glove in 1966.

Oliva's numbers dropped off rapidly after the 1971 campaign. Rod Carew, who roomed with Oliva while the team was on the road, remembered the aging right fielder being in constant pain. Carew often wondered how Oliva could continue playing with his knee in that condition. After the 1976 campaign, Oliva finally decided to call it quits. After his retirement as a player, he worked as a Twins coach. He is the only on-field member of the club to serve in three World Series (1965, 1987, and 1991). In 2014, the Golden Era Committee narrowly overlooked him for the Hall of Fame. He missed induction by a single vote.

Rafael Palmeiro

First Baseman

Of all the players currently outside the Hall of Fame, Rafael Palmeiro has some of the most impressive numbers—more than 3,000 hits, 500 homers, and 1,800 RBIs. But in 2014, he was eliminated from the ballot after receiving less than 5 percent of the vote (the minimum requirement). Baseball writers were responding to the regrettable events of 2005, when Palmeiro appeared before a congressional panel and unequivocally denied using steroids. He later tested positive and was suspended for 10 days. Palmeiro contended that he unknowingly ingested the banned substance in a tainted vitamin B-12 injection and even passed a polygraph test. But there were those who presumed him to be less than innocent. Palmeiro was one of several players implicated in Jose Canseco's controversial autobiography *Juiced*. He was also named in the infamous Mitchell Report. Shortly after Mitchell's findings were made public, pitcher Jason Grimsley—in a sworn affidavit—fingered Palmeiro as an amphetamine user. At present, Palmeiro stands little chance at being enshrined in baseball's hallowed Hall.

Long before the controversy, Palmeiro was one of baseball's most consistent players. Born in Havana, he later graduated from Jackson High School in Miami. He moved on to Mississippi State University. In 1985, he was the Cubs' first-round draft pick. While playing in the Eastern League in 1986, he hit .306, earning a brief call-up from the Cubs. He began the 1987 season with Iowa of the American Association but was again summoned to Chicago to play backup to Jerry Mumphrey in left field and Leon Durham at first base. Palmeiro would spend the entire 1988 campaign as a full-time outfielder before making a permanent switch to first base the following year.

Palmeiro won three Gold Gloves during his career, although the third was controversial. He was an excellent choice in 1997 and 1998, but won the award the following year with Texas despite playing only 28 games at first base (he served mainly as a DH). Numerous sources sounded off about the apparent oversight, including an Associated Press writer, who remarked, "Seems like some managers and coaches weren't paying much attention this year." Evan Grant of the *Dallas Morning News* quipped, "The offseason is becoming an embarrassment of riches for Rangers players. Tuesday, the emphasis was on embarrassment." Palmeiro himself was surprised by the honor. "When I heard about it, I laughed," he said. "I guess people are respecting me for what I've done in the past." It's true that Palmeiro's defensive play is worthy of respect. He currently ranks among the top ten of all time in assists and double plays. His .994 lifetime fielding percentage is also one of the top marks.

Palmeiro's batting feats were even more remarkable. While he generated little power early in his career, he collected more than 30 homers each year from 1995 to 2003. He reached the century mark in RBIs in each of those seasons. A four-time All-Star, he received serious MVP consideration three times—especially in 1999, when he put up career-high numbers in multiple categories, including homers (47) and RBIs (148).

Palmeiro never played in another major-league game after the ill-fated 2005 slate. He is one of only four players with 500 homers and 3,000 hits. After learning that he had been dropped from the Hall of Fame ballot, he told a CBS reporter that he was disappointed. "I was hoping to stay on it as long as I could, maybe gain some momentum. But it went the other way." Palmeiro will be eligible again via the Veterans Committee in 2026. Refreshingly, he made no further excuses for the 2005 incident. "I take full responsibility, accountability for my mistake. It cost me tremendously in my life," he said. "Some lessons are harder than others, and this one I'll pay for the rest of my life."

Palmeiro spent 10 years with the Rangers, 7 years with the Orioles, and 3 years with the Cubs. He has the dubious distinction of playing in the most major-league games without appearing in a World Series. After his retirement, he gained some notoriety for appearing in Viagra commercials.

Camilo Pascual

Pitcher

Born in Havana, Camilo Pascual originally wanted to be a shortstop. Signed by the Senators in 1951, scout Joe Cambria convinced him that pitching would be his ticket to the majors. Pascual's older brother Carlos played briefly for Washington, earning the nickname "Potato," which was a bastardized form of the Spanish word *patato*—meaning "short" (Carlos was listed at 5-foot-6). While he was five inches taller than his brother, Camilo ended up carrying the nickname "Little Potato."

Camilo left Cuba at the age of 17 and joined Oklahoma's Sooner State League. He played for three Class C teams in 1951, two of which were composed almost entirely of Cambria's Cuban prospects. Pascual was the most successful of the bunch, although he struggled early in his career. After puttering in the minors for three seasons, he was called to Washington. Manager Bucky Harris used him exclusively in relief at first, but when he logged three consecutive scoreless appearances, he was inserted into the starting rotation. Two rocky outings later, he was back in the bullpen.

The Senators were a poor team in those days, finishing at the bottom of the pack each year. Pascual was equally ragged, posting a 5.98 ERA in 1955–1956, while averaging close to five walks per nine innings. The Senators hung onto him because of his moderately high strikeout totals. Pascual had an excellent fastball and changeup. He also threw one of the sharpest-breaking overhand curves in the majors, later drawing comparisons to Sandy Koufax. His first successful campaign came in 1958, when he led the league in strikeouts per nine innings. Only Billy O'Dell of the Orioles posted a better strikeout-to-walk ratio that year.

During the offseason, Pascual played in Cuba with Cienfuegos. His six wins in the Caribbean Series are the most in history (tied with Jose Bracho and Ruben Gomez). Worried that year-round pitching would put undue stress on his arm, Senators owner Calvin Griffith offered Pascual a bonus if he quit playing winter ball. Pascual agreed.

During the next several seasons, the slender right-hander entered the prime of his career, winning no fewer than 15 games on five occasions. From 1959 to 1965, Pascual's ERA never exceeded 3.46. He was busy during that span, leading the league in complete games on three occasions and finishing second twice. He also outpaced his AL peers in strikeouts and shutouts three times. His best effort came in 1963, when he posted a 21–9 record, with a 2.46 ERA. In a puzzling turn of events, he was overlooked for the All-Star Team that year. He made the cut in five other campaigns.

When the Senators moved north to Minnesota, Pascual went with them. Fittingly, he started in the Twins' inaugural game at Metropolitan Stadium. Although Pascual wore a perpetual scowl on the mound, he was known for his pleasant temperament and dry sense of humor. Having more or less mastered English by the late 1950s, he told his roommate, catcher Hal Naragon, that he was experiencing difficulty with telephone conversations. Naragon grew tired of always having to answer the phone in their hotel room and demanded that Pascual share responsibilities. One morning, after the two had stayed up late into the night discussing game strategy, the phone awoke them. Pascual answered in Spanish. When the person on the other end of the line asked if he knew English, Pascual answered quite intelligibly, "Not at eight o'clock in the morning I don't." Then he hung up.

During Minnesota's pennant run in 1965, Pascual sustained a back injury and was out for the entire month of August. When he returned, Twins manager Sam Mele was forced to use him sparingly. He won nine of 12 regular-season decisions, with an economical 3.35 ERA, but fared rather poorly in his only World Series start against the Dodgers. The Twins had chased Drysdale and Koufax from the mound in the first two games and held a 2–0 Series advantage. Their offense sputtered in Game Three, as Pascual failed to make it past the fifth inning. It was his only appearance of the Series, which ended in a seven-game loss for the Twins.

Pascual's injury continued to plague him the following year, and he was traded to the "new" Senators. He experienced a brief career revival, winning 25 games, while posting a 2.95 ERA in a two-year span. Off to a poor start in 1969, he was traded to Cincinnati. He later played for the Dodgers and Indians before retiring in 1971. He accumulated 174 major-league victories.

After his playing days were over, Pascual worked as a coach for the Twins under manager Gene Mauch. In 1989, he became an international scout. He has worked for the A's, Mets, and Dodgers. His most notable signing was Jose Canseco. The moundsman has received numerous honors throughout the years. He is a member of four Halls of Fame (the Cuban, Caribbean, Latino, and Twins Halls).

Tony Perez

First Baseman

Tony Perez grew up in the Camaguey region, central Cuba's rural countryside. He worked in a sugar mill for a while and reportedly despised the job. While still a teenager, he got noticed by scout Tony Pacheco, who signed him for the cost of a plane ticket and a visa. He spent four years in the minors, reaching the century mark in RBIs twice before earning a permanent roster spot in Cincinnati. He became a full-time player in 1965.

Perez was tall, powerful, and quick, and always had a smile on his face. His value to the club went far beyond his contributions on the field. Johnny Bench remarked, "Tony cast a net over the entire team with his attitude. He was always up, always had a sense of humor." Pete

Rose echoed that sentiment, describing Perez as a "fatherly type in the clubhouse, especially to the Spanish ballplayers. They looked up to him, as well as relating to him through his background and language." Statistics show that Perez was good with a bat as well. In his book *Game Six*, author Mark Frost writes, "[I]n even the most pressurized situations, [Perez] possessed an almost unearthly calm." Second baseman Joe Morgan considered Perez to be the most important member of the club. "Nobody was better with men on base than 'Doggie' (as he was known to teammates). Some of us may have gotten more attention, but he was the guy that made the 'Big Red Machine' go."

The "Machine" was a dominant force during the 1970s, capturing 6 division titles, 4 pennants, and 2 World Series. Perez's RBI totals during that decade were second only to teammate Johnny Bench. His most productive season at the plate occurred in 1970, when he put up a career-best .317 batting average, with 40 homers. He finished third in MVP voting that year behind Bench and Billy Williams. Perez landed among the top 10 in MVP voting during three other seasons.

Primarily a first baseman, Perez split time at that position with several other players early in his career. He was shifted to third base in 1967, when Deron Johnson suffered an injury. He remained at the hot corner until Lee May was traded to the Astros before the 1972 slate. Although he never won a Gold Glove at either station, Perez led the league in multiple defensive categories at each corner.

Perez's success in the postseason was mixed. In the 1975 World Series, he got off to an 0-for-15 start. But his bat came alive in Game Five, as he slammed a pair of homers and drove in four runs. He added another clout in Game Seven. During 11 postseason series, he reached base by hit or walk 56 times.

When Perez's regular-season numbers dropped off a bit in 1976, he was traded to Montreal for pitchers Woodie Fryman and Dale Murray. It was a lopsided transaction, as Fryman went 5–5, with a clumsy 5.38 ERA. Murray wasn't much better, posting a 4.94 ERA. Meanwhile, Perez remained consistent, driving in 91 runs. Reds manager Sparky Anderson commented years later, "We would have won at least two more championships with Perez."

In 1980, the clutch-hitting first baseman had his best season outside of Cincinnati, collecting 105 ribbies and gathering 59 extra-base hits for Boston. He went into decline after that. Reunited with the Reds in

1984, he continued with the club until he was 44 years old. He retired after the 1986 slate. In October of that year, he launched his last career homer (number 379), tying him with Orlando Cepeda for the most by a Latin player. That record has since been broken.

Perez served as a Reds coach until 1993, when he was briefly installed as manager. He had a second managerial stint with the Marlins in 2001, replacing John Boles with 114 games to go in the season. The Marlins finished fourth that year. Perez was elected to Cooperstown in 2000. A life-sized sculpture of him resides outside of Great American Ballpark in Cincinnati.

Cookie Rojas

Second Baseman

Cookie Rojas was born to a moderately well-to-do family in Havana. His mother gave him the nickname "Cuqui," which means "charming" or "adorable." It was later anglicized to "Cookie." Ignoring his father's wishes (his dad was a doctor), Rojas pursued a professional baseball career. Bespectacled and slight in stature at 5-foot-10, 160 pounds, the odds were against him. But with hard work and determination, he ended up being signed by the Reds in 1956. Three years later, he helped the Havana Sugar Kings to an International League championship alongside fellow countryman Leo Cardenas.

With Johnny Temple and later Don Blasingame playing competently at second base, Rojas was prevented from being an everyday player in Cincinnati for many years. He caught a break before the 1962 slate, when the Reds traded him to the Phillies for pitcher Jim Owens. By 1964, he was appearing regularly in the Philly lineup.

Strictly a singles hitter, Rojas spent a significant portion of his career in the second spot of the batting order. He accrued a .263 lifetime average but hit 15 points higher with runners on base. With the bases loaded, he was even better, compiling a .314 average, with three grand slams. While he averaged just 21 extra-base hits per year during his 16 seasons, he could be a real pest on the basepaths, gathering a career-high 18 steals in 1973.

Rojas's primary value to the clubs he played for was his versatility and defensive excellence. By the time he entered his fifth major-league season, he had already played every position on the diamond except pitcher. He filled that void in 1967, when he took the mound in the ninth inning of a lopsided loss to the Giants. He completed the assignment without allowing a run and even retired Willie Mays on a fly ball to right field.

Rojas was a member of five All-Star Teams at his primary defensive station. He kept the bases clear with his diving stops and pinpoint throws to first. After he became a seasoned veteran, he inspired younger teammates with his enthusiasm. "No matter how down you are or tired you are, you gotta go out and play to win," he once said. "That's the tag you want to get—the tag of a winner."

Rojas didn't officially carry that tag until he was traded to the Royals midway through the 1970 campaign. In his first full season with Kansas City, he hit at an even .300 clip, while driving in 59 runs. The Royals were a young team with plenty of budding talent. After the addition of George Brett in 1973, things really turned around. By the time Kansas City captured the first division title in franchise history during the 1976 slate, Rojas was 37 years old and serving in a utility role. He filled that role admirably, hitting .242 during the regular season and .333 in the playoffs. He made one more postseason appearance in game five of the 1977 ALCS—a 1-for-4 performance against the Yankees.

Immensely popular with fans in Philadelphia and Kansas City, Rojas later reflected on his career, stating, "I came in with a reputation of not being able to hit, and I developed a reputation as a winning player who would do anything and play anywhere to help win." Rojas showed as much versatility after his playing career was over. He coached for the Cubs from 1978 to 1981, and then worked in the front office for the California Angels, also serving as a scout. When Gene Mauch stepped aside in 1988, for health reasons, Rojas took over as Angels manager, guiding a mediocre squad to a 75–79 record. He returned to the helm briefly with the Marlins in 1996. He later held coaching positions with the Mets and Blue Jays. He has served as a Spanish-language broadcaster for the Marlins since 2003. He is also a member of the Baseball Assistance Team, which strives to help former players, umpires, and team personnel who have fallen on hard times. Rojas was inducted into the Hispanic Heritage Baseball Museum Hall of Fame in 2011.

Tony Taylor

Second Baseman

Between 1902 and 1933, about 115,000 Jamaicans immigrated to Cuba, largely to work in the sugar industry. Tony Taylor's father was of Jamaican descent. Taylor spent his formative years in Central Alava, located in the province of Matanzas. In those days, the term *Central* referred to a socioeconomic system involving a network of affiliated sugar plantations geographically linked to one another by rail or sea. Taylor described Central Alava as a "quiet place" where there was nothing much to do aside from attending school and playing ball.

Taylor's parents were opposed to him pursuing a baseball career, but upon graduating from high school, he joined an amateur league in Matanzas. He was signed by the Giants and later drafted by the Cubs. Added to the Chicago roster in 1958, he would remain at the major-league level for 19 seasons. The first year was a rough one for Taylor due to the language barrier, but Cubs legend Ernie Banks reached out to him. "When I first joined the Cubs, I was so lonesome that Ernie tried to talk Spanish to me," Taylor reminisced years later. "Good guy, Banks—bad Spanish, but good guy."

In 1959, Taylor hit at a respectable .280 clip. The Cubs used him as trade bait the following season, and he ended up in Philadelphia. The personable infielder became immensely popular with fans there, prompting three different "Tony Taylor Days" to be held in his honor—the last one taking place at Veterans Stadium in 1975. "There is a big love affair between the fans and Tony Taylor—a great honor, indeed, for me," he remarked jovially in 1976. One writer observed that Taylor had a "special way with people. It doesn't matter who they are, other ballplayers, fans, or the press—he's to the Phillies what Ernie Banks was to the Cubs."

Taylor was a solid, if not outstanding, all-around player. He had good range at second base and made an excellent double-play partner. He currently ranks among the top 100 in putouts, assists, and double plays. He never had an outright poor season at the plate, although he did record a career-low .229 average in 1965, when he missed some time due to an injury. He collected more than 2,000 hits, retiring with a respectable .261 batting mark. He usually occupied the leadoff spot in the lineup, primarily because of his speed. He put up double-digit stolen-base totals 10 times and finished among the league leaders in that category during nine seasons.

Before each plate appearance, Taylor would make the sign of the cross. In spite of his strong faith, his teams never reached the World Series. A dubious claim to fame, he came out on the losing end of six no-hitters. To date, Johnny Callison and Bert Campaneris are the only other players to be victimized that many times.

When his playing days were over, Taylor served as a minor-league manager for several teams. He also coached for the Phillies and Marlins. He was inducted into the Cuban Baseball Hall of Fame in 1981, and added to the Phillies Wall of Fame in 2002. A baseball academy founded by his brother Jorge in 1972 still bears his name.

Luis Tiant

Pitcher

Baseball was in Luis Tiant's blood. His father was a renowned pitching star in the Cuban and Negro leagues for two decades. Having been denied a path to the majors, Luis Sr. didn't feel that there was any place for a black man in baseball. His wife Isabel felt differently and convinced the elder Tiant to stop discouraging their son. Young Luis came of age in Marianao, which is located in a range of high hills approximately six miles southwest of Havana.

After failing a tryout with the Havana Sugar Kings, Luis ended up with the Mexico City Tigers. He won 17 games at the age of 19, capturing the attention of the Cleveland Indians. Tiant toiled in four different minor leagues between 1962 and 1964. He found the experience incredibly difficult. "I couldn't speak English, but I understood racism," he said. "They treated me like a dog. I used to go back to my hotel room and cry." After posting a 15–1 record, with a 2.04 ERA, for Portland in 1964, he got his call to the majors. Tiant won 75 games for the Indians during a six-year span. The team wasn't very good, and his won–loss records suffered at times because of it. During the so-called "Year of the Pitcher" (1968), he enjoyed his finest season, going 21–9, with a league-leading 1.60 ERA. His nine shutouts were also tops in the AL that year.

Traded to the Twins before the 1970 slate, the veteran right-hander suffered a shoulder injury and missed most of the season. He lost a significant amount of velocity on his lively fastball and ended up being released by two teams during spring training the following year. "I had to do something to hide the ball better. I changed my delivery completely," Tiant later recalled. The altered pitching style became his trademark.

Reggie Jackson once described Tiant as the "Fred Astaire of baseball." His windup included a series of glove waggles intended to make hitters uncomfortable. When he was ready to throw, he would twist his body away from the plate and look at the sky before spinning and delivering. There was a stop motion just before the release. A writer from *Sports Illustrated* observed, "This delivery hides the ball from the batter until the instant it is released and has a psychological effect." One opponent described it as "disturbing." Tiant's approach varied from batter to batter. "The motion depends on how I feel, how I think the batter is thinking," he explained. "Sometimes I do nothing but throw the ball. You can't use the motions too much or they get used to it."

The "motions" kept batters off balance for several years. Broadcaster Curt Gowdy once remarked that Tiant's pitches seemed to "come from everywhere except between his legs." After the Twins and Braves passed on Tiant in the spring of 1971, the Red Sox picked up his contract. Although he struggled that season, he returned to top form the following year. Between 1972 and 1976, he won no fewer than 15 games, reaching the 20-win threshold three times. He finished among the top five in Cy Young voting twice in that span.

Tiant had a cheerful personality and enjoyed talking to reporters. He was known for his love of cigars. His ability to pitch in pressure situations endeared him to Fenway fans, who sometimes chanted his name. BoSox manager Darrell Johnson once said, "If a man put a gun to my head and said I'm going to pull the trigger if you lose this game, I'd want Luis Tiant to pitch that game." Tiant was 3–0 in postseason play, with an economical 2.86 ERA.

Granted free agency after the 1978 campaign, Tiant signed with the Yankees. At age 38, he assembled his last good season, winning 13 games. Traded by New York after the 1980 campaign, he lasted two more years in the majors with the Pirates and Angels before retiring. His 229 career victories are more than any Cuban-born hurler during the twentieth century. He ranks third among Latino players behind Dennis Martinez and Juan Marichal.

After his retirement, Tiant served as a Mexican scout for the Yankees and also coached in the minors for the Dodgers and White Sox. After spending four years as a college coach, he worked as a Spanish-language broadcaster for the Red Sox. He was inducted into the team's Hall of Fame in 1997. He was later elected to the Latino Baseball Hall of Fame.

Zoilo Versalles

Shortstop

Zoilo Versalles enjoyed a meteoric rise to fame before suffering an equally rapid descent into mediocrity. Dismissed by some as a flash in the pan, he was among the major league's top infielders for half a decade. In 1965, he assembled the most impressive offensive stats ever by a Cuban-born shortstop. Two years later, he was struggling to keep his average above the .200 mark.

Born in a poor section of Cuba's capital city, Versalles fought his way out of poverty by playing baseball. His father was an itinerant laborer who accepted whatever work he could get to support the family. Zoilo's big break came with the Fortuna Sports Club team in the Cuban Amateur Athletic Union League. During the winter of 1957, he established himself as one of the team's most reliable hitters. Signed by the Senators in 1958, he was sent to Elmira of the New York–Pennsylvania League. In 1959, he earned a call to the majors but failed to make the grade with a .153 batting average in 29 games. He began the 1960 campaign in the American Association, receiving a second summons to Washington. Despite a rather poor showing at the plate, he moved with the team to Minnesota and became the Twins' first starting shortstop.

According to multiple sources, Versalles struggled to adjust to life in the United States because of the language barrier and an almost debilitating fear of failure. He never learned to read or write English and was homesick throughout his career. In the minors, he was mislabeled as moody, overconfident, and incapable of taking instruction. Early in his career, club officials and members of the media took to calling him

"Zorro." When the nickname appeared on his 1961 Topps rookie card, it stuck.

In 1961, Versalles had a breakthrough season, hitting .280, primarily at the top of the batting order. Although he finished second in errors among shortstops, he ranked among the top 10 in stolen bases. The following season, he began to demonstrate some power, drilling 17 homers, while driving in 67 runs. Meanwhile, his defense improved dramatically, as he led the league in assists, putouts, and double plays. He received a handful of MVP votes that year. As Versalles began to blossom as a player, so did the Twins. The club finished second in 1962, and third the following season, after languishing in the second division (playing as the Senators) for nearly two decades.

Versalles emerged as a bona fide star in 1963, making an All-Star appearance and winning a Gold Glove. The award came in spite of the five errors he committed in a July doubleheader against the Orioles. He followed with another solid effort in 1964, slamming a career-high 20 homers and leading the league in triples for the second straight year. In 1965, Twins third-base coach Billy Martin took a special interest in Versalles. Under Martin's tutelage, the diminutive infielder (5-foot-10, 146 pounds) enjoyed his signature campaign, leading the league in numerous statistical categories, among them runs scored (126), extra-base hits (76), and total bases (308). Martin trumpeted Versalles's "arrival" by telling reporters, "He does it all now. Fields, hits, thinks—and most important, runs. He's got to be the most fearsome runner in the league." Versalles made his only World Series appearance that year against the Dodgers, hitting safely in six of seven games. His efforts could not prevent the Twins from losing the Series, although the AL MVP trophy and Gold Glove Award he received later must have come as a small consolation.

Before the 1966 campaign, Zorro received a significant pay increase. He suffered a back injury and was placed on the disabled list. He was never the same player afterward. In 1967, he struggled to keep his average above the Mendoza Line. The following year, he failed to do so, hitting just .196 in 122 games. Seeing the writing on the wall, the Twins traded him to the Dodgers. His struggles at the plate continued, and he found himself out of the majors in 1970. He played in the Mexican League before attempting a comeback the following year with the Braves. He hit below .200 in 66 games with Atlanta.

Life after baseball was not kind to Versalles. He worked as a manual laborer and ultimately lost his home. He ended up selling his awards and living on disability. Before his death in 1995, he underwent stomach surgery and experienced two heart attacks. He left six daughters behind. With everything he suffered through, it's sad to think that he wasn't around to see his name added to the Twins Hall of Fame in 2006.

NOTABLE ACTIVE PLAYERS

Jose Abreu

First Baseman

Jose Abreu was born in Mal Tiempo, a small neighborhood in Cruces. By the age of seven, he was a starting third baseman in Cuba's National School Games. He made his Cuban National Series debut at 16. In 2012, he was one RBI short of a Triple Crown. Realizing that he could improve his situation elsewhere, he made a decision to defect the following year.

In August 2013, Abreu escaped in a small boat to Haiti, where he established residency. The details of his journey have been kept under wraps, but sources close to him disclosed that he nearly drowned in 15-foot waves. From Haiti, Abreu moved to the Dominican Republic, where he trained at various parks and stadiums. He was signed by the White Sox and made his major-league debut without a shred of minor-league experience.

Abreu's Cuban National Series career spanned 10 seasons. He averaged 18 homers and 58 RBIs per year. His finest showing came with Elfantes de Cienfuego in 2010, when he hit .453 and drove in 93 runs in just 66 games. While his major-league numbers have not been quite as outlandish, he has fared exceptionally well so far.

In his rookie season of 2014, Abreu led the AL with a .581 slugging percentage. He not only made the All-Star Team, but also captured a Silver Slugger Award and was named Rookie of the Year. His 36 homers set a franchise record for freshmen.

Abreu's follow-up was nearly identical. He collected 67 extra-base hits (including 30 homers) and drove-in 101 runs. In 2016, he hit .293 while reaching the century mark in RBIs for the third straight season. Defensively, he placed second among AL first basemen in putouts and assists.

Asked about his harrowing escape from Cuba, Abreu said it was worth the risk to be free for the first time in his life. "In Cuba, people don't attain that," he remarked. "It's something I've never experienced, and I'm thankful for everything."

Yoenis Cespedes

Outfielder

Yoenis Cespedes was born in the town of Campechuela, which is in the Granma province. His father Cresencio was a former Cuban League catcher. His mother, Estela Milanes, was a softball pitcher who played for the Cuban national team. The two split when Cespedes was a year old. Extended family members took care of Yoenis when his mother was away at tournaments.

Milanes served as Cespedes's first coach, fashioning a bat out of a tree branch and polishing it with glass. At 10 years of age, she sent Yoenis to a state-run school that groomed players for the national team. Cespedes matured into a fine outfielder, hitting .458 in the 2009 World Baseball Classic. He played eight seasons in the Cuban Winter League before defecting.

Cespedes's journey out of Cuba was anything but smooth. After a series of preliminary mishaps, he left with 10 family members by boat. They landed in the Dominican Republic, where Cespedes split with the group upon signing with the A's. The rest of his family ended up stranded on a strip of sand 600 miles off the coast of Florida. With no food, water, or shade, dehydration set in rapidly. The group was miraculously rescued by a passing yacht, but their troubles were not over. By the time they reunited with Cespedes, their adventures included two trips to jail, an immigration raid, accusations of human trafficking, and a dispute with a Dominican baseball agent.

While his family members were struggling to find their way to the United States, Cespedes was making a name for himself in the majors.

Called to Oakland after just three games in the Pacific Coast League, he had a spectacular debut, with 23 homers, 82 RBIs, and a .292 average. He also stole 16 bases in 20 attempts, finishing second in Rookie of the Year voting to Mike Trout of the Angels.

Originally a center fielder, Cespedes was moved to left field during his rookie year. Although he hit just .240 in his sophomore campaign, he slugged 26 homers and drove in 80 runs, leading Oakland to a American League Division Series berth. He also won the 2013 Home Run Derby, beating Bryce Harper of the Nationals in the final round. In the ALDS, he batted .381, with three extra-base hits and four RBIs. The A's lost in spite of his efforts.

In July 2014, the A's traded Cespedes to the Red Sox. Although he hit well down the stretch, Boston slumped to last place in the AL East. Cespedes's travels continued in 2015, as he started the season with the Tigers and ended up with the Mets. He became a sensation in New York when he blasted 15 homers in a one-month span from late August to mid-September. He finished the season with his best numbers to date—83 extra-base hits and 105 RBIs. He also played sparkling defense, earning his first Gold Glove. While the Mets' World Series bid fell short, Cespedes contributed 12 hits in three playoff rounds with seven runs scored and eight driven in.

Cespedes enjoyed another fine season in 2016. Sidelined for 30 games with a leg injury, he still managed to crack 31 homers and drive in 86 runs for the Mets. Both were team highs. His selection to the All-Star Team was the second of his career.

Aroldis Chapman

Pitcher

Aroldis Chapman was born in Holguin, one of the largest cities on the island. His father was a boxing instructor who passed on the basic skills of the sport to him. Aroldis lived with his parents and two sisters in a three-room house. He wasn't invested in playing baseball until he reached his early teens. Initially used as a first baseman, his incredible throwing arm better suited him to pitching.

Chapman played for the Cuban national team, representing his country at the 2007 Pan American Games and 2009 World Baseball

Classic. In the spring of 2008, he engaged in a failed defection attempt. Cuban president Raul Castro suspended him for the remainder of the National Series and barred him from the 2008 Summer Olympics. Returning to the national squad in 2009, Chapman successfully escaped Cuba while playing in the Netherlands. He established residency in Andorra, a sovereign microstate in Europe.

In 2010, the hard-throwing left-hander signed a contract with the Reds. He spent portions of two seasons in the minors before catching on with Cincinnati full time. Nicknamed the "Cuban Missile," Chapman has been given credit for the fastest recorded pitch in history, at 105 miles per hour. Unconfirmed reports contend that his pitches have traveled even faster than that. He regularly hits 100 miles per hour on the radar gun. In 2015, he reached the 500-strikeout mark faster than any player in major-league history. The year before, he broke a record set by Bruce Sutter with at least one strikeout in 49 consecutive appearances.

Chapman uses a three-quarter delivery. He has a four-seam fastball and a slider. He also mixes in an occasional changeup. Joe Posnaski of *Sports Illustrated* marvels that, despite the amazing velocity of his pitches, Chapman has a smooth delivery. "He's the anti-Bob Gibson," writes Posnaski. "Just a slow beginning, a fluid motion, and *blammo*! The ball just fires out like the Batmobile rolling out of the cave."

Beginning in 2012, Chapman began a run of four consecutive seasons with at least 33 saves. He made the All-Star Team each year in that span, while averaging more than 15 strikeouts per nine innings. Traded to the Yankees before the 2016 campaign, he was suspended until May in the wake of a domestic dispute with his girlfriend. At the All-Star break, he had recorded 17 saves and three wins, with an economical 2.49 ERA. In late July, the Yankees traded him to the Cubs in exchange for four players. After saving 16 regular season games for Chicago, he added a pair of wins and 4 saves in the postseason, helping the Cubs break the longest championship drought in baseball history.

Kendrys Morales

First Baseman/Designated Hitter

Kendrys Morales hails from Fomento. As a teenager, he was a switch-hitting pitcher with power from both sides of the plate. When he joined the Cuban national team in 2002, he was the first teenager to make the squad in nearly two decades. His grand slam in the finale of the 2003 World Cup against Taiwan secured a tournament victory for his country. Prior to that, Morales had played for Industriales de La Habana in the Cuban National Series. He hit .350 in three seasons.

While participating in the 2003 Olympic Trials, he was removed from the team for consulting with a U.S. sports official. Embittered by the experience, he escaped Cuba on a raft in June 2004. It was reportedly his eighth defection attempt. He ended up in the Dominican Republic, where he was scouted by several teams. Eventually, he signed with Anaheim.

Morales labored in the minors for portions of four seasons before taking up permanent residence with the Angels. His breakthrough season came in 2009, when he hit .306, with 34 homers and 108 RBIs. He finished fifth in MVP voting that year. He was off to a great start in 2010 before a bizarre injury derailed his season. After hitting a walk-off grand slam in late May against the Mariners, he was met by an ecstatic horde of teammates at home plate. He jumped in the air and landed awkwardly on his ankle, fracturing it. The injury kept him out of action until 2012.

Morales hit .273 in his return, with 22 homers and 73 RBIs. Concerned about his diminished numbers, the Angels traded him to the Mariners. Morales had a decent season in 2013, but he got off to a slow start the following year. This prompted a trade to Minnesota. The Twins dished him back to Seattle when he hit just .234 in 39 games.

Morales realized his full potential in 2015, with the Royals. Serving mostly as a DH, he accrued a .290 batting average during the regular season, with 65 extra-base hits and 106 RBIs. Both marks were tops on the club. The Royals made it to the postseason, and Morales's three-run homer in the ALDS finale secured a 7–2 win. After an ALCS win over the Blue Jays, the Royals moved on to a Series victory over the Mets. Morales contributed four homers and 10 RBIs to the postseason cause.

As of 2016, Morales was still Kansas City's primary DH. He had an extremely productive year with 30 homers and 93 RBIs. A free agent at seasons' end, the Royals re-signed Morales for a reported $17 million.

Yasiel Puig

Outfielder

Yasiel Puig was born in Cienfuegos, the older of two siblings. His father Omar was an engineer in a sugarcane factory. Like most Cuban children, he was exposed to baseball early in his life. He started playing at the age of nine and began his road to the majors in the Cuban National Series eight years later. In his rookie season with the Elefantes de Cienfuegos, he hit .276 in 70 games. He was a star in the 2008 Central American and Caribbean Junior Championship but didn't play the following year. He returned to the National Series in 2010, tearing up the league by hitting .330, with 42 extra-base hits. In 2012, he enlisted the help of a petty criminal named Raul Pacheco to help him defect. The story of his escape reads like a pulp crime novel.

Puig's first several attempts were unsuccessful. He was caught by the Cuban police three times and the Coast Guard on another occasion. The fifth try was an unmitigated disaster. Puig left the country with a boxer, a pinup girl, and a priest. His smugglers had ties to Mexican drug cartels. While Pacheco negotiated with the smugglers, Puig was confined in a seedy hotel for weeks. The smugglers allegedly threatened to chop off his arm if they didn't receive payment. Puig was said to have been rescued from the hotel by a group of "fixers" hired by Pacheco, but the smugglers continued to seek compensation. One of them was later found dead in Cancun—the victim of an execution-style murder. Puig has remained largely mum on the topic but has been quoted as saying, "Sleep is when it's your time to die. For that reason, I sleep with one eye open."

Signed by the Dodgers in June 2012, Puig was assigned to an Arizona Rookie League team and quickly promoted to the Class A level. A staph infection in his elbow kept him out of action for months, and he played in the Puerto Rican Winter League to get back in shape. After a strong spring training in 2013, he was assigned to the Chattanooga Lookouts of the Southern League. He was called to the majors in June.

Puig has power at the plate. Although he has missed significant playing time in three of his four major-league seasons, his 162-game average includes 31 doubles and 21 homers. He strikes out at the distressing rate of once per four at-bats. He covers a lot of ground in the outfield and plays aggressively, which leads to occasional lapses. The same can be said of his baserunning. Appearing at every outfield station, he has spent a majority of time in right field. He has one of the strongest arms in the majors, leading the league in assists during the 2014 campaign. He set multiple franchise records that year, including most consecutive games with an extra-base hit and RBI. His three triples in a single game tied a team record set by Jimmy Sheckard in 1901. Puig finished second in Rookie of the Year voting during the 2013 slate.

During his brief and eventful career, Puig has been prone to injury. Hamstring problems kept him out for half the season in 2015. Those issues continued to plague him the following year. He has drawn negative attention to himself on more than one occasion. In 2013, he was arrested twice for reckless driving. In 2016, he was threatened with a suspension by MLB for wearing cleats that did not conform to standard uniform policy. Although Puig has yet to realize his full potential as a player, he is only 25 years old. There are many who believe he will have an MVP-caliber season at some point in the future.

Alexei Ramirez

Shortstop

Alexei Ramirez was born and raised in Pinar del Rio, which was also home to major-league standout Tony Oliva. Ramirez was 18 years old when he started playing for the Vegueras de Pinar del Rio in the Cuban National Series. He represented his country in multiple international tournaments, including the 2005 Baseball World Cup and the 2006 World Baseball Classic. He hit .375 in the latter tournament and finished his National Series career with a .332 batting mark.

After competing in the 2007 Pan American Games and helping Cuba to a gold medal, he moved to the Dominican Republic with his wife and two kids. He stated openly that he was not defecting. He had a brief stint in the Dominican Winter League but was released. Signed by the White Sox, manager Ozzie Guillen nicknamed him the "Cuban

Missile" for his tall, slender build and exceptional speed. He joined the club without any minor-league experience. At 26, he was fairly old for a rookie.

Ramirez's batting averages have been steady, ranging from .249 to .290 between 2008 and 2015. He has been highly durable, appearing in no fewer than 154 games in six consecutive seasons. As his nickname implies, he has speed on the bases. Entering the 2016 campaign, he had posted double-digit stolen-base totals seven times. Usually appearing in the bottom half of the batting order, he has moderate power, clubbing 15 or more homers on five occasions. He has captured two Silver Slugger Awards.

Ramirez's arm is so strong, manager Robin Ventura allowed him to pitch in the ninth inning of a lopsided loss to the A's during the 2015 slate. He hit one batter and allowed a double but held Oakland scoreless. Ramirez normally uses that strong arm to gun down baserunners. He has led AL shortstops in assists three times.

In January 2016, Ramirez brought his successful run with the White Sox to an end when he joined the Padres. He was released in September and signed by the Rays. After posting the lowest offensive numbers of his career, he was granted free agency at seasons' end.

5

PANAMA

ORIGINS OF BASEBALL IN PANAMA

The roots of Panamanian baseball cannot be traced specifically, but it is believed to have been introduced by American laborers during the construction of the Panama Railroad. The railroad was initially built to help facilitate traffic flow to California, which increased dramatically during the Gold Rush of 1849. Work began in 1850, and the span was completed by 1855. Still in existence today, the 48-mile railway runs parallel to the Panama Canal and connects the Atlantic Ocean to the Pacific Ocean. It was of vital importance to the canal's construction at the turn of the century.

One of the earliest accounts of an organized baseball game in Panama can be found in a newspaper blurb dated January 9, 1883. Few details of the game were provided aside from the fact that a Chiriqui provincial team took on the Panama Cricket and Baseball Club in Chiriqui Plaza. As baseball increased in popularity, teams began to appear throughout the country, taking on such colorful names as Swift Sure, Stars of the Pacific, and the Emerald of the Isthmus. In 1945, the Beisbol Profesional de Panama was formed. A national team began competing in the Caribbean Series four years later.

When baseball's color barrier was broken, Panamanian players began trickling into the major leagues. In 1955, three Panama natives made their debuts—Hector Lopez (utility man), Humberto Robinson (pitcher), and Webbo Clarke (pitcher). Dozens of others would follow.

Panama's professional league folded in the early 1970s. A new league known as Probeis was formed in 2001, but it was short-lived. It has been resurrected multiple times. The Panamanian national team has continued to participate in assorted tournaments. The club was recently eliminated in the qualifying round for the 2017 World Baseball Classic.

Panama's legacy in Major League Baseball has been rich and diverse. The following luminaries represent the cream of the crop.

MAJOR STARS OF THE PAST

Rod Carew

First Baseman/Second Baseman

Rod Carew came into the world under somewhat unusual circumstances. He was born on a segregated train in the town of Gatun, which was then considered part of the Panama Canal Zone. His pregnant mother—Olga Teoma—was obligated to sit in a rearward compartment because she was black. When she went into labor, the conductor stopped the train to find a doctor. Carew ended up being named after the man who presided over the emergency delivery (Dr. Rodney Cline).

Carew's father worked as a sign painter to support the family. He was a strict disciplinarian who sometimes resorted to corporal punishment. Carew and his four siblings relied heavily on their mother for guidance and support. Rod was in his second year of high school when his mother immigrated to New York City. Once she had established a home in Washington Heights, she summoned Rod and his brother Dickie (who was selected via a family lottery) to join her.

Carew enrolled at George Washington High—the same school attended by slugger Manny Ramirez. Rod had played baseball in Panama but chose not to try out for the team in the interest of keeping his grades up. He was determined to master the English language, which was new to him. He found his way back to the diamond in 1964, joining a sandlot club in the Bronx Federation League. A talented hitter, he caught the attention of Minnesota scout Herb Stein, who called Carew to Yankee Stadium for a tryout. Twins manager Sam Mele was suffi-

ciently impressed, and Carew was signed after his high school gradua-
tion.

While playing in the minors, Carew missed out on the Twins' 1965
World Series appearance. By the time he was called to the majors in
1967, the club was still in contention. Carew had a lot to do with that, as
he made the first of 18 consecutive All-Star appearances and captured
Rookie of the Year honors. The Twins finished just one game behind
the Red Sox that year.

Carew got his first taste of the postseason in 1969—the same year he
won his first batting crown. He flopped in the American League Championship Series, going 1-for-14 at the plate as the Twins were swept by
the Orioles. In 1970, Carew was off to another great start when a knee
injury sidelined him for three months. He made a pair of late-inning
appearances in the playoffs, which ended with another Baltimore
sweep.

During the course of his 19-year career, Carew gathered legions of
admirers for his hitting skills. Pitcher Ken Holtzman remarked, "He has
an uncanny ability to move the ball around as if the bat were some kind
of magic wand." Typically occupying the second spot in the order, the
lefty-swinging infielder collected just 92 homers in more than 10,000
plate appearances. But he knew how to find holes in the defense. "I got
a kick out of watching a team defense me," Carew once said. "A player
moves two steps in one direction, and I hit it two steps in the other
direction. It goes right by his glove, and I laugh."

He had plenty to laugh about throughout the years, as he won seven
batting titles and retired with more than 3,000 hits. His crowning
achievement came in 1977, when he was named American League
Most Valuable Player on the strength of his league-leading 128 runs,
239 hits, 16 triples, and .388 batting average. "There was a point at
which I thought I'd never get the MVP, especially the years I played at
Minnesota," Carew said years later. "We never won a pennant there, we
were far away from the big media centers of Los Angeles and New
York, and I wasn't a flashy power hitter, but a guy who hit to spots, who
bunted and stole bases." The Twins were in decline by 1977, and unable to meet Carew's salary needs, they traded him to the Angels after
the 1978 campaign.

Never known for his defense, Carew spent equal portions of time at
first base and second base during his career. Although he finished

among the league leaders in putouts and assists several times, he paced the loop in errors on multiple occasions. Overall, his strengths outweighed his weaknesses. Hall of Famer Catfish Hunter observed, "He has no weakness as a hitter. Pitch him on the inside, outside, high, low, fast stuff, breaking balls—anything you throw he can handle . . . he has no holes." Notorious spitballer Gaylord Perry was similarly dazzled by Carew's offensive talents. "Greaseball, greaseball, greaseball, that's all I throw him, and he still hits them. . . . He sees the ball so well, I guess he can spot the dry side," said Perry.

Carew spent his last seven years with the Angels, helping the club to a pair of postseason berths. In 1984, his batting average dropped below .300 for the first time in 16 years. He made the All-Star Team anyway. He retired after the 1985 campaign and was elected to the National Baseball Hall of Fame in his first year of eligibility. While he has been sufficiently recognized for his hitting exploits, Carew's fearlessness on the basepaths is sometimes overlooked. He stole home 17 times. This included seven successful attempts in 1969—just one short of Ty Cobb's single-season record.

After his retirement, Carew served as an Angels coach for eight seasons. The Brewers employed him in the same capacity in 2000 and 2001. In 2015, he suffered a massive heart attack and underwent a grueling round of surgery. According to one source, his life expectancy is rather short without a heart transplant. He remains a national hero in Panama, where Panama City's National Stadium was renamed in his honor.

After his retirement, Carew served as an Angels coach for eight seasons. He also coached for the Brewers. In 2015, he suffered a massive heart attack. His prognosis remained grim until December 2016, when he underwent successful heart and kidney transplants at Cedars-Sinai Medical Center in Los Angeles. The organs he received were donated by former NFL tight end Konrad Reuland, who died tragically of a brain aneurysm at the age of 29. On March 2, 2017, a grateful Carew met Reuland's parents and allowed them to listen to their son's heart beating inside his chest. Moved to the point of tears, Mary Reuland said to Carew: "You're part of our family now."

Carlos Lee

Outfielder/First Baseman

Although his name rarely surfaces in discussions of baseball's great sluggers, Carlos Lee was among the steadiest run producers of the early twenty-first century. He retired with more doubles, homers, and RBIs than any of his countrymen. And only six players in major-league history have hit more grand slams.

Lee grew up in Aguadulce, a small agricultural city in the province of Cocle. Located 190 kilometers from Panama City, the community is known for its sugarcane fields and salt flats. Lee's high school was named after a Liberal Party politician who served as president of Panama from 1924 to 1928. To date, Lee is the only Rodolfo Chiari alumnus to reach the majors.

Lee was discovered by White Sox scout Miguel Ibarra in 1994, and signed fresh out of high school. He spent portions of six seasons in the minors. Aside from his pro debut with the Gulf Coast White Sox, he hit .300 each year. Called to Chicago in May 1999, he got off to a prodigious start with a homer in his first major-league at-bat. He gathered 50 extra-base hits and 84 RBIs that year, finishing among the top 10 in Rookie of the Year voting.

A larger-than-life figure at 6-foot-2, 270 pounds, Lee served primarily as a left fielder but also spent more than 200 games at first base. He had limited range due to his size but was equipped with a strong arm and sure hands. In 2012, he posted the highest fielding percentage among National League first basemen. A few years earlier, he had completed 148 left-field assignments without an error. He was overlooked for a Gold Glove in both seasons.

Lee was far more industrious with a bat, gathering 80 or more RBIs each year from 1999 to 2011. He blasted no fewer than 26 homers in eight consecutive seasons. He had relatively low strikeout totals for a slugger, averaging one per every eight at-bats. After 2005, he never struck out more than 65 times a year. Highly durable, he remained injury free until 2008, when a broken finger ended his season in August. He was having a banner year, with a .314 batting average and 100 RBIs in 115 games.

Lee changed uniforms fairly often during his playing days. After spending six years with the White Sox, he had layovers in Milwaukee and Texas before landing in Houston. For a portion of his career, he was represented by agent Scott Boras, who has been widely blamed for driving player salaries into the stratosphere. In 2010, Lee's contract with Houston was listed among the 10 worst in baseball by multiple sources. At the time, he was making $19 million per year. Although he reached the 100-RBI threshold in three straight seasons for the Astros, his numbers began to taper off. He was traded to the Marlins in July 2012, before being granted free agency at season's end. He announced his retirement shortly thereafter.

A looming threat with the bases loaded, Lee hit .307 in that scenario during his 14-year tour of the majors. His 17 grand slams place him seventh on the all-time list—tied with Jimmie Foxx and Ted Williams. Three of Lee's slams came in extra innings, which is a major-league record. At the peak of his career, he had a fan club known as "Los Caballitos," which translates to "Little Horses." His sabermetric similarity scores compare him favorably to Hall of Famers Orlando Cepeda and Jim Rice.

In 2007, Lee purchased a mansion in Sugarland, Texas. He also owned and operated cattle ranches in Houston and Aguadulce. He sold his Sugarland mansion in 2014 for an estimated $1.6 million. He has remained active in baseball as a player for and manager of Panama's national team.

Hector Lopez

Infielder/Outfielder

Hector Lopez came of age in Colon, a sea-port city founded by Americans in the 1800s to serve as the Atlantic terminal of the Panama Railroad, during the late 1930s and early 1940s, when players of his color had no hope of making the major leagues. His father Manuel was a pitcher for various local teams, and Hector developed a passion for the game. The kids in Lopez's neighborhood would play using a broom handle for a bat and a ball made of tape and rubber. Even as a kid, Lopez was known for his hitting ability. But he knew the odds were against him. "Ever since I can remember, I wanted to be a ballplayer," he told a reporter in 1963. "Things didn't seem bright, though. Panama is crazy about baseball, but most of those few who had a chance in the majors were pitchers. I was a skinny little infielder."

During Lopez's formative years, the United States occupied the Panama Canal Zone. Lopez worked on a military base in a bowling alley. He emerged as a track star during high school and got his first opportunity in baseball while playing for an amateur team in a provincial league. After turning pro with the independent St. Hyacinthe Saints, he was discovered by A's scout Joe McDonald, who offered him a contract. Lopez's minor-league career began with Williamsport of the Eastern League. Serving primarily as a shortstop, he hit .270 and was promoted to Ottawa of the International League in 1954. He started the 1955 campaign at Columbus and was off to a hot start when the A's called him to Kansas City.

Lopez was a versatile defensive player; he played every position except pitcher and catcher. When he first arrived in the majors, the A's outfield was loaded with such veteran stars as Gus Zernial, Elmer Valo, and Enos Slaughter. Lopez was assigned to third base, where he led the league in errors for two straight seasons. He held his own at the plate, however, hitting at a cumulative .281 pace, with 33 homers and 137 RBIs during those two error-prone campaigns.

Playing under manager Lou Boudreau, Lopez established himself as one of the better infielders in the AL. His clutch hitting and persistent hustle endeared him to fans in Kansas City. Although there were some privileges that were denied him because of his skin color, he enjoyed his time with the A's. "It wasn't too bad in Kansas City," he said. "I got along with everyone, and they treated me well. . . . I can't complain." In those days, the A's served as a regular trading partner with the Yankees, exporting a steady stream of talent to the Bronx. "Kansas City was trying to build a ballclub, and they could get three or four players from the Yankees for every one or two players," Lopez explained. "There wasn't any draft at the time. Everybody wanted to play with the Yankees, so the Yankees signed a lot of ballplayers." In May 1959, Lopez and Ralph Terry were shipped to New York. Lopez would remain a staple in the Yankees lineup for the better part of eight seasons.

Casey Stengel was fond of using platoons, and Lopez was regularly inserted as a stopgap at second base and third base. He also appeared at every outfield station, spending the largest chunk of time in left field. He never remained at any one position long enough to receive Gold

Glove consideration. He likely would have been overlooked anyway. Lopez was never known for his defense. In fact, in *The Great American Baseball Card Flipping, Trading, and Bubble Gum Book*, one of the authors contends, "I would like to go on record right here and now as declaring that Hector Lopez was the all-time worst fielding major-league ballplayer." This is a bit of a stretch, although Lopez's cumulative fielding percentage in the outfield was 13 points below the league average.

Surrounded by all-time Yankee greats Mickey Mantle, Yogi Berra, and Whitey Ford, Lopez appeared in five World Series, winning two championship rings. Stengel employed him primarily as a pinch-hitter or defensive replacement, but he did participate in three games from start to finish. He made the most of his postseason opportunities, hitting .286 in 15 appearances, with four extra-base hits and seven RBIs.

By 1966, Lopez was 36 years old and fading. He played in 54 games that year and was released. He continued in the minors for two seasons before retiring. In 1969, he guided the Buffalo Bisons of the International League to a seventh-place finish, becoming the first black manager at the Triple-A level. He worked as a recreation director for 20 years in his hometown and also scouted for the Giants and Yankees. In 1994–1995, he took the reins of the Gulf Cost Yankees, guiding the club to an even .500 record. In 2009, he was appointed manager of the Panamanian national team in the World Baseball Classic. The club was badly overmatched, losing two games by a combined score of 16–0.

Lopez was the first Panamanian-born player to appear regularly in the majors. He was also the first to play on a world championship team and lead the league in a statistical category (sacrifice flies, 1958). He remains a revered figure in his native country.

Omar Moreno

Center Fielder

Omar Moreno was born in Puerto Armuelles, located on the Pacific Ocean in close proximity to Costa Rica. The town was built in 1927 by the United Fruit Company, later known as Chiquita Brands International. Aside from bananas and oil, Moreno is the most famous export to date.

In 1968, Moreno's high-school team competed in a national baseball tournament. He was used sparingly by his coach, prompting him to focus his energies on track and field thereafter. He became a high-jump champion. When the annual baseball tournament rolled around the following year, Moreno was asked to rejoin the team. He hadn't played or practiced that season and didn't want to go, but a local journalist convinced him that he might be of some value to the club. The long layoff had not eroded his skills, as he went 7-for-11 at the plate in three games, helping Chiriqui province claim its first championship. After the final game, he was approached by Herb Raybourn, a physical education teacher in the Panama Canal Zone and part-time scout for the Pirates. Raybourn informed Moreno that his parents had already signed a contract entering him into Pittsburgh's minor-league system. "I got really nervous," Moreno recalled. "I was barely 17, and I thought, 'I'm going to the U.S.'" He described it as one of the greatest moments of his life.

Putting his track-and-field skills to work, Moreno became a base-stealing terror in the minors, swiping more than 70 bases in 1973 and 1974. His .315 showing at Charleston during the 1976 campaign earned him a call to the majors. He got into 48 games with the Pirates and hit .270, with 15 steals. His performance prompted one writer to declare before the 1977 slate,

> Outstanding speed, durability, and the ability to make good contact at the plate are just some of Omar Moreno's credentials. If you tack on the fact that he is also an excellent outfielder and a seasoned veteran at the age of 23, then you have more reasons why the 1977 season is shaping up to be even more exciting than ever for the Pittsburgh Pirates.

Harding Peterson, vice president of player personnel for the Pirates, was equally optimistic about Moreno's future. Said Peterson, "We always had the confidence that Omar would someday blossom into a full-fledged major leaguer. In his case, it took longer than for most, but he never gave up on himself either. With his speed, he has a good chance to lead the major leagues in stolen bases." That statement proved prophetic, as Moreno was the NL's reigning stolen base king for two straight seasons (1978–1979). He swiped 37 or more bags seven times during his career, setting the Pirates team record on three separate occasions. His 96 steals in 1980 have not been equaled by any Pittsburgh alumnus to date.

Moreno's quickness aided him tremendously in center field, where he led the league in putouts twice. He had a strong arm, finishing with double-digit assist totals on four occasions. But despite his positive attributes, there were a few holes in his game. Primarily a line-drive hitter, he struck out way too often—more than 100 times in six campaigns. He set a dubious record in 1979, when he made 560 outs. After posting a collective .237 batting average in 1977–1978, Moreno worked with former NL batting champ Harry "The Hat" Walker to adjust his approach at the plate. Walker instructed Moreno to put the ball in play so he could take advantage of his speed. It worked out well for the lefty-swinging outfielder, as he gathered a career-high 196 hits in 1979—fifth best in the league.

The Pirates were a dominant force during the 1970s, winning a pair of world championships, while making six playoff appearances. The 1979 version of the club was among the best in history. Moreno was a sparkplug on the basepaths, stealing 77 bases (a league high) and scoring 110 runs. Thirty-nine-year-old veteran Willie Stargell (affectionately known as "Pops") served as a father figure to his teammates, fostering a warm, close-knit clubhouse atmosphere. The song "We Are Family"—popularized by the pop group Sister Sledge—became the celebratory anthem of Pittsburgh's championship season. After sweeping Cincinnati's "Big Red Machine," the Bucs took on the Orioles in the World Series. Down three games to one, they rallied to win the last three meetings by a combined score of 15–2. Moreno hit .333 in the Series and .311 overall in the postseason. It was his only appearance on the October stage.

Moreno was vastly underpaid during his prime, and before the 1983 slate he decided to test the free-agent market. He signed a contract with Houston but ended up being traded to the Yankees in August for Jerry Mumphrey. Moreno spent one full season in the Bronx, playing alongside corner outfielders Dave Winfield and Steve Kemp. The Yankees were mediocre in 1984, and so was Moreno, hitting .259 in 117 games. When he got off to a .197 start in 1985, he was released. He played in the Venezuelan Winter League that year, leading La Guaira to a pennant. He was less useful in major-league play, getting released by the Royals and Braves before retiring after the 1986 campaign.

Moreno hung around the game in various capacities—as a player in the short-lived Senior Professional Baseball Association and a baserunning instructor for the Medicine Hat Blue Jays of the Pioneer League. He worked for the Panamanian national team during the 1999 Pan American Games, later managing the club in the 2003 World Cup. He also managed Los Macheteros de Azuero in the 2001–2002 Panamanian Winter League.

Moreno has his own foundation that he runs with his wife—a youth baseball charity for underprivileged kids in Panama. In 2009, he accepted a position as secretary of sports from president-elect Ricardo Martinelli. He has a cameo appearance in the Mexican film *El Hombre de la Mandolina*, which was nominated for a prestigious Mexican Academy of Film award. He also did voice work for an episode of the cartoon parody *Space Ghost Coast to Coast*.

Ben Oglivie

Left Field

Ben Ogilvie was born in the city of Colon. Completion of the Panama Canal brought prosperity to Colon, but political unrest during the 1960s led to a series of destructive riots. The city's decline became complete during the military dictatorships of Omar Torrijos and Manuel Noriega.

Oglivie's family immigrated to the United States after the premature death of his father. A conscientious student and standout athlete, he graduated from Roosevelt High in New York City. He had initially planned to study electrical engineering at Bronx Community College but was noticed by a Red Sox scout. He was a late-round pick in the 1968 Amateur Draft.

Oglivie's breakthrough season occurred in 1971, at Louisville, where he hit .304 and drove in 86 runs. The following year, he played under Hall of Famer Larry Doby in the Venezuelan Winter League. Doby tagged him as a five-tool player, but the Red Sox were skeptical. "When I first came up, I was just happy to be there," said Oglivie of his early major-league experience. "I figured I'd wait my turn. My turn never came. I'd play two games and then I was back on the bench again. I couldn't comprehend that."

In his autobiography *The Wrong Stuff*, colorful moundsman Bill "Spaceman" Lee fondly remembers Oglivie's major-league arrival. Assuming he couldn't speak English, people had a tendency to speak to Oglivie slowly while making dramatic hand gestures. "It was a riot," Lee writes, "because the first thing I noticed about him was his ability to complete a *New York Times* crossword puzzle in about five minutes." The educated Oglivie attended several colleges, including Northeastern University in Boston and Wayne State University in Detroit.

After appearing in just 166 games for the BoSox in portions of three seasons, Oglivie was traded to the Tigers for Dick McAuliffe before the 1974 campaign. McAuliffe, who was in decline, played two more seasons before falling from the big-league ranks. Meanwhile, Oglivie blossomed into a fine offensive player.

Oglivie's power began to emerge during the 1976 slate. Playing in a career-high 115 games, he clubbed 15 homers—second on the club to first baseman Jason Thompson. He was outpaced by Thompson and designated hitter Rusty Staub the following year, although he appeared in far fewer games. After a lackluster finish in 1977, the Tigers were looking to retool their pitching staff. They sent Oglivie to Milwaukee in exchange for left-handed reliever Rich Folkers and right-handed starter Jim Slaton. Slaton won a career-high 17 games in 1978, as Oglivie had his best season to date, hitting .303, with 72 RBIs.

At 6-foot-2, 160 pounds, Oglivie didn't look much like a power hitter. But he fit the role in 1980, compiling a .304 batting average, while tying Reggie Jackson for the league lead in homers (41). Ogilvie earned the first of three All-Star selections that year. The Brewers had multiple stars in their lineup, including future Hall of Famers Paul Molitor and Robin Yount, but the team still finished third in the ultra-competitive AL East. During the strike-shortened 1981 campaign, Milwaukee made its first-ever playoff appearance, losing the American League Division Series in five games to the Yankees. The "Brew Crew" was back in business the following year, making it all the way to the World Series. The pennant race was tight, and Oglivie's acrobatic catch against the Orioles in game 162 forced a tiebreaker between the two clubs. The Brewers won, clinching the East. In the World Series, Milwaukee held a 3–2 advantage before suffering humbling losses to the Cardinals in the sixth and seventh games. Oglivie appeared in three postseason series with the Brewers during his career, reaching base 18 times in 16 games (excluding fielder's choices).

Oglivie had good speed for a slugger, finishing with double-digit stolen-base totals in five seasons. His swiftness worked to an advantage in the outfield, where he finished among the top five in putouts and range factor four times apiece. He led the AL in the former category during the 1982 slate.

In the mid-1980s, Oglivie saw increasingly less action. He continued to generate respectable batting averages, but the rest of his offensive numbers tapered off. He played his last major-league game in 1986, and spent two seasons with the Osaka Kintetsu Buffaloes of the Japanese Pacific League. He led the club in homers during the 1987 slate and reached the .300 mark in both campaigns. At the age of 40, he signed a minor-league contract with the Brewers organization but sustained a knee injury and ended up retiring. He later played in the Senior Professional Baseball Association.

After his playing days were over, Oglivie served as a hitting coach in the minors for multiple franchises, among them the Devil Rays and Padres. In 2010, he was hired by the Tigers to coach for the West Michigan White Caps. He was elected to the Latino Baseball Hall of Fame in 2012.

Mariano Rivera

Closer

It was a familiar scene at Yankee Stadium for nearly two decades: Mariano Rivera charging out of the bullpen accompanied by the ominous refrain of Metallica's power anthem "Enter Sandman." "I can't tell you how comforting it felt to have him come in when I left the game," said teammate Roger Clemens. Derek Jeter referred to him as the "most mentally tough person" he ever played with. For Rivera, it was simple. Describing his job to kids on the Yes Network television program *Yankees on Deck*, he said, "I get the ball, I throw the ball, and then I go take a shower."

Aside from Rod Carew, no Panamanian-born player has ever attained the same level of success. A 13-time All-Star and five-time World Series champion, Rivera won five AL Rolaids Relief Man of the Year awards and finished among the top 10 in Cy Young voting on six occasions, while setting the major-league record for saves (652, discounting the postseason). The accolades never went to his head, as he remained accommodating and approachable throughout his career. "I don't wait for people to give me respect," he once said. "I always give them respect." He demonstrated an almost eerie calm on the mound, never showboating after his numerous triumphs. "I'm a simple guy," he explained. "If I do something, it's not going to be 'look at this, look at that.' It just happens."

It all began in Puerto Caimito, the poor fishing village where Rivera grew up. Although soccer was Rivera's favorite sport as a boy, he remembered playing baseball on the beach during low tide using milk cartons for gloves and tree branches for bats. He received his first real glove at the age of 12. After dropping out of school in ninth grade, he worked on a commercial fishing boat with his father, who was captain. It was hard work, and Mariano gave it up after his uncle died from wounds sustained at sea. A series of ankle and knee injuries prompted Rivera to quit soccer and turn his attention to baseball.

In 1988, Mariano played for a local amateur team as a shortstop. Overlooked by scout Herb Raybourn, he got a chance to pitch the following year when the team's starter fared poorly in a playoff game. With virtually no experience, Rivera mowed down the opposition. Two weeks later, he was invited to attend a tryout in Panama City. Having heard about Rivera's positional switch, Raybourn decided to attend. At the time, Rivera weighed 155 pounds and threw at a relatively uninspiring 87 miles per hour. But Raybourn was enamored with his smooth delivery. In February 1990, Rivera accepted a modest $2,500 signing bonus. He entered the Yankees organization as a "fringe prospect."

During his debut with the Gulf Cost Yankees, Rivera worked mostly in relief, compiling a ridiculously efficient 0.17 ERA. He was allowed to start the last game of the season to qualify for the league ERA title. According to manager Glenn Sherlock, Rivera's seven-inning, no-hit performance "put him on the map with the organization." He was groomed as a starter after that, making his major-league debut in May 1995. After several rocky outings, manager Buck Showalter transferred him to the bullpen, where he would remain for the rest of his career. In 1996, Rivera served as a setup man for Yankees closer John Wetteland. He won eight of 11 decisions, while averaging 10.9 strikeouts per nine frames. In three rounds of postseason play, he allowed just 10 hits and one run in 14.1 innings of work, as the Yankees captured their first world championship in nearly two decades. For Rivera, it was the beginning of a long, fruitful October career.

With the departure of Wetteland after the 1996 slate, Rivera took over closing responsibilities. Although he blew nine opportunities in his debut, he posted a 1.88 ERA and finished second to Baltimore's Randy Myers in the save department. During the next 16 seasons, Rivera's ERA would exceed the 3.00 mark just once. He would finish among the top 10 in saves on 15 occasions, leading the league three times. Had he not been sidelined for most of the 2012 season Because of a freak injury (he ruptured a ligament shagging fly balls during batting practice), he would have raised his lifetime mark for saves considerably.

Rivera's success was somewhat surprising considering he only had three pitches in his arsenal—each a variation of his fastball. He threw a cutter, a two-seamer, and a four-seamer. According to Rivera, all of his pitches had a cutting motion. He learned to control them by adjusting the amount of pressure in his grip. His effortless delivery was deceptive to batters, and his pitches exhibited late movement. Catcher John Flaherty remarked, "The ball explodes on you."

The postseason was often Rivera's finest hour. In 32 series, he was 8–1, with a 0.70 ERA and 42 saves—another all-time record. His only loss came during an ill-fated appearance in Game Seven of the 2001 World Series against the Diamondbacks. He had far better days in the October spotlight, earning MVP honors in the 1999 World Series and 2003 ALCS. Ninety percent of his postseason appearances were scoreless.

Rivera announced his impending retirement prior to the 2013 campaign. There were numerous farewell ceremonies during his final tour of the majors. He made his last postseason appearance against the Tampa Bay Rays on September 26, at Yankee Stadium, pitching 1.1 perfect innings. Fittingly, he was greeted by fellow "Core Four" members Andy Pettitte and Derek Jeter, with whom he had captured five World Series titles. The fourth member—Jorge Posada—had retired after the 2011 slate. Rivera broke down in tears as he embraced Jeter and Pettitte, before continuing to cry as the crowd chanted his name. "I was bombarded with emotions and feelings that I couldn't describe," Rivera said later. "Everything hit at that time. I knew that that was the last time, period. I never felt something like that before."

The Yankees paid homage to Rivera in 2014 with a spring training visit to Panama. That same year, the AL named the annual award for best reliever after him. It was a good year all around, as Rivera's autobiography *The Closer* became a national bestseller. He served as a spring training instructor for the Yankees in 2015. The following season, a plaque was dedicated to him in Yankee Stadium's prestigious Monument Park. He will almost certainly be a first-ballot Hall of Famer in 2018.

Manny Sanguillen

Catcher

Manny Sanguillen was born in Colon, Panama's second largest city. He was one of 13 children. Manny's father worked as a fisherman to support the family. As a youth, Sanguillen was drawn more to soccer and basketball. He also boxed competitively. He didn't start playing baseball until he was in his early 20s. When scout Herb Raybourne first discovered Sanguillen playing with an amateur team composed of men who were much older, Manny was rough around the edges. "When I finally started to play, I didn't know what I was doing," Sanguillen recalled. "The first fly ball I tried to catch hit me in the eye." This happened during his initial Pirates tryout, which was presided over by "super scout" Howie Haak, who came to Panama to evaluate Raybourne's prospects. Sent to Batavia in 1965, Sanguillen hit well at every minor-league stop, earning a call to the majors in 1967. He was sent back down the following year but earned a permanent roster spot in 1969.

Sanguillen was lively, outspoken, and quick with a smile. He had a broad, gap-toothed grin that people found contagious. Accused by some of being a "hot dog," frequent batterymate Steve Blass explained, "He just enjoys playing, and he shows it." Sanguillen's teammates felt that he was the best catcher in the league aside from Johnny Bench. Bench had more power and was superior defensively, but Sanguillen hit for average and ran the bases more adeptly. Pirates announcer Bob Prince took to calling Sanguillen the "Road Runner" because of his surprising speed. He finished among the top 10 in triples three times, peaking at nine in 1970. His three bases-loaded triples in 1971 are a team record.

Sanguillen worked hard to improve his defense. In his first full season, he committed 17 errors but never matched that total in any other season. He was equipped with a strong, accurate arm, foiling no less than 41 percent of attempted steals for five straight campaigns. He kept up a running dialog with batters even if a pitch was on the way. He felt that the chatter distracted them.

Sanguillen developed a strong attachment to Roberto Clemente, who he idolized. Manny was slated to be on Clemente's humanitarian mission to Nicaragua in December 1972, but he reportedly misplaced his car keys and missed the ill-fated flight. While other team members attended an island memorial, Sanguillen joined a group of volunteer divers in search of Clemente's remains. According to one source, he nearly died while inspecting the caverns beneath the coral reefs. The team recovered pilot Jerry Hall's body, but Clemente's remains were never found. Sanguillen had logged some outfield experience playing winter ball in Puerto Rico, and when the 1973 season opened, the Pirates penciled him into Clemente's vacant right-field slot. Sanguillen returned to catching after making eight errors in 59 assignments.

The Pirates maintained a strong team throughout Sanguillen's career, winning two World Series and six division titles. "Danny Murtaugh (Pirates manager) would tell us that no team could beat us after the seventh inning," Sanguillen said. "If we were ahead at that point or tied, we were going to win. And we came back in the late innings a lot of times." Sanguillen was a consistent October performer, hitting .282 in seven postseason series. He compiled a .375 batting average in World Series play. His ninth-inning pinch-hit single in Game Two of the 1979 Fall Classic was the game-winner.

Sanguillen most often appeared sixth in the order. He used a long bat to reach pitches off the plate. He liked to put the ball in play, drawing relatively few walks. He attributed his impatience to a lack of instruction early in his career. "When I started, nobody told me what a strike zone was. They gave me a bat, and I swung at the ball." Sanguillen swung his hefty bat well throughout the years. During his peak seasons (1969–1973), he hit .305 and averaged 67 RBIs per year. He was named to three All-Star Teams and received MVP consideration on four occasions.

Aside from one season with Oakland (1977), Sanguillen spent his entire career with the Pirates. He was traded to the Indians after the 1980 campaign but failed to make the club out of spring training. He continued in the Mexican League for one season before retiring. Sanguillen owns a restaurant on the Riverwalk at PNC Park—home of the Pirates. In 2003, the team honored him with a bobblehead doll. Sanguillen was pleased, remarking, "I think I'm the first player, other than the Hall of Famers, to have one in Pittsburgh." In 2013, he was inducted into the Latino Baseball Hall of Fame. Two years later, a room dedicated to Sanguillen was added to the Roberto Clemente Museum in Lawrenceville. Sanguillen has served as a Pirates spring training instructor for several years.

Rennie Stennett

Second Base

Whenever Rennie Stennett's name surfaces, the focus invariably shifts to his hitting exploits on September 16, 1975. On that date, the Panamanian-born infielder had one of the best days ever by a major leaguer, going 7-for-7, with two doubles and a triple, tying a record (most hits in a nine-inning game) that had stood for more than eight decades. After collecting his seventh hit off of Cubs reliever Paul Reuschel, he was replaced with a pinch-runner—a little-known rookie named Willie Randolph (who would have a spectacular career with the New York Yankees). To date, no one has duplicated Stennett's feat, a fact that the former Pirates star finds surprising. "I've seen games with 20, 30 runs scored. I'm sure each time I see one of those that someone will have seven hits," he said in 2009. "That's the thing: Your team has to score a lot for you to get up to the plate that many times. The other thing that has to happen is your manager has to leave you in the game." Bucs skipper Danny Murtaugh rested Willie Stargell, Al Oliver, and Manny Sanguillen in the 22–0 rout but must have had a sense of what Stennett was about to accomplish, sending him to the plate a seventh time. While the rest of Stennett's career was not so flamboyant, he had a good run for several years.

Born in Colon, Stennett's full name is Renaldo Antonio Stennett Porte. He was still a teenager when scout Howie Haak signed him in

1969. Primarily a second baseman, Stennett was also adept as a third baseman and outfielder. He was often used as a leadoff man, although he never adopted a table-setter's philosophy. Never the type to sit around waiting for a walk, Stennet had an inside-out swing and liked to put the ball in play. He was hitting .344 at Charleston when the Pirates added him to their roster.

When Stennett joined the club in August 1971, the Bucs were embroiled in a close pennant race. Third baseman Jose Pagan was out with a fractured wrist, and Dave Cash had been pressed into obligatory military duty. The unproven Stennett was immediately inserted into the lineup. Surpassing expectations, he compiled a .353 batting average down the stretch, hitting safely in 18 straight games. In the field, he displayed exceptional range and played with great enthusiasm. At 20 years of age, Stennett was already drawing comparisons to Roberto Clemente. But Murtaugh was concerned about his lack of experience and left him off the postseason roster. Returning to action, Pagan gathered four hits in the World Series and drove in the deciding run in Game Seven. Meanwhile, Cash compiled a feeble .133 average in 30 at-bats. Stennett was reportedly "deeply hurt" by Murtaugh's decision.

During the next several seasons, Stennett blossomed into one of the better hitters on the team. Impressed with his progress, the Pirates traded Cash before the 1974 slate to make room for Stennett at second base. In 1974–1975, Stennett hit .289, with 173 runs scored. His batting average stood at .336 in August 1977, when a gruesome injury altered his career trajectory. During a game at Three Rivers Stadium, he shattered his ankle while sliding into second base. The image of him writhing on the ground in agony still haunts many who witnessed the game. Stennett was not only forced to sit out the rest of the season, but he also narrowly missed out on a batting title, falling short of the minimum requirements. Teammate Dave Parker grabbed the crown with a .338 mark.

Stennett was never the same after his injury, hitting .241 in the next four seasons. By 1981, he was serving mostly as a pinch-hitter or defensive replacement. When the Giants released him in April 1982, he still had $2 million left on the blockbuster contract he had signed prior to the 1980 campaign. He was one of the first flops of the free-agent era. He migrated to the Mexican League before attempting a comeback with the Expos in 1983. He hit .309 at Wichita but was never called to the majors.

In 1989, Stennett returned to baseball, signing a minor-league contract with the Pirates. He was released before the season began and ended up playing for the Gold Coast Suns of the Senior Professional Baseball Association. Competing against players his own age, he returned to form, hitting .323 in 55 games. After his retirement, Stennett settled in Florida. His brother Fernando was a minor leaguer in the Pirates organization.

NOTABLE ACTIVE PLAYERS

Carlos Ruiz

Catcher

Carlos Ruiz shares a name with a New York City photographer and a Guatemalan soccer player. He grew up in David, which is the capital city of the Chiriqui province. It is a fairly prosperous city, and Ruiz's parents were gainfully employed. His father was a police officer and his mother a school teacher. When Carlos was seven, his father was killed in the line of duty. As soon as he was old enough, he went to work on a coffee farm to help support the family. He excelled in secondary school and was on his way to a college degree when he dropped out to attend the Phillies' baseball academy.

A natural leader, Ruiz organized baseball games in his community. He acquired the necessary equipment, sorted players into teams, and assigned players positions. His ability to take charge suited him well to catching.

Ruiz's professional career began in 1999. By the time he got the call to Philadelphia in 2006, he was 27 years old. He saw little playing time his first year but became a first-stringer in 2007. He maintained that status for the next nine seasons.

Ruiz works exceptionally well with batterymates. Veteran Jamie Moyer commented, "I see a real assuredness to his body language. He's not cocky or brash. He just seems very confident in what's going on." In 2010, Ruiz caught two of Roy Halladay's no-hitters—the first one being a perfect game against the Marlins. Halladay labeled Ruiz a "rock" behind the plate and, after receiving the Cy Young Award that year, gave Ruiz a replica of the trophy. Ruiz is one of only two catchers in history to catch four no-hitters (Jason Varitek is the other).

Offensively, Ruiz is among the more productive catchers in the NL. A lifetime .266 hitter, his best season at the plate came in 2012, when he collected 48 extra-base hits and 68 RBIs while hitting .325—all career highs. For three consecutive seasons, he walked more than he struck out, a relatively unusual occurrence nowadays.

Although the Phillies have fallen on hard times lately, Ruiz has played on two pennant-winning squads. He hit .375 in Philly's World Series victory over Tampa Bay in 2008. He reached base in each of the club's 15 postseason games the following year, justifying his nickname "Senor Octubre." One writer refers to Ruiz as a "number-eight hitter who hits like John Buck in the regular season then turns into Johnny Bench come autumn."

In November 2012, Ruiz was suspended for 25 games after testing positive for an amphetamine known as Adderall. He claimed he used it to treat his ADHD disorder, although he had neglected to get proper medical authorization. In a prepared statement, he apologized for his actions and accepted the penalty. He has kept his record clean since.

In August 2016, Ruiz was traded to the Dodgers. He appeared in seven postseason games, scoring and driving in a combined total of 6 runs. In November 2016, the 38-year-old backstop became property of the Mariners.

Returning to his roots, Ruiz played for the Panamanian National Team in the qualifying round of the 2017 World Baseball Classic. Panama was eliminated by Colombia in the finale, 2–1.

6

MEXICO

ORIGINS OF BASEBALL IN MEXICO

Although some historians believe that baseball arrived in Mexico during the 1840s, it is more commonly believed that the game was introduced by U.S. soldiers three decades later. The sport would not be widely associated with Mexico until a Monterrey-based team won the Little League World Series in 1957. Known as the "Little Giants," the club received an invitation to the White House from President Dwight D. Eisenhower. The Dodgers also hosted the youngsters at Ebbets Field in Brooklyn.

Mexico's first professional league—the Liga Mexicana de Beisbol— was founded in 1925, by sportswriter Alejandro Aguilar Reyes and former player Ernesto Carmona. Through the 1930s, six teams played primarily in Mexico City with many Cuban imports. During the 1940s, the talent pool was expanded dramatically with the inclusion of Negro League and Major League Baseball stars. In 1946, millionaire Jorge Pasquel attempted to transform the Mexican League into a direct rival of MLB. Numerous contracts were offered to established stars, and although Pasquel's offers were rejected by the likes of Joe DiMaggio, Phil Rizzuto, and Ted Williams, several high-profile players were signed. Pasquel's efforts fell short when his league failed to generate sufficient revenue. The invitees returned to the United States, where they incurred penalties for their desertion.

In 1933, outfielder Mel Almada became the first Mexican-born player to reach the majors. Dozens of others would follow. The number of Mexican League teams grew to 20 in 1979, but fiscal problems reduced that number to 16. Today, baseball is thriving south of the border with an eight-team winter league (known as the Liga Mexicana del Pacifico) complementing summer play. Winners of the Liga Pacifico advance to the Caribbean Series to face other Latin American champions. In addition, a Mexican national team competes in the World Baseball Classic. To date, more than 100 Mexican natives have been involved in major-league action. The best and brightest are on the pages that follow.

MAJOR STARS OF THE PAST

Bobby Avila

Second Baseman

Bobby Avila was born in Veracruz, a port city located on the Gulf of Mexico. When he was a boy, bullfighting and soccer were popular pastimes in his hometown. Although the city has banned bullfighting, Veracruz is still home to professional soccer. Avila was a skilled soccer player before he turned his attention to baseball. He reportedly learned the finer points of the game from an instructional book authored by former A's pitching great Jack Coombs. Avila's father tried to discourage him from athletic pursuits, but young Bobby—known then as "Beto"—emerged as a star infielder during his high-school years.

While still a teenager, Avila joined a Veracruz winter league and was later added to the Puebla Parrots roster. Although he managed a feeble .229 average in his professional debut, he raised that mark by more than 100 points the following year. In 1946, when millionaire executive Jorge Pasquel lured numerous major-league stars to Mexico in an attempt to compete with the American League and National League, Avila had one of his best seasons ever, compiling the third highest batting average in the circuit, at .359. He turned down multiple offers to play in the United States, winning the 1947 Mexican League batting title with a .346 mark. Before the 1948 campaign, the Cleveland Indians outbid the

Dodgers for his services. Avila signed a lucrative contract worth $17,500 (an attractive figure in those days).

Avila's minor-league career was brief. He spent one season in the International League before bonus rules compelled the Indians to promote him. He saw little playing time, with Hall of Famer Joe Gordon at second base, but learned how to speak English with the help of teammate Mike Garcia. Gordon retired after the 1950 slate, and manager Lou Boudreau penciled Avila into the vacant slot. Avila secured the starting job with 10 homers, 58 RBIs, and a .304 batting average.

Avila had decent speed and was a daring baserunner, finishing with double-digit stolen-base totals during four seasons. He was a skilled bunter as well, placing among the top three in sacrifices on six occasions. He also hit for average, capturing a batting crown in 1954, with a .341 mark. He played part of the season with a broken thumb. The city of Avila, California, named him honorary mayor that year.

During his prime years (1950–1955), Avila's lowest batting average was .272. Dizzy Dean once commented that Avila could be the next .400 hitter. "If I ever hit .400, they'd make me president of Mexico," Avila joked. Recognized as one of the top second basemen in the league, he was the first Mexican-born player to make the All-Star Team. He earned three selections during his career.

Avila appeared in the 1949 baseball film *The Kid from Cleveland*, alongside Cooperstown greats Bob Feller, Tris Speaker, and Hank Greenberg, among others. Greenberg, who served as Cleveland's general manager, was one of Avila's biggest advocates, commenting, "[Avila] has that extra something that makes a great hitter. Call it the competitive instinct. In a tough spot, I'm always glad to see Bobby Avila at the plate."

Avila had an off year in 1956, hitting just .224. While he rebounded in 1957, he began to share second-base responsibilities with Billy Moran the following year. Traded by the Indians prior to the 1959 campaign, he was waived by the Orioles and Red Sox before landing in Milwaukee. In 1960, he returned to the Mexican League and hit .333, while setting a league record for walks, with 124. It was his last pro season.

After retiring as a player, Avila purchased the Veracruz Eagles and aspired to the presidency of the Mexican League. His celebrity status helped him become mayor of Veracruz. Two Mexican League stadiums were named in his honor. He was elected to the Latino Baseball Hall of Fame in 2010.

Vinny Castilla

Third Base/Shortstop

Vinny Castilla was born in Oaxaca, located in the southwestern part of the country and renowned for its rich archaeological history. He completed his secondary education at the Carlos Gracita Institute and moved on to Benito Suarez University in Oaxaca. Castilla was playing for Saltillo of the Mexican League when the Braves purchased his contract in 1990. He later commented on his rise to the majors, saying, "Scouts were always looking for pitchers. They wanted another [Fernando] Valenzuela. So if you were a positional player, you could really get lost."

Castilla had stiff competition in Atlanta with Chipper Jones also vying for a spot at third base. In 1992, he was left unprotected in the Expansion Draft. The Rockies signed him despite protests from manager Bobby Cox. Braves assistant GM Chuck LaMar said of the transaction, "No one in the organization predicted [Castilla] would ever hit more than 15 home runs." Castilla began his major-league career at shortstop, moving to third base in 1995. An underrated defensive player, he led the NL in assists, double plays, putouts, and fielding percentage twice. His lifetime range factor is among the top marks of all time. But despite those impressive stats, he never captured a Gold Glove.

Castilla's breakthrough season came in 1995, when he hit 32 homers—the most ever by a Mexican-born player. He would surpass that mark four times. Prospering greatly in hitter-friendly Coors Field, he averaged 27 home runs per year during his nine seasons with the Rockies. He enjoyed his most productive campaign in 1998, when he gathered 206 hits (including 46 long balls) and 144 RBIs. His efforts were eclipsed by the dramatic home-run race between Mark McGwire and Sammy Sosa that year. Coupled with the ongoing Coors Field bias, Castilla ended up finishing 11th in Most Valuable Player voting.

The righty-swinging slugger earned two All-Star selections and three Silver Slugger Awards. If he had one weakness, it was the fact that he was slow afoot. He grounded into plenty of double plays and also struck out a lot, as power hitters often do. After a fourth consecutive 100-RBI campaign in 1999, Castilla was traded to Tampa Bay. He joined Greg Vaughn, Jose Canseco, and Fred McGriff to form a tandem dubbed the "Bay Bombers." The quartet performed below expectations, as Castilla was hit by injuries, ending up on the disabled list three times. Before the 2001 slate, he bragged that he would be the Comeback Player of the Year. He failed to back up the boast and ended up being released in May. The Astros picked up his contract, and he got back on track, slamming 12 homers in June and July. He finished the season with 25.

Traded to Atlanta in 2002, Castilla put up ordinary numbers for two straight seasons. Returning to Colorado in 2004, he led the league with 131 RBIs, while slamming 35 homers—his highest total in six years. Entering the 2005 campaign, he was 37 years old and nearing the end of his playing career. He announced his retirement after the 2007 Caribbean Series, taking a job as special assistant to Rockies GM Dan O'Dowd. He remained with the organization through 2015.

Castilla managed the Mexican national team in the 2007 Pan American Games, guiding the club to a bronze medal. In 2009, he piloted Mexico again, with less dramatic results. He later became a spokesman for Alliance Charities, which helps enrich the lives of children and families in need. Specifically, Castilla helped raised awareness about the importance of organ donorship. Castilla is the all-time leader among Mexican players in four major statistical categories—home runs, RBIs, extra-base hits, and total bases.

Jorge Orta

Second Base

Jorge Orta's father Pedro was a player of note in Cuba and Mexico. He helped the Cuban national team win an Amateur World Series in 1940. Seduced by a lucrative contract offer, Pedro joined the Mexican League in 1946. Born four years later in the city of Mazatlan, Jorge developed a passion for the sport. "Baseball has always been my life, from the very first when I was a boy growing up in Mexico," he told *Baseball Digest* in 1988.

Jorge made his professional debut at the age of 17, with Fresnillo Mineros of the Mexican Central League (a Class A circuit). He was a part-time player until 1971, when he hit .423 for Tuneros de San Luis Potosi. By that time, the White Sox had him on their radar, assigning him to the Knoxville Smokies in 1972. While Orta's fielding left something to be desired, he hit .316, with 41 runs scored, in 53 games. He would spend the rest of his career in the majors.

During his 16-year big-league tenure, Orta was almost always overshadowed by the higher-profile second basemen in the league, among them Rod Carew, Frank White, and Lou Whitaker. The White Sox were noncontenders during Orta's eight years in Chicago, and that also served to obscure his accomplishments. He accomplished little with a glove, compiling a lifetime fielding percentage below the league average. Statistical giant Bill James once rated Orta as the "worst-fielding second baseman per innings played among the top 250 guys in innings played at second base." But James also refers to Orta as an "excellent left-handed line-drive hitter" and saw fit to assign him an all-time ranking of 87th among players at his position.

Orta had good speed, gathering seven or more triples on five occasions. In 1975–1976, when his managers turned him loose on the basepaths, he stole 40 bases in 57 attempts. He enjoyed his peak years with the White Sox between 1974 and 1977, when he averaged 46 extra-base hits per year and hit at a cumulative .293 clip. His lowest RBI total in that span was 67.

After the 1979 slate, Orta opted to test the free-agent market. He spent two seasons with Cleveland, earning his second All-Star berth during the 1980 campaign. His first selection had come in 1975. After the strike-shortened 1981 campaign, he landed in Los Angeles, joining fellow countryman Fernando Valenzuela. The Dodgers lineup was loaded with stars, and Orta saw limited playing time. After a brief layover in Toronto, he was added to the Royals roster in 1984. Serving mostly as a designated hitter, he had his best season in years, hitting .298, with 50 RBIs. He would finish his career in Kansas City.

Orta is perhaps best remembered for the controversial play he was involved in during Game Six of the 1985 World Series. The Royals were trailing three games to two and were locked in a scoreless tie with the Cardinals through seven innings. When St. Louis broke through for a run, Orta was called upon to pinch hit for Pat Sheridan leading off the ninth. He hit a slow roller to first baseman Jack Clark, who fielded it and relayed to pitcher Todd Worrell in time. But umpire Don Denking-er blew the call. Although TV replays showed that Orta was out, um-pires were not allowed to review footage in those days. The inning continued to unravel for the Cardinals when Steve Balboni hit a catch-able foul pop that dropped between Clark and catcher Darrel Porter. On the next pitch, Balboni singled, sending Orta to second. While Orta was erased at third on a failed sacrifice bunt attempt, a passed ball, an intentional walk, and a two-run single followed. The Royals won, 2–1, and carried that momentum into Game Seven, which ended in an 11–0 blowout. It was the first world championship in Kansas City history. The consequences of Denkinger's blown call have been debated for years. In 1987, Balboni became the Royals' full-time DH, and Orta was released in June. It was his last major-league season.

Orta played in Italy during the 1994 slate, fashioning an uninspiring .241 batting average. He went on to a long career as a minor-league coach for the Astros, Reds, and Rangers. He managed the Martinsville Astros from 2001 to 2003. In the latter season, the club made it to the league finals but lost. Orta was elected to the Salon de la Fama (Mexi-can Professional Baseball Hall of Fame) in 1996.

Aurelio Rodriguez

Third Baseman

Aurelio Rodriguez was born in Cananea, a mining community in the northern part of the country near the U.S.–Mexican border. He began his professional career at the age of 17, with the Fresnillo Mineros of the Mexican Center League, drilling 25 homers while driving in 104 runs. The following season, he led the Mexican League with 16 triples and was signed by the Angels.

When Rodriguez arrived in the United States, he could barely speak English. He spent a couple of seasons bouncing up and down from the majors to the minors before the Angels installed him at third base full time. A 1970 trade landed him in Washington. The change of scenery suited him well, as he reached career-high marks in multiple offensive categories. In October of that year, he was dealt to the Tigers in a massive eight-player swap. He would spend nine seasons in Detroit, establishing himself as one of the best third basemen in the majors.

Rodriguez was never much of a hitter, compiling a lifetime .237 batting average. He had only moderate power and was slow afoot. But there were few who compared to him defensively. During his career, he led AL third basemen in assists, double plays, and fielding percentage twice apiece. His lifetime range factor per nine innings is second on the all-time list, behind Darrell Evans. His wizardry at the hot corner prompted one writer to remark, "Rodriguez could do it all defensively. He had lockdown hands and superior lateral movement. His range was so good, he played shortstop at times and played it acceptably." Hall of Famer George Brett once joked about Rodriguez, stating, "Remember that guy?! He would toy with you and pound the ball into his glove and you were still out by 10 feet."

Rodriguez's throws to first base actually had a rising action, prompting Yankees broadcaster Phil Rizzuto to comment repeatedly throughout the years, "There's that arm. If I had an arm like that . . ." Rodriguez's career coincided with those of Brooks Robinson, Graig Nettles, and Buddy Bell—three of the most defensively gifted third basemen in history. Aside from 1976, when Rodriguez finally won a Gold Glove, the award was monopolized by the aforementioned players for more than 20 years.

Off the field, Rodriguez had a warm, engaging personality. Tigers broadcaster Ernie Harwell described him as the "kind of person everyone took to." Rodriguez had a cultural impact in Detroit, often venturing into the community during the season to conduct baseball clinics or talk to young fans. He continued the practice even after his retirement. Tigers community relations director Fred Feliciano said, "[Rodriguez] was really the first prominent Hispanic figure in the Detroit community."

The slick-fielding third baseman is remembered by some for his 1969 Topps baseball card, which features a picture of Angels batboy Leonard Garcia. For years, the cause of the error was a source of debate. As it turns out, the players union advised members not to pose for pictures with Topps photographers in 1968, after the company failed to adequately compensate subjects. Topps representatives were forced to dig into their archives, where a picture of the batboy had been mislabeled. The card went into circulation, and the mistake was not even spotted until 1973.

Rodriguez's career in Detroit came to an end before the 1980 campaign, when he was traded to the Padres. He hit just .200 in 89 games and was sold to the Yankees, who found him to be a useful retread. In three postseason series with New York, Rodriguez hit .389. His .417 mark in the 1981 World Series against the Dodgers was second on the club to Lou Piniella. He made several dazzling stops at third base as well. Rodriguez would later play for the White Sox and Orioles before falling from the major-league ranks in 1983. He continued in the Mexican leagues for several years, finally retiring at the age of 41. He was inducted into the Salon de la Fama (the Mexican Professional Baseball Hall of Fame) in 1995.

In September 2000, Rodriguez was in Detroit for a card show. While walking up the street with a female friend, a car veered onto the sidewalk and hit both of them before striking a utility pole. The 52-year-old Rodriguez was pinned under the car. He died later at Henry Ford Hospital. The woman behind the wheel was operating the vehicle with a suspended license. She had been instructed not to drive due to an aneurism she had suffered years earlier. The condition directly caused the accident, as she suffered a seizure at the wheel. She was charged with felony manslaughter and ended up on probation. Rodriguez's funeral was attended by Mexican president Ernesto Zedillo. His tomb is located inside Emilio Ibarra Almada, a stadium in Los Mochis, Sinaloa. In 2012, he was elected to the Latino Baseball Hall of Fame.

Fernando Valenzuela

Pitcher

No Mexican-born pitcher has ever accomplished as much as Fernando Valenzuela during his 17-year career. Entering his third major-league season, he was already a world champion, Rookie of the Year, and Cy Young Award recipient. Completing a stellar resume, he added a no-hitter several years later.

Valenzuela was one of 12 children born to a farming family in Etchohuaquila, a small town in the state of Sonora. Although his age was officially listed as 19 in his major-league debut, he was believed to be much older. He began his professional career in 1977, with Mayos de Navojoa of the Mexican Pacific League. He moved to the Mexican Central League (at the Class A level) the following year. When the circuit was absorbed into the Liga Mexicana de Beisbol in 1979, Fernando was elevated to Triple-A status.

The Dodgers felt that Valenzuela would be more effective with an off-speed pitch in his repertoire and assigned pitcher Bobby Castilla to teach him how to throw a screwball. It turned his career around. He led the Texas League with 162 strikeouts in 1980, earning a late-season call to Los Angeles.

Many words have been used to describe the affable left-hander throughout the years, among them "pudgy," "jovial," and "moonfaced." Known for his flamboyant windup and skyward glance before delivery, one writer remarks that Valenzuela was "built like a bull on its hind legs." A durable performer, he carried the nickname "El Toro," which literally translates to "The Bull."

After allowing no earned runs in his debut, Valenzuela followed with a spectacular rookie campaign, gathering legions of fans worldwide. The international movement known as "Fernandomania" was born in April 1981, when an injury to staff ace Jerry Reuss made Valenzuela an Opening Day starter. His five-hit shutout against the Astros turned a few heads, but his next seven starts made him a celebrity. From April 9 to May 14, he tallied 8 wins, 7 complete games, and 5 shutouts. He finished the strike-shortened regular season at 13–7, before winning a game in each round of the playoffs, including a gutsy 147-pitch effort in the World Series on short rest. After receiving baseball's top pitching honor, the hurler admitted he had never heard of Cy Young. "I do not know who he was," said Fernando, "but a trophy carries his name so he must be someone very special to baseball."

By the time his rookie season was over, Valenzuela had become an inspiration to Hispanic people in both Mexico and the United States. According to one researcher, he "changed the face of baseball in Los Angeles." By the mid-1980s, Latinos comprised roughly 40 percent of paid admissions. And Valenzuela's sphere of influence had spread to three continents. "He created interest in baseball among people who did not care about baseball," wrote one scribe.

Whenever Valenzuela warmed up before home games, the giddy refrain of Abba's "Fernando" could be heard blaring from the PA system. Although his starts were festive occasions for the hordes of Latinos who flocked to the ballpark, opponents had far less reason to be cheerful. From 1981 to 1987, Valenzuela won more games than any NL hurler. He worked more than 250 innings in six consecutive seasons and completed 10 or more of his starts on half a dozen occasions. He pitched in five All-Star Games during that span, allowing no runs. In the 1986 Midsummer Classic, he struck out five batters in a row, tying a record set 32 years earlier by another screwball master—Hall of Famer Carl Hubbell.

In 1988, the heavy workload took its toll, as Fernando's arm went dead. He lasted two more seasons in LA, cementing his legacy with a no-hitter against the Cardinals in 1990. Released in the spring of 1991, he held a long-standing grudge against the Dodgers, refusing to attend home games or participate in events even though he lived just minutes from the stadium. When the Dodgers invited him to spring training in 1999, he refused.

Valenzuela traveled extensively after LA cast him adrift. He pitched poorly for the Angels in 1991 before joining the Mexican League the following year. Between 1993 and 1997, he wore four different uniforms. His best effort came in 1996, when he posted a 13–8 record for the Padres. After nearly a decade of inactivity, he returned to the Mexican Pacific League, going 6–3, with an unwieldy ERA in portions of two seasons. He called it quits for good after that.

Valenzuela coached for the Mexican national team in the 2006, 2009, and 2013 World Baseball Classics. In 2003, he put his differences with the Dodgers aside, accepting a job as a color analyst for the Dodgers' Spanish network. He received numerous accolades throughout the years, being inducted into the Hispanic Heritage Baseball Museum Hall of Fame and the Caribbean Baseball Hall of Fame. He was also named as one of three starters on MLB's Latin Legends Team. In 2015, Fernando officially became a U.S. citizen, joining 8,000 others at a ceremony in downtown Los Angeles.

NOTABLE ACTIVE PLAYERS

Yovani Gallardo

Pitcher

Yovani Gallardo was born in Penjamillo de Degollado, located in the Mexican state of Michoacan. His family moved to Fort Worth, Texas, when he was four years old. Gallardo's father and cousins played in an adult recreational baseball league, and Yovani developed a love of the sport. He started playing at about age 10. By the time he reached high school, he was mowing down batters with remarkable precision. During his senior year at Trimble Tech, he struck out 25 opponents in an 11-inning start. He had planned on attending college at Texas Christian University but changed his mind when the Brewers selected him in the 2004 MLB Draft.

Gallardo spent portions of four seasons in the minors before getting called to Milwaukee in 2007. In his debut game, he turned in a quality start versus the Giants and ended up with a win. He finished the season at 9–5, with a 3.67 ERA.

In March 2008, Gallardo tore the lateral meniscus in his left knee. He returned to action in April and tore his ACL during an early May start. He was out until September. He faced the Phillies twice in the National League Division Series, and despite being charged with no earned runs in seven innings of work, he was saddled with a loss.

Gallardo's most productive stretch to date occurred between 2009 and 2013. He averaged 14 wins per year in that span, peaking at 17 victories in 2011. Gallardo has five pitches in his arsenal. His fastball generally travels in the mid- to low 90s. He complements it with a slider, curve, cutter, and changeup. He is a strikeout pitcher, sometimes generating high pitch counts. He has averaged more than eight strike-outs per nine innings but rarely goes deep into games. Entering the 2017 slate, he had just four complete games and three shutouts to his credit.

Gallardo hits well for a pitcher. He had gathered 21 doubles and 12 homers in 424 at-bats at the time of this writing. His best offensive showing came in 2010, when he hit .254, with eight extra-base hits and 10 RBIs. Those numbers earned him a Silver Slugger Award.

Traded to Texas in 2015, Gallardo attained a goal his mother had set for him as a boy. "I achieved the one thing my mom wanted me to achieve, and that was to play for the Rangers," he said excitedly. "I can't believe it. It's something I've always wanted to do." He posted the lowest ERA among Texas starters that year, at 3.42, and finished second to staffmate Colby Lewis with 13 wins as the Rangers advanced to the ALDS. Gallardo started the first game against Toronto and got the win. As of 2017, his lifetime postseason ERA was 2.32.

Gallardo didn't stay in Texas for long. Granted free agency before the 2016 campaign, he signed with the Orioles. In April, he was placed on the disabled list due to tendinitis in his right shoulder. He finished the season with 6 wins and a 5.42 ERA. He is one of five Mexican-born players to win 100 games in the majors. He may soon be joined by fellow countryman Jorge De La Rosa on that list.

Joakim Soria

Pitcher

Joakim Soria was born in Monclova, Mexico's principal producer of steel. Signed by the Dodgers at the age of 18, he was released three seasons later. The Padres held his contract until the Royals acquired him in the 2006 Rule 5 Draft. Soria appeared in two different Mexican leagues and was given multiple trials as a starter. In 2006, he tossed the third perfect game in the history of the Mexican Pacific League, joining Vicente Romo and Jesus Moreno. By 2007, the Royals felt he was ready for prime time.

In his debut, Soria filled various bullpen roles, serving as a closer, setup man, and middle reliever. In addition to the 17 saves he gathered, he was unofficially credited with nine holds. His 2.48 ERA in 62 appearances landed him among the top 10 in Rookie of the Year voting.

Soria's follow-up season was spectacular. He assembled a string of 13 consecutive saves, breaking a team record held by Al Hrabosky. Named to the All-Star Team, he pitched 1.2 scoreless frames in a game that was ultimately won by the AL in 15 innings. Soria finished second in the league with 42 saves that year, while accruing a marvelously efficient 1.60 ERA.

Soria's success continued in 2009 and 2010. He posted a cumulative ERA of 1.97, while recording 73 saves. In the latter campaign, he received his second All-Star selection, along with Cy Young consideration.

After a subpar season in 2011, it was discovered that Soria had damaged the UCL in his right elbow. He missed the entire 2012 campaign and ended up signing with the Rangers. He didn't return to form until 2015, when he compiled a 3–1 record, with 24 saves and a 2.53 ERA for the Tigers and Pirates.

During the offseason, Soria returned to the Royals. Used primarily as a setup man, he struggled with control problems at times. He hit a rough patch in late-July, but got back on track the following month with 11 consecutive scoreless appearances. He finished the season with 5 wins and 20 holds.

A right-hander, Soria relies heavily on a standard fastball and a cut fastball, both of which consistently hit the low to mid-90s on the radar gun. In addition, he uses a slider, changeup, and curve, which is even slower than his change, at roughly 70 miles per hour. Prior to the 2011 slate, Soria picked up the nickname the "Mexicutioner." He publicly stated that he wanted the nickname dropped due to the persistent violence in his native country. He is the all-time saves leader among Mexican-born players.

7

COLOMBIA

ORIGINS OF BASEBALL IN COLOMBIA

Located in the northwestern region of South America, Colombia is one of the most ethnically blended nations in the world. It is geographically diverse as well, with portions of the country comprising the Amazon rainforest and Caribbean/Pacific coastlines. A major producer of oil and exporter of emeralds, Colombia currently supplies the United States with a majority of its cut flowers.

Although soccer, cycling, and motor sports have a larger following, Colombians have a passion for baseball as well. The national team, which recently qualified for the 2017 World Baseball Classic, has a rich tradition dating back to 1944, when the club competed in its first World Cup. To date, Colombia has won two gold, two silver, and a pair of bronze medals in World Cup action.

The first Colombian player to reach the majors was Luis Castro, who made his debut with the Philadelphia A's in 1902. While Castro's family originated in Colombia, there has been some debate as to whether Luis was born there himself. He attended Manhattan College in New York City when it also served as a high school. Although he later claimed to have been born in New York, it is likely he did so in response to a prevailing prejudice against immigrants. Recently uncovered evidence strongly suggests that Castro landed in NYC with his family during the 1880s. Based on the year of his birth, this would place him at elementary or middle school age when he arrived. His baseball career was somewhat unremarkable, spanning one major-league season and nine minor-league campaigns. His best effort came in 1903, when he played for the Baltimore Orioles of the Eastern League alongside Hall of Famers Hughie Jennings and Wilbert Robinson. He hit .328, with 21 triples in 111 games.

The Colombian Professional Baseball League was established in 1948, and currently has six teams. The season stretches from October to January and ends with a best-of-seven series between the top two clubs. Colombian ballparks are rather small, with the largest, Estadio Once de Noviembre (located in Cartagena), having a seating capacity of 12,000. Given that professional baseball is relatively new to the country (at least in comparison to other Latin American nations), Colombia's contributions to the major leagues have been minimal. Entering the 2016 campaign, fewer than 25 Colombian-born players have worn big-league uniforms. Two of those players had distinguished careers. A handful of standouts are active in the majors today, at least two of whom bear mentioning.

MAJOR STARS OF THE PAST

Orlando Cabrera

Shortstop

Orlando Cabrera was born and raised in Cartagena, the capital of the northern-lying department of Bolivar. His older brother Jolbert got a head start in the minors, although Orlando appeared in the big leagues first and had a far more distinguished career. Signed by the Expos at the age of 18, Orlando hit .315 in his Gulf Coast League debut. With Wil Cordero and Mark Grudzielanek at shortstop, Montreal waited until 1999 to promote Cabrera to full-time status. An ankle injury ended his season in early August, but the Expos were sufficiently impressed, handing him the job again in 2000.

Cabrera had excellent range and a steady glove at short, leading both leagues in assists and fielding percentage on multiple occasions. He won two Gold Gloves. He was intimately familiar with the artificial surface at Olympic Stadium, expertly playing the erratic hops and using the turf to aid his throws to first base.

In July 2004, Cabrera was involved in a four-team trade that sent him to Boston. He had big shoes to fill there, replacing the popular but frequently injured Nomar Garciaparra. In 58 regular-season games, he hit .294, with 26 extra-base hits. The Red Sox had been stonewalled by the Yankees in postseason play for many years, and Cabrera helped end the curse, scoring five runs and driving in five more against the Bombers in the American League Championship Series. He added three more RBIs during a Series sweep of the Cardinals, which ended a championship drought in Beantown dating back to 1918.

Cabrera appeared throughout the batting order, spending the least amount of time in the ninth slot. He most often appeared second, compiling a lifetime .290 average in that capacity. He had moderate power, peaking at 17 homers in 2003, and gathering 40 or more doubles on four occasions. He also possessed remarkable speed, finishing with double-digit stolen-base totals in 10 straight seasons. He had a knack for making productive outs, leading the league in sacrifice flies three times. He was second or third during two other campaigns.

The Red Sox failed to resign Cabrera in 2005, and he was faced with the task of replacing another tremendously popular player—Anaheim's David Eckstein. He played well with the Angels, earning a Gold Glove in 2007—the first by an Angels shortstop in 40 years. In 2006, he compiled a 63-game on-base streak, among the top five streaks of its kind. He also executed a successful steal of home that season, scoring without a throw.

In 2008, Cabrera began a brief stint with the White Sox. He was extremely unhappy in Chicago, generating controversy by arguing with management, snubbing reporters, and hounding staff in the press box to have errors overturned. During the first game of the American League Division Series, he kicked dirt at Tampa Bay pitcher Grant Balfour. Cabrera traveled extensively after that, wearing five different uniforms in a three-year span. In Cincinnati, he showed his lighter side by dressing up as a batboy and fulfilling the role for one game while on the disabled list.

In 2011, Cabrera became a naturalized U.S. citizen, and in 2012 he announced his retirement during a radio interview. He was invited to play for the Colombian national team in the 2013 World Baseball Classic. Cabrera is the all-time leader among Colombian-born major leaguers in doubles and triples. He collected more than 2,000 hits during his career and is second to Edgar Renteria (whom he played against in the 2004 World Series) in that category.

Edgar Renteria

Shortstop

Edgar Renteria was a member of the upstart 1997 Marlins, who surprised the baseball world by becoming the first wild card team to win a World Series. More than 60 percent of the players on Florida's roster that year were younger than 30. Renteria's game-winning RBI in the bottom of the ninth of the opener of the National League Division Series prompted him to proclaim, "This is the happiest moment of my life!" The declaration was a bit premature, as he ended up delivering a bases-loaded single in the 11th inning of the World Series finale, giving the Marlins a championship. He was later voted Colombia's "man of the year" in an opinion poll and awarded the nation's highest honor—the San Carlos Cross of the Order of the Great Knight. While it was a tough act to follow, Renteria had several more great seasons in the majors.

Renteria grew up in Barranquilla, located in one of Colombia's smallest states (known as "departments"). He was just 16 years old when he entered the Marlins minor-league system. Despite his diminutive age, he hit .288 in his Gulf Coast League debut. After spending portions of five seasons on the farm, he was invited to Florida in May 1996. His 22-game hitting streak helped elevate him to second place in Rookie of the Year voting, behind Todd Hollandsworth.

Renteria had many talents. Blessed with good speed, he stole at least 17 bases in eight consecutive seasons. He also hit for average, peaking at .332 in 2007, and retiring with a respectable .286 lifetime mark. He was a three-time Silver Slugger Award recipient. Defensively, he was adept around second base and had a strong arm, capturing back-to-back Gold Gloves in 2002 and 2003.

Renteria didn't stay in Florida for long. The front office staged a dramatic fire sale after the 1997 championship season, and he ended up with the Cardinals in 1999. A stable presence in the lineup, he helped the club reach the postseason four times. This included a World Series appearance in 2004, which ended in a sweep at the hands of the Red Sox. The Fall Classic was often Renteria's finest hour. He hit .333 in the 2004 edition and captured Most Valuable Player honors in the 2010 Series while playing for the Giants. His fifth-inning homer in Game Two of that Series held up as the game-winner. In Game Five, he drove in all three of San Francisco's runs as the Giants clinched.

After the 2004 slate, Renteria became a gun for hire, spending time with the Red Sox, Braves, Tigers, and aforementioned Giants. In 2011, the five-time All-Star took a dramatic pay cut, signing with the Reds. He sat out a significant portion of the season, and his offensive numbers tapered off. Although multiple teams expressed interest in him before the 2012 campaign, he declined the offers. In March 2013, his retirement was made official.

Among Colombian-born players who have reached the majors, Renteria is the statistical leader in runs scored (1,200), hits (2,327), home runs (140), RBIs (923), and stolen bases (294). He also has the highest batting average of players with a minimum of 1,000 at-bats. He is likely to hang on to those records for quite some time.

NOTABLE ACTIVE PLAYERS

Jose Quintana

Pitcher

In June 2016, sportswriter Jim Margalus posted a facetious Cooperstown plaque online "honoring" Jose Quintana. It read as follows:

> Jose Guillermo Quintana "Poor Jose" 2012–2030. Talented left-hander who rose from obscurity to befuddle hitters with impeccable command over 19 seasons despite lack of run support. Only starter enshrined in Cooperstown with a losing record. MLB record-holder for no decisions, or "Quintana Wins," as they are now known.

Although Margalus was putting the proverbial cart ahead of the horse, he had a point.

Through 2016, Quintana had a 46-46 record with a serviceable 3.42 ERA. He had held opponents to a collective .258 batting average. Forty percent of his starts were no decisions and he had been staked to 2 runs or less in more than a third of his appearances.

Quintana hails from Arjona, located in the northern department of Bolivar. Signed by the Mets in 2006, he started his pro career in the Venezuelan Summer League at the age of 17. Released in 2007 after violating Major League Baseball's drug policy, he was signed by the Yankees and subsequently released in 2011, despite his 10–2 record in the Florida State League. The White Sox scooped him up and promoted him the following year.

Quintana has command of several pitches. He relies heavily on his four-seam fastball, which typically travels at about 93 miles per hour. He also uses a curve, change, and cutter. A scouting report on Quintana states that his cutter is "thrown at a speed that's borderline unfair" and is an "extreme fly ball pitch" with "good rise." Quintana has pinpoint control, averaging just two walks per nine innings during his four-plus seasons in the majors.

Since 2012, Quintana has won 10 games in a season just once, largely due to inadequate run support. He has finished among the top 10 in starts three times and ERA on two occasions. He is also a fine defensive pitcher, posting two errorless seasons. In 2016, he was finally recognized as an All-Star. He pitched a scoreless fifth inning in a game won by the American League, 4–2. Nearly 60 percent of his lifetime appearances have been quality starts.

Julio Teheran

Pitcher

Born in Cartagena, Julio Teheran was 17 years old when he threw his first professional pitch for Danville of the Appalachian League. His uncle was a Braves scout and helped negotiate an $850,000 contract. Although he got hit hard in his 2008 Danville debut, Teheran was ranked ninth among Braves prospects. He improved at every level of minor-league play, working his way up to an overall rating of fifth. He appeared briefly with Atlanta in 2011, and again in 2012, before becoming a permanent member of the rotation the following year.

In his first full season, Teheran made 30 starts, winning 14 games, while fashioning a superb 3.20 ERA. His strikeout-to-walk ratio was among the top 10 in the National League. Showing off his superior defensive skills, he handled 37 chances without an error. Recognized for his efforts, he finished fifth in Rookie of the Year voting.

Teheran's follow-up season was even better. He lowered his ERA by more than 30 points and posted a 14–13 record despite questionable run support from the sub-.500 Braves. Teheran received his first All-Star selection, although he didn't appear in the game.

In 2015, Teheran remained the ace of the Braves staff. On a club that lost 95 games, the right-hander still managed to win 58 percent of his decisions. While he yielded a career-high 90 earned runs, he averaged close to eight strikeouts per nine innings and gave up far fewer hits than innings pitched.

The Braves were a mediocre team in 2016 and Teheran's won/loss record suffered because of it. He posted a 7–10 record in spite of his 3.21 ERA. He was strapped with a loss or no-decision in a significant number of quality starts. In one particularly frustrating outing, he pitched eight scoreless innings in a game the Braves lost due to an 11th-inning bullpen lapse. Although trade rumors abounded at the All-Star break, the Braves hung onto their ace.

Teheran's favorite pitch is his four-seam fastball, which averages 92 miles per hour. He complements it with a two-seamer, slider, and change—all of which travel much slower. Occasionally, Teheran throws a screwball, which frustrates hitters at 65 miles per hour. He has an excellent move to first and has picked off 22 runners over the last four seasons. His 14 pickoffs in 2013–2014 were the most by any pitcher during that span. His selection to the All-Star Team in 2016 was the second of his career.

8

NICARAGUA

ORIGINS OF BASEBALL IN NICARAGUA

Located in Central America between Costa Rica and Honduras, there are roughly 6 million inhabitants of Nicaragua. According to one source, nearly all of them play baseball. A writer from the *Toronto Star* observes, "To say Nicaraguans are baseball crazy seems ludicrously inadequate. The game is part of the air people breathe. The crack of the bat permeates hot, tropical nights."

The game was introduced in the nineteenth century by a U.S. retailer named Adolf Adlersberg, who supplied locals with equipment transported from New Orleans. Teams were created, with the first official game taking place in 1891, between Managua and Granada. The first continuous team was founded by Carter Donaldson, a U.S. consul, in 1904. The U.S. Marines helped popularize the sport as well.

Professional baseball was played in Nicaragua until the late 1960s, when financial constraints and political unrest brought the sport to a temporary halt. It returned in the 1970s, with the national team capturing a bronze medal in the Intercontinental Cup. To date, the Nicaraguan team has claimed seven silver and 10 bronze medals in tournament play. The club has never qualified for the World Baseball Classic, however, despite multiple attempts.

Although the policy in Nicaragua has long been to discourage the recruitment of players to the major leagues, more than a dozen Nicaraguans have made it to "The Show." Only one has made a lasting impression on the sport. His biography is included in this chapter.

MAJOR STAR OF THE PAST

Dennis Martinez

Pitcher

A model of durability, Dennis Martinez began his major-league career at the age of 22 and pitched until he was in his mid-40s. He made four All-Star appearances after his 35th birthday and reached the 200-inning mark in nine seasons—six of them consecutive. By the time he appeared in his final game, he was a grandfather.

Martinez was the first Nicaraguan-born player to reach the majors. While his 245 lifetime victories (the most by a Latin American pitcher) are a triumph in themselves, the resilient right-hander won a personal battle against alcoholism early in his career. After establishing himself as one of the most reliable Orioles pitchers during the late 1970s, he began to lose his form. "Coming to this country from Nicaragua, learning a new language, the different lifestyle, it was a lot of pressure," Martinez told a *Los Angeles Times* reporter in 1987. "Honestly, the way I reacted to it wasn't good. Nobody could tell me what to do. I was a big shot. Those things can destroy you, send you downhill." Saddened by the civil war in his native country and the death of his father, Martinez's drinking nearly spiraled out of control. But he entered a rehabilitation program before the 1984 campaign and got sober.

Martinez's home of Granada is one of Nicaragua's most populous cities. It lies on the western shore of Lake Nicaragua near the Pacific Ocean. Martinez was the last of seven children. With 10 years separating him from the next youngest sibling, he described his childhood as lonely. By his own report, he was a "rascal" who "grew up in the streets." He remembered playing pickup games using balls made from socks. He didn't grip a real baseball until the age of 13. He started out as an infielder. Eventually converted to a pitcher, he led his team, Prego Junior, to a juvenile championship. He moved on to the First Division—an amateur summer league—in 1972. In August of that year, he helped the Nicaraguan national team win a bronze medal in the Amateur World Series. The following year, the Nicaraguan squad took a silver medal, and Martinez was signed by the Orioles.

From 1977 to 1982, Martinez posted an 81–55 record. In 1979, he led the American League with 18 complete games. During the strike-shortened 1981 campaign, he paced the loop with 14 wins. But as he descended into alcoholism, his pitching suffered. For three straight seasons, he posted an ERA above the 5.00 mark. In 1986, the Orioles gave up on him, dealing him to Montreal. It turned his career around.

In seven full seasons with the Expos, Martinez won 97 games—an average of 14 per year. He made three consecutive All-Star appearances from 1990 to 1992. His best season came in 1991, when he led the National League in complete games (9) and shutouts (5), while capturing an ERA title with a 2.39 mark. The most memorable moment of that season occurred on July 28, when Martinez pitched a perfect game against the Dodgers. The Los Angeles lineup was loaded with dangerous hitters that day, including sluggers Darryl Strawberry and Eddie Murray. Martinez helped his own cause with a spectacular play on a bunt by speedy second baseman Juan Samuel. He used just 95 pitches to complete the gem. Martinez remembered feeling a little anxious and isolated when his teammates avoided him in the dugout as the game progressed (a customary practice during no-hitters). "I was looking for somebody, anybody, to come up beside me and talk to me," he said.

Before the 1994 campaign, Martinez signed with the Indians. He was credited with the win that clinched the pennant for Cleveland the following year. Then, with his team facing elimination in Game Six of the 1995 World Series, he pitched 4.2 scoreless innings. It wasn't enough, as the Braves emerged with a 1–0 win. Martinez made his final postseason appearance with Atlanta in 1998, allowing no runs in four National League Championship Series assignments.

Shortly after his 40th birthday, Martinez finished first in a popularity poll in Nicaragua and was encouraged to run for president. He chose not to but carried the nickname "El Presidente" thereafter. He retired as a player at the end of the 1998 campaign and managed the Nicaraguan national team in the 1999 Pan American Games. He also piloted the national squad in the 2011 World Cup and 2013 World Baseball Classic qualifiers. He was elected to the Latino Baseball Hall of Fame and the Canadian Baseball Hall of Fame. A baseball stadium in Managua bears his name.

9

CURACAO

ORIGINS OF BASEBALL IN CURACAO

The island territory of Curacao is located in the South Caribbean Sea roughly 40 miles off the Venezuelan coast. A constituent country of the Netherlands, it was formerly a member of the Netherlands Antilles, a collection of island territories. The union was dissolved in October 2010. Curacao includes the main island and another uninhabited atoll known as Klein Curacao. The territory spans approximately 170 square miles and has a population of about 170,000.

Baseball was introduced to the Netherlands in 1911, by an English teacher named J. C. Grase, after a visit to the United States. Dutch children turned to baseball in defiance of German occupiers during World War II, and the game caught on. Today, it places a distant second to soccer in popularity but flourishes in overseas territories—especially Curacao.

Curacao is known more for windsurfing. Baseball is not an official high-school sport, nor are there any baseball academies on the island (at least there weren't at the time of this writing). Most games take place on weekends in organized amateur leagues. Nevertheless, the Netherlands Antilles team won a Little League World Series in 2004. By 2014, seven Curacaoans were in the majors. The most successful by far was Andruw Jones.

MAJOR STAR OF THE PAST

Andruw Jones

Center Fielder

Early in his career, there were those who believed that Andruw Jones was a one-hit wonder. Signed by the Braves as a nondrafted free agent in 1993, he was later named Minor League Player of the Year by *Baseball America*. Called to Atlanta in August 1996, he hit just .217 in 31 games but still made the postseason roster. At 19 years of age, he hit home runs in consecutive innings during Game One of the World Series, replacing Mickey Mantle as the youngest player to go deep in a Fall Classic. He finished the Series with a .400 batting average and six RBIs, making him an overnight sensation. Jones's first full season was disappointing. He hit .231 and posted a fielding percentage below the league average. While he had his share of detractors, he would prove them all wrong, blossoming into one of the premier outfielders in the majors.

Jones grew up in Willemstad, Curacao's capital city. His father Henry played for the Royal Scorpions during the 1960s and 1970s. Known for his speed, Henry taught his son the finer points of the game. Curacao had never been a hotbed for major-league talent, and Andruw received only modest attention from scouts. The Braves ended up signing him at a bargain basement price. Proving he was worth every penny and then some, Jones worked his way up to a number-one rating among major-league prospects.

In 1998, Jones began improving in all areas of the game. He captured his first Gold Glove that year and retained the honor for 10 consecutive seasons. Only Willie Mays was more decorated in center field. Jones had a habit of positioning himself shallow and making difficult catches look routine. His persistent grin and casual manner led some to believe that he wasn't taking his job seriously.

From 1998 to 2007, Jones hit no fewer than 26 homers. His lowest RBI total in that span was 84. He reached the peak of his offensive prowess in 2005, when he led the National League with 51 homers and 128 ribbies. He finished second to Albert Pujols in Most Valuable Player voting. He was the fourth youngest player to reach the 300-

homer threshold, surpassed by Ken Griffey Jr., Alex Rodriguez, and Jimmie Foxx.

Traded to the Dodgers in 2008, Jones's numbers began to rapidly decline. He remained a defensive asset to each of the three clubs he played for between 2009 and 2012. When the Yankees opted not to renew his contract before the 2013 slate, he signed with the Rakuten Golden Eagles of the Japanese Pacific League. He helped the club to a Japan Series title with 26 homers and 94 RBIs as a designated hitter/first baseman.

Jones still ranks among the top 10 Braves players of all time in multiple statistical categories. In 17 postseason series with Atlanta, he carried his weight offensively, scoring and driving in a combined total of 76 runs. Despite his efforts, the Braves never won a World Series with him in the lineup. Jones waited until the spring of 2016 to announce his retirement. In March of that year, he was hired by the Braves as special assistant to baseball operations.

NOTABLE ACTIVE PLAYERS

Kenley Jansen

Pitcher

Kenley Jansen was born in Willemstad. He was the youngest of three boys. Jansen's father worked construction until a stroke left him incapacitated. Jansen's mother worked in the travel industry to support the family.

Jansen excelled at baseball from an early age. In 2004, the Dodgers signed him as an amateur free agent. He began his minor-league career as a catcher and, after demonstrating his strong arm, was converted to pitching. Beginning in 2009, he was groomed as a reliever. He took to the role so naturally that he became a fixture in the Dodgers bullpen by 2010. In his last 11 appearances of the season, he allowed just four hits and no runs. He finished the year with a 0.67 ERA.

Jansen didn't officially qualify as a rookie until 2011. He set a single-season record when he averaged more than 16 strikeouts per nine innings. His 2.85 ERA in 51 appearances drew some Rookie of the Year consideration. He finished seventh in the balloting.

Jansen has a three-pitch repertoire that features an explosive cutter that has been known to travel in the upper 90s. His sinker generates a high number of swings and misses in the 95-mile-per-hour range, while his slider travels at a glacial pace by comparison, at 82 miles per hour.

Jansen began the 2013 season as a setup man but ended up replacing Brandon League as the Dodgers' principal closer. He was excellent in the role, finishing the year with 28 saves and a 1.88 ERA. In the playoffs, he shut down the Braves in three National League Division Series appearances. He fared moderately well in the National League Championship Series, although he was hit hard in game five. Fortunately, the Dodgers had the offense to back him up that day. Through 2015, Los Angeles had won eight of the 10 postseason games Jansen appeared in.

By 2014, Jansen had emerged as one of the premier closers in the NL. He finished third in saves, with 44, during the 2014 slate and seventh the following year, with 36. He almost certainly would have collected more had he not undergone surgery, which shortened his season. In 2016, Jansen made his first All-Star appearance and collected a career-high 47 saves. Against the Cubs in the NLCS, he struck out 10 and allowed just one hit in 6.1 innings of work.

Because of his role as a closer, Jansen rarely gets a chance to hit. When the opportunity arises, he knows how to swing the bat. He hit .229 in 316 minor-league games, with 58 extra-base hits and 97 RBIs.

Jonathan Schoop

Second Base

Jonathan Schoop was born in Willemstad. He was on the Curacaoan team that won the Little League World Series in 2004. A thin, undersized kid, he eventually grew into a 6-foot-1, 225-pound slugger. He played against fellow Curacaoan major leaguer Andrelton Simmons while growing up. "He was always a good player," said Simmons in 2014. "But playing with him last year for the Dutch national team, I really saw what he was capable of on the big stage." In the 2013 World Baseball Classic, Schoop tied for the team lead in homers and RBIs.

Schoop was discovered in 2008 by Orioles scout Ernst Meyer. He bounced around several minor leagues, attaining a high ranking at the lower levels. In 2011, Frederick Keys manager Orlando Gomez moved Schoop from shortstop to second base. Faced with the task of learning a new position, Schoop's stock dropped considerably. Prior to 2014, *Baseball America* had assigned him a ranking of number 82.

Although Schoop plays strong defense and has considerable power at the plate, he doesn't always hit for high average. Such was the case during his first full season in the majors. After a September call-up in 2013, he was the Orioles' starting second baseman the following year. He posted the fourth-highest fielding percentage in the American League but hit just .209. He also struck out with alarming regularity.

Schoop made numerous adjustments in 2015, raising his average by 70 points while cutting his strikeouts nearly in half. He gathered 32 extra-base hits in 86 games, helping the O's to a division title—their first in more than a decade. Schoop hit .300 in the American League Division Series but fizzled in the American League Championship Series against the Royals, which ended in a Baltimore loss.

In 2016, Schoop was among the league leaders in assists, fielding percentage, and range factor. He gathered 64 extra-base hits (including a career-high 25 homers) and drove-in 82 runs. After a game-winning RBI against the Angels, he told a reporter, "The more at-bats you get the more you learn. I wasn't trying to do too much. My first year, the situation, I would have tried to hit a sac [fly] or something. Now I said let me get a pitch I can hit hard somewhere and find a hole." The Orioles hope that Schoop can keep finding those holes as his career progresses.

Andrelton Simmons

Shortstop

Andrelton Simmons was born in Mundo Nobo. Although he was also fairly skilled at basketball and soccer, he ultimately chose to pursue a career on the diamond. He played alongside future major leaguers Kenley Jansen and Didi Gregorius while growing up and received little attention from scouts until he began to excel at Western Oklahoma College. He helped the team to a Division II World Series berth in

2010. Enamored with his potential, the Braves drafted him in the second round that year.

Simmons had a relatively brief minor-league career that spanned portions of three seasons. He hit at a cumulative .299 pace before earning a call to Atlanta in June 2012. The Braves advanced to the wild-card round with Simmons in the lineup and handed him the starting shortstop job the following year.

During his four-plus seasons in the majors, Simmons has drawn glowing praise from contemporaries for his defensive wizardry. Longtime Atlanta beat writer David O'Brien proclaimed, "I've never seen any shortstop as good defensively as Andrelton Simmons, and I can say that with absolute certainty." Hall of Famer Don Sutton, now an Atlanta broadcaster, agreed with that assessment. "He has things you're born with," said Sutton. "I think you can only refine those things. . . . He has a sense that's more astounding than a sixth sense in that he does things you can't anticipate."

Entering the 2016 slate, Simmons had led the league in putouts three times and assists twice. He earned two consecutive Gold Gloves and was a finalist for the award in 2015, before narrowly losing out to Brandon Crawford of the Giants. He was having another excellent defensive campaign in 2016 before a hand injury sidelined him for more than a month. He returned to action in mid-June, finishing among the top five in fielding percentage and range factor.

Typically appearing in the lower third of the batting order, Simmons is capable of hitting home runs. He peaked at 17 long balls in 2013, but has not finished in double digits since. "I don't see myself as a power hitter," he once said. "I just try to be a line-drive guy—to square it up and hit it hard."

In November 2015, Simmons was traded to the Angels for Erick Aybar and a pair of minor-league prospects. There are many who feel that the Angels got the better end of the deal. Simmons is signed through the 2020 campaign. In 2016, he hit .281 with 44 RBIs in 124 games.

10

HONDURAS

ORIGINS OF BASEBALL IN HONDURAS

Honduras is located in Central America and bordered by Guatemala, El Salvador, and Nicaragua. Formerly home to the Mayans, it has a rich archaeological past. Although a majority of the country's 8 million inhabitants are soccer fans, baseball is fairly popular as well. Honduras's national baseball team made its first Amateur World Series appearance in 1950. Since then, the club has competed in seven international tournaments, failing to place higher than sixth. Only a handful of Honduran-born players have been scouted by major-league clubs, and at the time of this writing, only two have seen action at the big-league level. Chito Martinez was born in British Honduras a few years before it was officially renamed Belize. Primarily a right fielder, he spent portions of 11 seasons in the minors and three in the majors (1991–1993), failing to make a lasting impression with his bat or glove. Martinez was preceded in the majors by Gerald Young, who had a far more distinguished career. His biography follows.

MAJOR STAR OF THE PAST

Gerald Young

Center Fielder

Gerald Young was born in Tela, a small town on the northern Caribbean coast in the department of Atlantida. The beaches of Tela attract sun worshippers from throughout the world. While most of the town is equipped with modern amenities, some of the outlying dwellings are bamboo thatch huts with no running water or electricity.

Young's family moved to the United States when he was in his formative years, and he attended high school in California's Santa Ana Valley. The school also sent Cardinals standout Garry Templeton to the majors. Drafted by the Mets in the fifth round of the 1982 Amateur Draft, Young began his pro career as an infielder. The Kingsport Mets tried him out as a shortstop in 1982, but when he committed 38 errors in 54 games, he was moved elsewhere. He eventually found a home in the outfield, where he was far more competent.

In August 1984, Young was traded to the Astros, along with Manuel Lee, in exchange for infielder Ray Knight. Among his best qualities, Young had exceptional speed. He stole 54 bases in the minors during the 1986 campaign and 43 the following year. The Astros had several speedsters in their lineup already, and looking for an extra spark, they called Young to Houston in July 1987. The switch-hitting outfielder had an exceptional debut, hitting .321 in 71 games, with 26 steals. He finished fifth in Rookie of the Year voting.

Young's follow-up campaign was equally successful. Although his batting average fell considerably, he stole 65 bases (second to Vince Coleman of the Cardinals) and scored 79 runs. Defensively, he was among the league leaders in putouts, assists, and range factor. Only three center fielders posted a higher fielding percentage than Young in 1988. Two of them (Robin Yount and Kirby Puckett) are in the Hall of Fame.

Young had another good season in 1989, although he was less successful as a basestealer. He got caught in 42 percent of his attempts, leading the league in that dubious category for the second straight year. While his batting average dropped to .233, he drew a career-high 74 walks. Defensively, he led the NL in fielding percentage, assists, put-outs, double plays, and range factor. In a curious decision, the Gold Glove went to Andy Van Slyke of the Pirates, who had compiled a fielding percentage far inferior to Young's. The speedy Young dazzled observers throughout the year by making 412 putouts with just a single error.

After the 1989 slate, Young began to suffer from an assortment of injuries. He sat out more than 200 games from 1990 to 1993. Granted free agency after the latter campaign, he signed with the Colorado Rockies. He was property of the Reds, Mariners, and Cardinals before falling from the major-league ranks for good in 1994. The Cardinals were the last team to cut him loose despite his .317 average in 16 games. Young remained active in the independent Northern and Atlantic leagues through the 2000 slate.

Young's Baseball-Reference page speculates that he may have played in an era that did not suit his skill set. His similarity scores compare to multiple players of the Deadball Era—a time when walks, stolen bases, and the ability to put the ball in play were highly valued. He stole a total of 471 bases at various professional levels during his career.

11

BRAZIL

ORIGINS OF BASEBALL IN BRAZIL

Brazil is relatively new to the baseball scene, having sent just three players to the majors at the start of the 2016 campaign. More than a century ago, a quarter-million Japanese nationals immigrated to Brazil, bringing their love of baseball with them. Most of them settled in Sao Paulo, Brazil's largest city and baseball capital. Today, a sizeable number of Japanese descendants comprise the country's national team, which upset Panama in the qualifying round of the 2013 World Baseball Classic.

Soccer is Brazil's most popular sport, and that is not likely to change anytime soon. More than 2 million Brazilians play soccer on roughly 29,000 teams scattered throughout the nation. "Soccer will never diminish in Brazil," said Indians catcher Yan Gomes. "It's like asking Americans not to watch football on Sundays." True, but with a population of more than 200 million (the largest in Latin America) it stands to reason that the door will remain open in the future. Gomes was the first to appear in the majors during the 2012 slate. He was followed by pitcher Andre Rienzo in 2013 and outfielder Paulo Orlando in 2015. Rienzo has yet to prove himself, but Orlando put forth a commendable effort in 2016, hitting .302 in 128 games. Even so, Orlando's alarming strikeout rate and lack of power left many questioning his value to the Royals. To date, Gomes is the most successful of all the Brazilian imports.

NOTABLE ACTIVE PLAYER

Yan Gomes

Catcher

Growing up, Yan Gomes had never heard of Ruth, Gehrig, or Mantle. The first time he was able to hit the ball in a practice game, he ran the bases backward. But he has come a long way since then. Born in Sao Paulo, Gomes's family moved to the United States when he was 12. After graduating from Miami Southridge High School, he enrolled at the University of Tennessee, where he played Division I ball. Highly versatile, he appeared at every infield station except shortstop.

In 2008, Gomes was drafted by the Red Sox but opted to stay in college. After two years of service with the University of Tennessee Volunteers, he transferred to Barry University. He set multiple school records and was named an All-American. When the Blue Jays chose him in the 2009 MLB Draft, he accepted their offer.

Gomes spent portions of four seasons in the minors before earning a promotion. The Blue Jays brought him up in May 2012, but were disappointed with the results. Prior to the 2013 campaign, he was traded to Cleveland, along with infielder Mike Aviles, for right-handed reliever Esmil Rogers. Gomes served as backup to Carlos Santana, hitting at a highly competent .294 pace in 88 games. Demonstrating some power, he collected 31 extra-base hits and drove in 38 runs.

By 2014, Gomes was the primary catcher for the Indians. He distinguished himself as the top offensive backstop in the American League, capturing a Silver Slugger Award with 21 homers and 74 RBIs. Defensively, he placed among the top five in assists, double plays, and fielding percentage. He led the league in putouts.

In April 2015, Gomes sustained a MCL sprain when Rajai Davis of the Tigers slid into his leg at home plate. He missed 67 games but remained the Indians' most-used catcher. He managed 34 extra-base hits, while driving in 45 runs in limited duty.

At the All-Star break in 2016, Gomes was mired in a horrendous slump. To break him out of it, teammates organized a "sacrificial ceremony" to the fictional baseball god Jobu. During the mock ceremony, teammate Mike Napoli offered a "blessing" intended to "absolve

Gomes of any wrongdoings." The ritual—borrowed from the popular 1980s comedy film *Major League*—concluded with Gomes slicing a store-bought chicken. He sustained a separated shoulder shortly thereafter and was placed on the disabled list. When healthy, Gomes is equipped with a powerful arm behind the plate. Entering the 2017 slate, Gomes was ranked seventh among active catchers in caught stealing percentage.

BIBLIOGRAPHY

"All Golden Era Candidates Fall Short." *ESPN.go.com*, December 8, 2014, http://www.espn. com/mlb/story/_/id/11999830/all-10-golden-era-candidates-fall-short-hall-fame-induction?ex_cid=espnapi_public (retrieved March 3, 2016).

"Altuve Thrilled to Be Astros' All-Star." *CBSSports.com*, July 2, 2012, http://www.cbssports. com/mlb/gametracker/recap/MLB_20140629 (retrieved July 5, 2016).

Anderson, R. J. "The Indians Counter Yan Gomes' Slump with a Chicken Offering to Jobu." *CBSSports.com*, July 16, 2016, http://www.cbssports.com/mlb/news/watch-the-indians-counter-yan-gomes-slump-with-a-chicken-offering-to-jobu/ (retrieved July 19, 2016).

Arangure, Jorge, Jr. "A Man, a Time, Intertwined." *Sportsonearth.com*, May 1. 2013, http://www.sportsonearth.com/article/46220706/ (retrieved May 10, 2016).

Armour, Mark. "Felipe Alou." *SABR.org*, http://sabr.org/bioproj/person/b79ab182 (retrieved May 10, 2016).

———. "Luis Tiant." *SABR.org*, http://sabr.org/bioproj/person/2212deaf (retrieved May 10, 2016).

———. "Matty Alou." *SABR.org*, http://sabr.org/bioproj/person/3d8b257b (retrieved May 10, 2016).

Axisa, Mike, "Cubs' Maddon on Manny Ramirez as Coach: 'I Love Having Him Here.'" *CBSSports.com*, October 17, 2015, http://www.cbssports.com/mlb/news/cubs-maddon-on-manny-ramirez-as-coach-i-love-having-him-here/ (retrieved March 4, 2016).

———. "Leaderboarding: Best Hitting Catchers in Baseball History." *CBSSports.com*, January 1, 2013, http://www.cbssports.com/mlb/news/leaderboarding-best-hitting-catchers-in-baseball-history/ (retrieved March 4, 2016).

———. "Rafael Palmeiro Says Falling off Hall of Fame Ballot Is 'Disheartening.'" *CBSSports.com*, January 9, 2014, http://www.cbssports.com/mlb/news/rafael-palmeiro-says-falling-off-hall-of-fame-ballot-is-disheartening/ (retrieved March 4, 2016).

Baggarly, Andrew. "In an Era of Fast-Paced Bullpens, Javier Lopez Just Keeps on Cruisin' for the Giants." *Blogs.mercurysports.com*, February 29, 2016, http://blogs.mercurynews. com/giants/2016/02/29/era-fast-paced-bullpens-javier-lopez-just-keeps-cruising-giants/ (retrieved July 4, 2016).

Berg, Ted. "Yasiel Puig's Coming-to-America Story Is Dark and Complicated." *USA Today*, April 14, 2014, http://ftw.usatoday.com/2014/04/yasiel-puig-los-angeles-dodgers-cuba-defection-mexico (retrieved July 4, 2016).

Berra, Lindsay. "Yadier Molina Knows Squat." *ESPN.com*, August 10, 2009, http://www. espn.com/espn/magazine/archives/news/story?page=magazine-20090810-article22 (retrieved July 4, 2016).

"Best MLB Players from the Kingdom of the Netherlands." *ESPN.com*, June 16, 2015, http://www.espn.com/mlb/story/_/id/13082214/best-mlb-players-kingdom-netherlands (retrieved April 14, 2016).

Bjarkman, Peter C. "Dolf Luque." *SABR.org*, http://sabr.org/bioproj/person/29c1fec2 (retrieved April 14, 2016).

———. "Zoilo Versalles." *SABR.org*, http://sabr.org/bioproj/person/273cca73 (retrieved April 14, 2016).

Bostrom, Dan. "Abreu Admits to Using Creatine, but Not Steroids." *Morning Call*, April 12, 2005, http://articles.mcall.com/2005-04-12/sports/3611058_1_creatine-baseball-and-steroids-first-baseman-rico-brogna (retrieved May 6, 2016).

Boyd, Brendan C., and Fred C. Harris. *The Great American Baseball Card Flipping, Trading, and Bubble Gum Book*. Boston: Ticknor and Fields, 1973.

Brown, Ian. "Papi Confirms He Will Retire after 2016 Season." *MLB.com*, November 18, 2015, http://m.mlb.com/news/article/157514386/david-ortiz-to-retire-after-2016-season/ (retrieved May 6, 2016).

Brunt, Stephen. "One-on-One with Toronto's Edwin Encarnacion: The Best-Kept Secret in the Game." *Sportsnet.ca*, March 29, 2014, http://www.sportsnet.ca/baseball/edwin-encarnacion-on-home-turf/ (retrieved July 2, 2016).

Bush, David. "Where Are They Now? Campy Campaneris/Playing the Lead Role/Campy Likens the Current A's to His Title Teams." *Sfgate.com*, May 4, 2003, http://www.sfgate.com/sports/article/where-are-they-now-campy-campaneris-playing-2650441.php (retrieved July 2, 2016).

"Camilo Pascual." *Cooloftheevening.com*, http://www.cooloftheevening.com/camilo_pascual.htm (retrieved March 6, 2016).

Clair, Michael. "Bartolo Colon Continues to Be a Source of Pure Joy in the Universe, Flips behind the Back for the Out." *MLB.com*, September 5, 2015, http://m.mlb.com/cutfour/2015/09/05/147633376/bartolo-colon-adds-to-mixtape-on-behind-the-back-flip-for-out (retrieved April 25, 2016).

Connolly, Dan. "With Orioles' Jonathan Schoop and Others, Curacao Becoming a Baseball Hotbed." *Baltimore Sun*, March 25, 2014, http://www.baltimoresun.com/sports/orioles/bs-sp-orioles-curacao-0324-20140323-story.html (retrieved April 25, 2016).

Costello, Rory. "Dennis Martinez." *SABR.org*, http://sabr.org/bioproj/person/05148239 (retrieved April 25, 2016).

———. "Sandy Amoros." *SABR.org*, http://sabr.org/bioproj/person/4f02bbd8 (retrieved April 25, 2016).

Costello, Rory, and Jose Ramirez. "Tony Gonzalez." *SABR.org*, http://sabr.org/bioproj/person/859e2b7d (retrieved April 25, 2016).

———. "Tony Taylor." *SABR.org*, http://sabr.org/bioproj/person/bc362446 (retrieved April 25, 2016).

Craig, Mark. "Yankees' Mariano Rivera Is More Than Just His Cutter." *Star-Ledger*, September 20, 2011, http://www.nj.com/yankees/index.ssf/2011/09/yankees_mariano_rivera_is_more.html (retrieved April 23, 2016).

Della Costa, Morris. "Colorful Bell Swung a Mighty Bat." *London Free Press*, June 24, 2013, http://www.lfpress.com/2013/06/24/colourful-bell-swung-a-mighty-bat (retrieved April 23, 2016).

DiGiovanna, Mike. "Matty Alou Dies at 72: One of Three Baseball-Star Brothers." *Los Angeles Times*, November 4, 2011, http://articles.latimes.com/2011/nov/04/local/la-me-matty-alou-20111104 (retrieved April 23, 2016).

Dominguez, Robert. "The Forgotten All-Star Game: Fifty Years Ago, Baseball's Latin Legends Played in Polo Grounds' Last Game." *New York Daily News*, July 10, 2013, http://www.nydailynews.com/news/national/forgotten-all-star-game-50-years-baseball-latino-legends-played-polo-grounds-game-article-1.1395064 (retrieved April 23, 2016).

Emert, Rich. "Where Are They Now? Manny Sanguillen." *Pittsburgh Post-Gazette*, April 10, 2003, http://old.post-gazette.com/sports/other/20030410where0410p7.asp (retrieved April 23, 2016).

Espinoza, Alex. "Herrera Hero as Colombia Set for '17 Classic." *MLB.com*, March 21, 2016, http://mlb.mlb.com/pa/news/print.jsp?ymd=20160321&content_id=168318270&vkey=mlbpa_news&fext=.jsp (retrieved April 23, 2016).

Feinsand, Mark. "Mariano Rivera Says Goodbye in an Emotional Final Appearance at Yankee Stadium." *New York Daily News*, September 27, 2013, http://www.nydailynews.com/sports/baseball/yankees/e-mo-tional-tearful-goodbye-rivera-yankee-stadium-article-1.1469041 (retrieved April 23, 2016).

"Forgotten Yankees: Raul Mondesi." *Pinstripealley.com*, August 15, 2015, http://www.pinstripealley.com/yankees-editorials-opinions-analysis/2015/8/15/9132731/yankees-raul-mondesi-dodgers-angels (retrieved May 4, 2016).

Frost, Mark. *Game Six: Cincinnati, Boston, and the 1975 World Series: The Triumph of America's Pastime*. New York: Hyperion, 2003.

"Galarraga Says He's Overcome Second Bout with Cancer." *USA Today*, May 25, 2004, http://usatoday30.usatoday.com/sports/baseball/2004-05-25-galarraga-cancer_x.htm (retrieved April 23, 2016).

"Giants Trade Benitez for Messenger." *MLB.com*, May 31, 2007, http://m.giants.mlb.com/news/article/1997941 (retrieved April 23, 2016).

Gillette, Gary, Peter Gammons, and Pete Palmer, eds. *The 2005 ESPN Baseball Encyclopedia*. New York: Sterling, 2005.

Gonzalez Echeverria, Roberto. *The Pride of Havana: The History of Cuban Baseball*. New York: Oxford University Press, 1999.

Gordon, Peter M. "Cookie Rojas." *SABR.org*, http://sabr.org/bioproj/person/0c6cd3b5 (retrieved April 23, 2016).

Graczyk, Wayne. "Batista's Numbers Didn't Justify His Massive Salary." *Japan Times*, December 18, 2005, http://www.japantimes.co.jp/sports/2005/12/18/baseball/batistas-number-didnt-justify-his-massive-salary/ (retrieved April 23, 2016).

"Guillen Speaks His Mind." *Denver Post*, May 1, 2010, http://www.denverpost.com/2010/05/01/guillen-speaks-his-mind/ (retrieved April 23, 2016).

Harrison, Doug. "Remembering El Presidente: Dennis Martinez's Perfecto." *CBC Sports*, July 28, 2014, http://www.cbc.ca/sports/baseball/mlb/remembering-el-presidente-dennis-martinez-s-el-perfecto-1.2720692 (retrieved April 23, 2016).

Harrison, Ian. "How Carlos Delgado Fell Short of Cooperstown." *Sports.vice.com*, June 12, 2015, https://sports.vice.com/ca/article/how-carlos-delgado-fell-short-of-cooperstown (retrieved June 9, 2016).

Hayes, Marcus. "Yankees Pitcher Chamberlain Learns from Mistakes." *Philadelphia Daily News*, November 3, 2009, http://www.philly.com/philly/sports/20091103_Yankees_pitcher_Chamberlain_learns_from_mistakes.html (retrieved July 12, 2016).

Hernandez, Lou, and Rory Costello. "Chico Carrasquel." *SABR.org*, http://sabr.org/bioproj/person/76069a18 (retrieved July 12, 2016).

Hopkins, Jared S. "Jose Abreu's Mysterious Journey." *Chicago Tribune*, July 11, 2016, http://www.chicagotribune.com/sports/baseball/whitesox/ct-abreu-chicago-cuba-spt-1102-20141107-story.html (retrieved July 12, 2016).

Hughson, Callam. "Baseball in Nicaragua." *Mopupduty.com*, November 15, 2012, https://mopupduty.com/baseball-in-nicaragua-111512/ (retrieved April 5, 2016).

———. "Mexican Baseball." *Mopupduty.com*, February 13, 2007, http://mopupduty.com/mexican-baseball/ (retrieved April 5, 2016).

Hurd, Jay. "Ben Oglivie." *SABR.org*, http://sabr.org/bioproj/person/6eb958b1 (retrieved July 12, 2016).

Hurte, Bob. "Manny Sanguillen." *SABR.org*, http://sabr.org/bioproj/person/b675d587 (retrieved July 12, 2016).

Ingraham, Jim. "Indians: Omar Vizquel Reflects on Career in Cleveland during Tribe Fest." *Morning Journal and News-Herald*, January 26, 2014, http://www.morningjournal.com/article/mj/20140126/news/140129315 (retrieved April 5, 2016).

James, Bill. *The New Bill James Historical Baseball Abstract*. New York: Simon and Schuster, 2001.

"Joakim Soria Wants to Drop Nickname." Associated Press, February 3, 2011, http://www.espn.com/mlb/spring2011/news/story?id=6151322 (retrieved April 5, 2016).

"Jose Canseco." *Biography.com*, http://www.biography.com/people/jose-canseco-17180940 (retrieved February 21, 2016).

"Jose Canseco Pitching in 1993." *Miscbaseball.wordpress.com*, https://miscbaseball.wordpress.com/2009/09/08/jose-canseco-pitching-in-1993/ (retrieved February 21, 2016).

"Julio Franco a Player-Manager in Japan: 'I Don't See Myself Out of Baseball.'" *USA Today*, May 10, 2015, http://www.usatoday.com/story/sports/mlb/2015/05/10/former-pro-franco-stays-busy-in-japan-as-player-manager/27078711/ (retrieved February 21, 2016).

Kepner, Tyler. "Indians Catcher Hopes to Spread His Sport in Brazil." *New York Times*, February 23, 2014, http://www.nytimes.com/2014/02/24/sports/baseball/indians-yan-gomes-hopes-to-spread-his-sport-in-brazil.html?_r=0 (retrieved February 21, 2016).

Klapisch, Bob. "Will Brazil Be Baseball's Next Frontier?" *Foxsports.com*, http://www.foxsports.com/mlb/just-a-bit-outside/story/baseball-in-brazil-next-big-thing-mlb-yan-gomes-paulo-orlando-andre-rienzo-092415 (retrieved April 16, 2016).

Kraval, David. "Jose Cardenal: The Latin Connection." *MSBLNational.com/Hardball-Archive*, http://www.msblnational.com/HardBall-Archives/Blog/Jose-Cardenal-The-Latin-Connection-39-249.htm (retrieved February 24, 2016).

Kurkjian, Tim. "A Scout's Life in Colombia." *ESPN.com*, January 20, 2011, http://www.espn.com/mlb/columns/story?id=6038291&columnist=kurkjian_tim (retrieved February 24, 2016).

Langosch, Jenifer. "For Molina, No Greater Influence Than Father." *MLB.com*, June 19, 2015, http://m.mlb.com/news/article/131277324/for-molinas-no-greater-influence-than-father/ (retrieved June 16, 2016).

Lawson, Earl. "Spindly Cardenas Peppers Pill in Strong Stretch Run." *Sporting News*, September 22, 1962.

Lee, Bill "Spaceman," and Richard Lally. *The Wrong Stuff*. New York: Three Rivers Press, 2006.

"Livan Hernandez, Mom Reunited." Associated Press, October 28, 1997, http://www.christusrex.org/www2/fcf/momandlivan102797.html (retrieved April 18, 2016).

"Looking Back at . . . Cesar Cedeno." *Astrosdaily.com*, http://www.astrosdaily.com/history/cedeno.html (retrieved April 18, 2016).

Lopez, Javy, and Gary Caruso. *Behind the Plate: A Catcher's View of the Braves Dynasty*. Chicago: Triumph, 2012.

Loverro, Thom. *The Encyclopedia of Negro League Baseball*. New York: Checkmark Books, 2003.

Luciano, Mike. "Julio Franco's Batting Stance Should Be Inducted into Baseball Hall of Fame." *Mic.com*, January 9, 2013, https://mic.com/articles/22379/julio-franco-s-batting-stance-should-be-inducted-into-baseball-hall-of-fame (retrieved April 27, 2016).

Manzullo, Brian. "Ex-tigers Ordonez, Guillen Reunite in Puerto Rico." *Detroit Free Press*, February 8, 2015, http://www.freep.com/story/sports/mlb/tigers/2015/02/08/detroit-tigers-magglio-ordonez-carlos-guillen/23081085/ (retrieved April 27, 2016).

Maraniss, David. *Clemente: The Passion and Grace of Baseball's Last Hero*. New York: Simon and Schuster, 2006.

Margalus, Jim. "Jose Quintana's Hall of Fame Plaque." *Southsidesox.com*, June 17, 2016, http://www.southsidesox.com/2016/6/17/11967950/jose-quintanas-hall-of-fame-plaque (retrieved April 27, 2016).

Markusen, Bruce. "Card Corner: 1973 Topps: Rico Carty." *Hardballtimes.com*, February 22, 2013, http://www.hardballtimes.com/card-corner-1973-topps-rico-carty/ (retrieved April 24, 2016).

———. "Cooperstown Confidential: Where Are the All-Black Nine Now?" *Hardballtimes.com*, September 2, 2011, http://www.hardballtimes.com/cooperstown-confidential-where-are-the-all-black-nine-now/ (retrieved March 31, 2016).

———. "Recalling the Death of Aurelio Rodriguez." *Detroitathletic.com*, July 23, 2015, https://www.detroitathletic.com/blog/2015/07/23/recalling-the-death-of-aurelio-rodriguez/ (retrieved April 1, 2016).

McCarron, Anthony. "Former Mets Second Baseman Felix Millan, Key Piece of '73 Mets Series Team, Can Still Handle a Bat." *New York Daily News*, April 30, 2011, http://www. nydailynews.com/sports/baseball/mets/mets-baseman-felix-millan-key-piece-73-world-series-team-handle-bat-article-1.115921 (retrieved April 1, 2016).

McCarthy, Charlie. "Jose Fernandez Set to Make MLB Debut Sunday." *Fox Sports Florida*, April 5, 2013, http://www.foxsports.com/florida/story/jose-fernandez-set-to-make-mlb-debut-sunday-040513 (retrieved October 1, 2016).

McGuire, Kevin. "MLB Asks Yasiel Puig to Stop Wearing His Vin Scully Cleats." *Yardbark-er.com*, July 27, 2016, http://awfulannouncing.com/2016/mlb-asks-yaisel-puig-stop-wearing-vin-scully-cleats.html (retrieved October 1, 2016).

McManis, Sam. "Martinez Has Fought Own Battle, Won." *Los Angeles Times*, August 28, 1987, http://articles.latimes.com/1987-08-28/sports/sp-2873_1_sandinistas (retrieved April 1, 2016).

Megdal, Howard. "Off to See the Wizard?" *Sportsonearth.com*, April 24, 2014, http://www. sportsonearth.com/article/73100358/undefined_15 (retrieved July 19, 2016).

Melewski, Steve. "Jonathan Schoop on His Go-Ahead Hit, Plus Other Clubhouse Quotes." *Masnsports.com*, July 9, 2016, http://www.masnsports.com/steve-melewski/2016/07/jonathan-schoop-on-his-go-ahead-hit-and-other-clubhouse-quotes.html (retrieved July 19, 2016).

Merkin, Scott. "Uribe Clears Name, and His Head." *MLB.com*, February 23, 2007, http://chicago.whitesox.mlb.com/news/print.jsp?ymd=20070223&content_id=1813166&vkey=spt2007news&fext=.jsp&c_id=cws (retrieved July 4, 2016).

Mooney, Patrick. "Cubs' Catcher Miguel Montero Is Going to Do It His Own Way." *Csnchi-cago.com*, April 12, 2015, http://www.csnchicago.com/chicago-cubs/cubs-catcher-miguel-montero-going-do-it-his-way (retrieved July 4, 2016).

Mooney, Roger. "Jose Fernandez, Marlins Ace and Alonso Grad, Dies in Boating Accident." *Tampa Bay Times*, September 25, 2016, http://live.tampabay.com/Event/Marlins_ace_Alonso_grad_Jose_Fernandez_dies_in_boating_accident?Page=0 (retrieved October 1, 2016).

Morris, Frank. "Pedro Guerrero." *SABR.org*, http://sabr.org/bioproj/person/7e530bab (retrieved October 1, 2016).

National Baseball Hall of Fame and Museum. *The Hall: A Celebration of Baseball's Greats*. Boston: Little, Brown and Company, 2014.

Neft, David, et al. *The Sports Encyclopedia: Baseball*. New York: St. Martin's Griffin, 2000.

Newhan, Ross. "Upper-Deck Home Run Doesn't Measure up for Canseco." *Los Angeles Times*, October 8, 1989, http://articles.latimes.com/1989-10-08/sports/sp-435_1_home-run (retrieved October 1, 2016).

Nightengale, Bob. "Jose Fernandez, Embodiment of American Dream, Had Irrepressible Spirit." *USA Today*, September 26, 2016, http://www.usatoday.com/story/sports/mlb/columnist/bob-nightengale/2016/09/25/jose-fernandez-killed-boating-accident/91077800/ (retrieved October 1, 2016).

O'Brien, David. "Simmons' Instinct and Arm Separate Braves' Shortstop from Rest." *Atlan-tabravesblog.ajc.com*, May 19, 2015, http://atlantabraves.blog.ajc.com/2015/05/19/simmons-instincts-and-arm-separate-braves-ss-from-rest/ (retrieved July 19, 2016).

O'Leary, Daniel. "Yasiel Puig's Defection from Cuba, Journey to Dodgers Is a Sordid Tale." *New York Daily News*, April 15, 2014, http://www.nydailynews.com/sports/baseball/report-chronicles-incredible-secretive-defection-dodgers-puig-article-1.1757713 (retrieved July 19, 2016).

"Omar Moreno: How He Was Discovered." *Vimeo.com*, 2012, https://vimeo.com/33308158 (retrieved July 19, 2016).

"On the Pirates: Stennett Reflects on Sweet Seven." *Pittsburgh Post-Gazette*, May 31, 2009, http://www.post-gazette.com/sports/pirates/2009/05/31/On-the-Pirates-Stennett-reflects-on-sweet-seven/stories/200905310172 (retrieved July 19, 2016).

Ortiz, Jorge L. "As Vladimir Guerrero Eyes Hall of Fame, His Family Tree Strengthens in Dominican." *USA Today*, February 11, 2016, http://www.usatoday.com/story/sports/mlb/

2016/02/11/vladimir-guerrero-eyes-hall-fame-his-family-tree-strengthens-dominican/ 80218052/ (retrieved July 19, 2016).

Otis, John. "Baseball's Venezuelan Talent Pool Dries up amid Poverty and Discord." *Time*, March 24, 2016, http://time.com/4270487/baseball-venezuela/ (retrieved May 23, 2016).

"Ozzie Guillen of Marlins Suspended for Five Games." *ESPN.com*, April 10, 2012, http:// www.espn.com/mlb/story/_/id/7795152/ozzie-guillen-miami-marlins-suspended-five-games (retrieved May 23, 2016).

Pietrusza, David, et al. *Baseball: The Biographical Encyclopedia.* London: Sport Media Publishing, 2003.

Plano, Josh. "Why Johnny Cueto Has Become the Giants' Ace after Struggling with the Royals." *Washington Post*, June 1, 2016, https://www.washingtonpost.com/news/fancy-stats/wp/2016/06/01/why-johnny-cueto-has-become-the-giants-ace-after-struggling-with-the-royals/ (retrieved July 11, 2016).

Plaschke, Bill. "Fifty Years after Giants' Juan Marichal Hit Dodgers' John Roseboro with a Bat, All Is Forgiven." *Los Angeles Times*, August 22, 2015, http://www.latimes.com/sports/ dodgers/la-sp-roseboro-marichal-plaschke-20150823-column.html (retrieved July 11, 2016).

Posnanski, Joe. "Thirty-Two Fast Pitchers." *SI.com*, September 7, 2010, http://www.efastball. com/about-us/press/backupdocs/2010-09-27-joeposnanski-si-com.pdf (retrieved July 11, 2016).

Reid, Lydia M. "Baseball's Roots in Panama." *Silverpeople.com*, January 31, 2010, https:// thesilverpeopleheritage.wordpress.com/2010/01/31/baseballs-roots-in-panama/ (retrieved March 26, 2016).

Rhoden, William C. "Delgado Makes a Stand by Taking a Seat." *New York Times*, July 21, 2004, http://www.nytimes.com/2004/07/21/sports/sports-of-the-times-delgado-makes-a-stand-by-taking-a-seat.html?_r=0 (retrieved March 26, 2016).

Rivera, Brandon. "An Interview with Vinny Castilla." *Lavozcolorado.com*, April 29, 2015, http://www.lavozcolorado.com/detail.php?id=8056 (retrieved March 31, 2016).

Rodriguez, Angel. "Jose Fernandez's Death Is Especially Heartbreaking for Cubans and Cuban Americans." *Los Angeles Times*, September 25, 2016, http://www.latimes.com/ sports/mlb/la-sp-fernandez-cuban-perspective-20160925-snap-story.html (retrieved March 26, 2016).

Salisbury, Jim. "Ruiz Give Phils the Feeling They Hit the Lottery." *Philadelphia Inquirer*, March 29, 2008, http://articles.philly.com/2008-03-29/sports/25259829_1_carlos-ruiz-adam-eaton-phillies+&cd=1&hl=en&ct=clnk&gl=us (retrieved July 12, 2016).

"Salvador Perez Sticks with Perfume." Associated Press, October 24, 2014, http://www.espn. com/mlb/playoffs/2014/story/_/id/11754714/2014-world-series-salvador-perez-kansas-city-royals-wearing-perfume-good-luck-charm (retrieved July 12, 2016).

Sanchez, Jesse. "Uncertainty Swirls around Luis Castro." *MLB.com*, April 23, 2007, http://m. mlb.com/news/article/1925446/ (retrieved July 12, 2016).

Santon, Jeffrey. "Jose Canseco Outs Magglio Ordonez." *Bleacherreport.com*, January 24, 2008, http://bleacherreport.com/articles/7445-jose-canseco-outs-magglio-ordonez (retrieved May 23, 2016).

Sargent, Jim. "Hector Lopez." *SABR.org*, http://sabr.org/bioproj/person/048dfeef (retrieved July 12, 2016).

Schoenfield, David. "The Cautionary Tale of Cesar Cedeno." *ESPN.com*, August 8, 2012, http://www.espn.com/blog/sweetspot/post/_/id/27814/the-cautionary-tale-of-cesar-cedeno (retrieved April 18, 2016).

Sexton, Joe. "Fernandez Doesn't Dwell on Health." *New York Times*, February 26, 1993, http://www.nytimes.com/1993/02/26/sports/baseball-fernandez-doesn-t-dwell-on-health. html (retrieved April 18, 2016).

Skrbina, Paul. "Ozzie Guillen: 'I Miss Baseball.'" *Chicago Tribune*, July 8, 2015, http://www. chicagotribune.com/sports/baseball/whitesox/ct-ozzie-guillen-misses-baseball-spt-0709-20150708-story.html (retrieved April 18, 2016).

Slusser, Susan, and Demian Bulwa. "The Yoenis Cespedes Chronicles: While the Cuban Defector Broke in with Oakland A's, His Family Endured a Harrowing Struggle to Reach the U.S." *San Francisco Chronicle*, http://www.sfchronicle.com/sports/cespedes/ (retrieved August 2, 2016).

Snyder, Matt. "From Childhood Friends to All-Stars: Salvador Perez, Jose Altuve." *CBSSports.com*, July 4, 2014, http://www.cbssports.com/mlb/news/from-childhood-friends-to-al-all-stars-salvador-perez-jose-altuve/ (retrieved July 5, 2016).

"Speed Whiz Boosts Bucs Flag Hopes." *Sunday Grit: National Edition*, November 28, 1976.

Stankevitz, J. J. "Cubs Honor Aramis Ramirez as 18-Year Career Nears Its End." *CSNChicago.com*, September 27, 2015, http://www.csnchicago.com/chicago-cubs/cubs-honor-aramis-ramirez-18-year-career-nears-its-end (retrieved May 14, 2016).

Stewart, Mark. "Minnie Minoso." *SABR.org*, http://sabr.org/bioproj/person/796bd066 (retrieved May 14, 2016).

Sullivan, Jeff. "Searching for a Defense of Rafael Palmeiro's 1999 Gold Glove." *SBNation.com*, December 2, 2011, http://www.sbnation.com/2011/12/2/2604446/rafael-palmeiro-1999-gold-glove (retrieved March 5, 2016).

Sullivan, T. R. "Emotional Sierra Enters Rangers Hall." *MLB.com*, August 2, 2000, http://m.rangers.mlb.com/news/article/6190610/ (retrieved June 19, 2016).

Taylor, Phil. "No-no Regrets: Johan Santana Would Rather Not Alter a Thing. Terry Collins Might." *SI.com*, June 1, 2015, http://www.si.com/mlb/2015/05/31/johan-santana-no-hitter-anniversary-new-york-mets-terry-collins (retrieved June 19, 2016).

Thornley, Stew. "Roberto Clemente." *SABR.org*, http://sabr.org/bioproj/person/8b153bc4 (retrieved June 19, 2016).

"Turmoil with the White Sox, as Cabrera Feels Lack of Support." *ESPN.com*, May 10, 2008, http://www.espn.com/mlb/news/story?id=3415430 (retrieved April 7, 2016).

Underhill, Nick. "The Ten Best 'Manny Being Manny Moments.'" *Masslive.com*, April 9, 2011, http://www.masslive.com/sports/2011/04/the_10_best_manny_being_manny.html (retrieved May 16, 2016).

Vizquel, Omar, and Bob Dyer. *Omar! My Life on and off the Field*. Cleveland, OH: Gray and Company, 2003.

Waldstein, David. "A Speck on the Map Gushes Talent: Curacao Unlikely Supplier of Major League Players." *New York Times*, December 14, 2014, http://www.nytimes.com/2014/12/15/sports/curacao-becomes-unlikely-supplier-of-major-league-players.html?_r=0 (retrieved May 16, 2016).

Wancho, Joseph. "Rod Carew." *SABR.org*, http://sabr.org/bioproj/person/0746c6ee (retrieved May 16, 2016).

———. "Vic Power." *SABR.org*, http://sabr.org/bioproj/person/fc3d3b7b (retrieved May 16, 2016).

"When Things Get Bad, Royals Managers Say and Do the Darndest Things." *Kansas City Star*, May 29, 2015, http://www.kansascity.com/sports/spt-columns-blogs/k-zone/article320075/When-things-get-bad-Royals-managers-say-and-do-the-darndest-things.html (retrieved May 16, 2016).

Wilker, Josh. "Luis Tiant, Perpetual Motion." *Theclassical.org*, July 19, 2012, http://theclassical.org/articles/luis-tiant-perpetual-motion (retrieved March 9, 2016).

Wilson, Jeff. "Yovani Gallardo: 'I Don't See Myself Ever Leaving Fort Worth.'" *Fort Worth Star-Telegram*, February 19, 2015, http://www.star-telegram.com/sports/mlb/texas-rangers/article10678964.html (retrieved July 14, 2016).

Wilson, V. C. "Fernandomania." *SABR.org*, http://sabr.org/research/fernandomania (retrieved July 14, 2016).

Zigler, David. "Tony Bautista: A Man on a Mission." *Minnesotapublicradio.org*, April 13, 2006 (retrieved April 20, 2016).

Websites

Baseball Almanac: http://www.baseball-almanac.com
Baseball Cube: http://www.thebaseballcube.com/
Baseball Page: http://www.thebaseballpage.com

Baseball-Reference: http://www.baseball-reference.com/
BrainyQuote: https://www.brainyquote.com/
JockBio: http://www.jockbio.com/
Minoso: http://www.minoso.com/
Roberto Alomar: http://www.robertoalomar.com/

INDEX

ABOUT THE AUTHOR

Jonathan Weeks has published six books on the topic of baseball, including *Baseball's Dynasties and the Men Who Built Them*; *Mudville Madness: Fabulous Feats, Belligerent Behavior, and Erratic Episodes on the Diamond*; and *Cellar Dwellers: The Worst Teams in Baseball History*. Originally from Schenectady, New York, he currently resides in Malone. When baseball is not in season, he moonlights as a hockey fan.